A MODERN PENTECOST:
EMBRACING A RECORD OF THE
SIXTEENTH NATIONAL CAMP-MEETING
For the Promotion of Holiness,
Held At
LANDISVILLE, PA.,
July 23d to August 1st, 1873

B. L. Fisher Library Camp Meeting Series ; vol. 3.
Series editor: Robert A. Danielson, Ph.D.

A MODERN PENTECOST:
EMBRACING A RECORD OF THE
SIXTEENTH NATIONAL CAMP-MEETING
For the Promotion of Holiness,

Held At

LANDISVILLE, PA.,
July 23d to August 1st, 1873

Edited By
ADAM WALLACE

First Fruits Press
Wilmore, Kentucky
c2016

A modern Pentecost: embracing a record of the Sixteenth National Camp-Meeting for the Promotion of Holiness held at Landisville, Pa., July 23d to August 1st, 1873.
Edited by Rev Adam Wallace.

First Fruits Press, ©2016
Previously published by the Methodist Home Journal Publishing House, 1873.

ISBN: 9781621715580 (print), 9781621715597 (digital) 9781621715603 (kindle)

Digital version at http://place.asburyseminary.edu/firstfruitsheritagematerial/134/

A modern Pentecost : embracing a record of the Sixteenth National Camp-Meeting for the Promotion of Holiness held at Landisville, Pa., July 23d to August 1st, 1873 / edited by Adam Wallace. – Wilmore, Kentucky : First Fruits Press, ©2016.
    224 pages portraits ; 23 cm.--(B.L. Fisher Library camp meeting series ; volume 3)
    Reprint. Previously published: Philadelphia : Methodist Home Journal Publishing House, 1873.
    ISBN - 13: 9781621715580 (pbk.)
    1. National Camp-Meeting (16th : 1873 : Landisville, Pa.) 2. Camp meetings--Pennsylvania--Landisville. 3. Pennsylvania--Church history. I. Title. II. Asbury Theological Seminary. B.L. Fisher Library. Camp meeting series ; volume 3. III. Wallace, Adam.
BV3799.P67 R44 1896-1899

Cover design by Jon Ramsay

asburyseminary.edu
800.2ASBURY
204 North Lexington Avenue
Wilmore, Kentucky 40390

First Fruits
THE ACADEMIC OPEN PRESS OF ASBURY SEMINARY

First Fruits Press
The Academic Open Press of Asbury Theological Seminary
204 N. Lexington Ave., Wilmore, KY 40390
859-858-2236
first.fruits@asburyseminary.edu
asbury.to/firstfruits

A MODERN PENTECOST;

EMBRACING A RECORD OF THE

Sixteenth National Camp-Meeting

FOR THE PROMOTION OF HOLINESS,

HELD AT

LANDISVILLE, PA.,

July 23d to August 1st, 1873.

"And they were all filled with the Holy Ghost."—Acts 2, 4.

EDITED BY

Rev. ADAM WALLACE.

METHODIST HOME JOURNAL PUBLISHING HOUSE, 14 NORTH SEVENTH ST.

1873.

CONTENTS.

———

CONTENTS.

CONTENTS.

EIGHTH DAY.

LAST GREAT DAY OF THE FEAST.

INTRODUCTORY.

To PRESENT SOMETHING in the form of a full and complete representation of at least one of the National Camp-meetings for the promotion of Holiness, has for some years past been the ardent wish of the compiler of these pages.

When the first of this wonderful series was determined upon at Vineland, in 1867, we had arrangements made to embody its varied exercises in a book. Had we succeeded, no volume in all the range of our spiritual literature, it is thought, would be more interesting to-day and for many years to come, than such a compendium of practical doctrine and experience.

Through the columns of our paper, THE METHODIST HOME JOURNAL, we have endeavored to furnish the best synopsis possible, of every meeting of this character that has transpired; but to thousands of our readers, unable to participate in the high and holy privileges of these renowned occasions of re-union and spiritual power, the reports sent forth only excited a desire to have more ample and accurate details of the order, incidents and daily scenes of these gatherings of the Lord's people, with their witnessing words, and kindling songs, relating to Jesus and his great salvation.

The volume entitled "Penuel, or Face to Face with God," published a few years ago by W. C. PALMER, JR., New York; and another, more recently issued, from the graphic pen of Rev. GEORGE HUGHES—"Days of Power in the Forest Temple," by JOHN BENT & Co., Boston, Mass., give, respectively, a pretty thorough *resume* of this movement, and the material elements which have characterized its rise and progress.

To portray one meeting, however, working up its actual history, and sketching its daily services, yet remained a purpose to be accomplished. Correspondents in remote sections of the country, and some in other lands, have urged upon our attention the propriety and usefulness of such a work. They want, in some such form, a model of the management, an exhibit of its genius and force—and to this end we have attempted the task of putting a National Camp-meeting in a book.

When Landisville, in the heart of Eastern Pennsylvania, was designated as the place for one of the National Meetings of 1873, we immediately conceived the purpose of gratifying our friends, by placing on record the story of its Pentecostal manifestations from the presence of the Lord.

A great meeting was expected—and none who prayed and waited for the result, were disappointed. So confident were we that God would baptize the assembled people with the Holy Ghost and fire sent down from heaven, that the plan of our prospective book embraced the title, " Pentecost Repeated." After the lapse of time, and some interchange of thought, we have modified this title so as to avoid questioning and criticism as far as needful, and the Landisville National Camp-meeting of 1873 we now set forth as " A Modern Pentecost." We hold that the remarkable days described in Acts ii, did not end, but opened a glorious dispensation of the Spirit, and are being repeated in these times.

It may not be inappropriate just here to make an apology and explanation, due on account of delay in the issue of this publication. After a careful survey of our facilities, we supposed it would be in the hands of its eager readers in ten days after the meeting closed ; but full that many weeks of weary work rolled over us, and found our preparation, in the way of an entire set of stereotype plates, unfit for the press. In the hurry of office business and the ceaseless demands of editorial duty, we for a time gave way to discouragement, and abandoned the enterprise. Appeals from sources entitled to consideration and respect, then revived our energies, and in a form entirely different from the original, we have re-printed the whole book.

That it is not all we designed, or half up to the ideal of excellence we entertained, we may be allowed frankly to admit. The stenographers engaged to aid us, failed to attend, and the personal supervision required, from a combination of occurrences surrounding us, we were not able fully to render at the meeting.

It would have been a matter of impossibility with us to have followed the entire routine of services during the successive days of devotion, but for the aid and assiduous application of Rev. G. A. PHOEBUS, who, with a few generous helpers, and the assistance of members of the National Association, placed at our disposal the material we could not otherwise have obtained. To bring it within portable compass required considerable abbreviation. What in our judgment is profitable for doctrine and edification, we have carefully retained.

The series of sermons, given mostly entire, the extended reports of testimony, and all the incidental features embraced, will, we hope, not merely allow its readers to enjoy a "feast of tabernacles" at their own firesides, making "December as pleasant as May," but quicken desire after God, convert souls that are temporizing in sin, and pour light on the pathway of those who are seeking a deeper baptism, and a richer experience in the life of faith and love. Every possible phase of the doctrine, enjoyment and duties of Holiness will be found illustrated here. May the Divine blessing rest on every page, and every reader!

A. WALLACE.

BRIEF SKETCH

OF THE

REVIVAL OF CAMP-MEETINGS IN LANCASTER CO., PA.

FOR TWENTY YEARS prior to 1867, we are informed, no camp-meeting, under the exclusive control of the M. E. Church, had been held in Lancaster county, Pa.

The usage had been kept up, however, by one or two denominations, whose manner and doctrine were adapted to this peculiar mode of worship.

The crowds attending these meetings, especially on the Sabbath day, and a prevailing sentiment among the people that the occasion was little else than a pic-nic, created such disorder, and tended so largely to demoralization, that Methodists were excusable in withholding the sanction of their presence from all such scenes of desecration as cast odium on religion, although they were always willing to lend a helping hand in every effort to advance the gospel and save souls.

In the revival of the camp-meeting spirit, which, by coincidence, occurred soon after the starting of the METHODIST HOME JOURNAL, the communities respectively of the cities of Lancaster, Harrisburg, Reading, Lebanon and Columbia, (all in a group), began to agitate the subject, and it was proposed to hold a district meeting. The difficulties in the way were serious enough to intimidate any but men of large experience and indomitable energy. Such men were found, and led by Rev. C. I. Thompson, then stationed in Lancaster. Brother T. had succeeded, on the Peninsula, in conducting the largest meetings with a degree of nerve, resolution and success that gave him confidence in this attempt to rally the forces and maintain order, even among the most stolid and obstinate of the German population.

MANHEIM.

A fine grove near the old town of Manheim, was with some difficulty secured, and the meeting commenced August 8th, 1867. Vineland had scattered "live coals" all over the country. The working force at Manheim were inspired with new zeal, and converting and sanctifying grace came upon the people.— Father Boehm, in his 93d year, preached one of the sermons, addressing the grandchildren of his own early associates in that vicinity.

Referring to a report of the first Manheim meeting, published in the HOME JOURNAL of August 17, 1873, written by Rev. T. B. Miller, we find the following brethren named as having preached on the ground : Messrs. Isett, Kessler, J. F. Meredith, Pugh, J. P. Miller, Hurlock, O'Neill, S. H. C. Smith, T. B. Miller, G. Cummins, Pancoast, Rakestraw, Lindamuth, W. L. Gray, P. Elder, J. W. Jackson, Freund, Wiggins, Cookman, J. A. Wood, J. F. Chaplain, C. I. Thompson and Wm. Major, then pastor at Columbia.

The order was good, although a few refractory cases had to be dealt with in a manner admonitory to others ; rowdyism was met, and, on its own chosen field, completely conquered.

When, in 1868, the question arose as to a site for the Second National Camp-Meeting, Manheim became immortal in being selected as the most central and suitable place to be found.

The Presiding Elder, Rev. W. L. Gray, gave personal co-operation to the movement, and his preachers threw their influence into the scale, largely contributing to the overwhelming spiritual power and signal results of the meeting.

Men and women on that ground received such power from on high that their labors, although previously of little account in the church, have subsequently been instrumental in the salvation of thousands of souls. We might refer, for example, to R. Pearsall Smith and his excellent and laborious wife, who, at Manheim as never before, received a commission from God which has absorbed their being, and proved an untold blessing to all the churches through their abundant labors.

In 1869 the encampment was moved to the vicinity of Lebanon, Pa., and, referring to our visit and reports published that year, we find that it was an occasion of great interest. Father Boehm was again present, talking to the people in demonstration of the Spirit, and with power.

Several converts, as we remember, in bearing testimony in the experience meetings, poured forth their praises in the German tongue, and the venerable patriarch stood up and translated their burning words to those who did not understand the language.

At this meeting (in 1869) a proposition to select and purchase a permanent camp-ground, obtained general concurrence. A committee was appointed, consisting of Messrs. Thompson and Glover, Harrisburg ; Myers and Sampson, Lancaster ; Patton and Grove, Columbia, with other brethren whose names have escaped us, and who, after a thorough examination of numerous available places, found at

LANDISVILLE

a grove which, in their judgment, could not be surpassed for accessibility and all the pre-requisites both of a first-class camping ground and a summer residence. The features of the grove are thus described :

THE MEANS OF ACCESS

to the ground are direct—it being situated at the junction of the Pennsylvania

Central and the Reading and Columbia Railroads, connecting with all the great lines North and South, East and West.

THE LOCATION

is very beautiful and picturesque, being in the most fertile and best cultivated part of Lancaster county.

THE ATMOSPHERE

is pure, free from miasmatic influence, and conducive to health—a desirable resort for invalids.

THE GROUND

is a splendid park of about twenty-five acres of majestic oak, walnut and hickory trees, towering over one hundred feet, free from underbrush, and affording a perfect circulation of air. The supply of water is abundant, and deliciously cool.

An association was formed, the ground purchased and enclosed, and the first meeting was held there, commencing July 26, 1870. It was under the control of the Presiding Elder of Harrisburg district, Rev. Dr. Pattison, and continued as a district camp-meeting during the seasons of 1871 and 1872. Of the exercises at each of these meetings, we have given reports from year to year in the HOME JOURNAL.

Meanwhile the grounds were improved, surveyed and apportioned off in lots to suit purchasers, and the blessing of God, invoked in earnest prayer, had come on the place and people, consecrating Landisville forever as a leafy temple in which devout souls might worship the Lord in the beauty of holiness.

Referring to the attractions and adaptation of the grounds, in our notes of 1872, we remember having said :

" After greatly enlarged experience since we first called attention to the extraordinary advantages of this noble forest, we can heartily endorse the opinion expressed by all who visit it, that a finer location for camp-meeting purposes could not be desired.

" The interlacing branches of these tall trees form a refreshing shade, the supply of water is ' abundant, free and clear,' and for area and general convenience, we submit that the National Camp-Meeting for 1873, or one of the series to be held next year, could not find a better place than Landisville. The prestige and holy memories of Manheim have not paled in contrast with the many great meetings held in other places since 1868, and thousands would experience a thrill of pleasurable anticipation if it should please the National Association to appoint another Manheim meeting, only in a better grove, and where every preparation is already made for such a gathering of the Lord's people, on the most extensive scale."

The Board of Control, through their President, Rev. C. I. Thompson extended an invitation to the National Association in accordance with the above suggestion, and the latter, at their annual meeting in New York, October 16, 1872, accepted it, and placed Landisville on the list for July 23d, 1873, one meeting—Cedar Rapids, Iowa, preceding, and two, Moundsville, West Va., and Knoxville, Tenn., following this date.

Early in the season, the local Board of Control began their forecasting, to have all preliminary arrangements completed before the appointed day. Committees were designated, to whose judgment was assigned the different departments of work. In this connection we present the minutes of a meeting held on the camp ground May 14, 1873. There were present, Rev. C. I. Thompson, President; Wm. Paton, Vice President; G. F. McFarland, Secretary; E. Hershey, Treasurer; Samuel Grove, John W. Glover, George M. Brubaker, Jos. Samson, John B. Good, S. M. Myers, Jacob Shaffer, D. Beideman and W. K. Bender, Managers; also Rev. C. F. Turner, P. E., Rev. A. Wallace, of the METHODIST HOME JOURNAL, Messrs. Wilhelm, and Holt, and Rev. John C. Gregg.

To Bros. Patton, Grove, J. W. Awl and E. Hershey, was assigned the charge of erecting and superintending lodging houses and boarding arrangements.

Messrs. Hershey, Grove and Samson were appointed a committee to provide tent accommodations.

Committee on Tabernacle, Messrs. Glover, Crouse, Brubaker, Grove and Myers.

To Rev. C. I. Thompson, President, was assigned the duty of arranging with railroad companies for a reduction of fare to and from the National Camp-meeting.

The re-arrangement and enlargement of the ground was committed to Bros Hershey, Glover, Good and Grove.

The police and sanitary departments were placed in charge of Messrs. Glover, Samson, Holt, Myers and Patton.

The transfer of passengers and baggage from depot to camp ground was committed to Bros. Patton and Myers.

All applications for tents to be made to Samuel Grove, and the postal and book arrangements to be left in the hands of the President. After correspondence with the National Association, they assumed the entire control of the book and periodical business, and secured the services of Rev. C. A. Maulsbury, of New Jersey Conference, to attend to it. The reception and forwarding of all mail matter was carefully attended to by Rev. C. C. McLean.

Bros. Ellenberger, of Harrisburg, and Prof. J. R. Sweeney, of the Penna. Military Academy, were on hand to render aid in conducting the singing.

J. Wesley Awl, Esq., after the departure of Col. McFarland to Europe, was appointed Secretary of the Board, in the further preliminary business, and during the camp-meeting.

To the Editor of the HOME JOURNAL was assigned all needed space for tents in rear of the stand, and facilities for reporting the exercises of the meeting.

Pursuant to these appointments, the buildings were erected, tents put up, seating arranged, and people far and near invited to attend the meeting, and meanwhile pray for its success.

OPENING DAY

OF THE SIXTEENTH NATIONAL CAMP-MEETING.

WHERE the review of the wonderful work of God at fourteen National Camp-meetings, in the book entitled "Days of Power in the Forest Temple," by Rev. George Hughes, closes, we would like to resume the history, and repeat the incidents of the Fifteenth, which was held in Iowa, closing July 4, 1873; but that would comprise a volume in itself, as thrilling as any ever written. The tidings of victory from the western banks of the Mississippi, coming eastward, inspired the hosts of Israel to pray and believe for a Pentecost at Landisville. Repeatedly, through the HOME JOURNAL, the trumpet was sounded, and the people called upon to "come up to the help of the Lord." Rev. C. I. Thompson, in his general circular issued the following bugle note:—

"COME TO THIS FEAST OF TABERNACLES.

"Come from the North; come from the South; come from the East; come from the West! Come fully marshalled for the conflict, with banners flying, having inscribed upon them—

'HOLINESS TO THE LORD.'

"Come, expecting the baptism of power; come, praying that God may send an influence out from the meeting, that will cause the powers of hell to retreat, and righteousness to prevail. Let all churches that love holiness come, that being baptized together in the spirit of love, they may no more vex each other, but battle unitedly for Christ and his great salvation."

While some were providentially enabled to obey the invitation, thousands, whose hearts were stirred within them with desire to be present, had to forego the privilege, and remain at home, or turn to other paths of duty. A word for both classes appeared from the pen of brother Hughes in the HOME JOURNAL at the beginning of the exercises:—

"ONCE MORE TO THE FRONT!"

"WHEN these lines greet the eyes of the thousands of our readers, the great convocation of the friends of holiness at Landisville, will have been opened; the old 'battle-hymn' will have been sung, holy hands uplifted, and ardent supplications breathed into the Divine ear, and the introductory words of counsel and exhortation spoken.

"There are two classes of our readers at this hour, sustaining vital relations to this meeting:—

"First. Those privileged to attend it. Happy are the eyes that will look upon its scenes, and happy are those hearts that may be under the droppings from above at Landisville. But we would remind all such that the enjoyment of these extraordinary Christian privileges, involves vast responsibilities. Ten days' tenting in the forest, under such circumstances, will call for a solemn reckoning in the Judgment. Be apprised of this; let it rest upon your hearts, ye dwellers for these wonderful days at Landisville! The songs, and prayers, and sermons of this festival of 1873, should stir your hearts to their profoundest depths—draw out your holiest aspirations, and give your whole character a more Christ-like impress; and then remember, dear friends of Jesus, that you are in the forest temple not only to be like Christ, but to do like Christ; and what do we mean by doing like Christ? Doing! Why he was, during each hour of the day, doing the will of his Father in saving erring men. Suffer us then to exhort you lovingly and earnestly—

"1. *Keep your blessed Bible near you at Landisville.* Find time each day to read and ponder it. It is a lamp to your feet, and a light to your path. Hold it well in hand.

"2. *Be sure to pray in secret.* Don't merge private into public devotion. Have some time each day alone with God, in the tent, or at the foot of a tree in some secluded spot. Attendance upon the public meetings will not meet the whole case; be alone with God; speak to your Father when no one else is nigh except the beloved of the family.

"3. *Be eager to win a soul for Jesus.* Be after some one; track him through the forest by day and night, if need be: but be wise in your movements; study the case well; follow up the matter steadily and determinedly, and take fast hold of the promise. *One soul for Jesus!* Let this be the universal motto on the ground. Brother! sister! I charge you to be instant in season and out of season, to win a soul. Souls are bought with blood divine. Jesus is in travail for them; angels are ministering unto them. Up! ye blood-washed people at Landisville—up to the work of winning souls! God help us!

"Second: Those who cannot be at the feast, but who are profoundly interested. We are sorry you cannot be there. God orders your absence—be submissive. Let no murmur escape your lips. Be calm, and sink into his will; but be present in spirit; let your prayer and faith be there in wondrous energy. You can help mightily though a thousand miles away. Perhaps on the coming

Sabbath, on some mountain slope or in an humble vale hundreds of miles away, in the quiet of your rural home, you will read what we are writing. We counsel you to be in close sympathy with us. While the five-o'clock meeting is progressing in the tabernacle, or the love-feast in front of the great stand at eight, or the man of God at ten, lifting up the glorious gospel standard, do you in spirit be in close connection with the work. Your faith may be the hinge of destiny—the conductor of life-forces to human souls. Men of Israel, help! Women of Zion, be much at the throne! See to it that the pentecostal fire is upon every head and heart at Landisville. The word of the Lord abideth forever. Prayer is mighty, and must prevail. Faith is prolific in spiritual results. Keep the angels busy in bearing tidings heavenward this week. O, for the days of the Son of Man and of the mighty descending of the Holy Ghost!"

SET UP THE TABERNACLE.

The morning of Wednesday, July 23d, dawned propitiously. Trains from the four cardinal points of the compass had deposited at the Landisville depot, hopeful companies and heaps of camp equipage. From Massachusetts, Rhode Island, Connecticut, New York and New Jersey, in the East; from Ohio, Indiana, Illinois, West Virginia, and Western Pennsylvania; Maryland, Delaware, and some of the Southern States; and down the Northern Central, from the region of the lakes, the people came, and were speedily transferred to their tents and temporary lodging places in the encampment.

The great National Tabernacle, the pride of Mr. Inskip, (if he has any of that article cleaving to him), was not yet up. Good brother Little, who had been expected from New York to superintend its erection, had gone across the Atlantic, and Mr. Inskip had to hurry forward and direct in the matter himself.

In due time the huge canvas superstructure rose into position on the edge of the outside circle of tents, and they who admiringly traced its history across the continent, its services in the cities and on the plains of the West, and remembered that thousands had been baptized with power under its canopy, greeted once more its symmetrical proportions as it became a feature of the meeting at Landisville.

We had time, during the day, to glance at the topography of the ground, study the sublimity of sunlight on the leafy bower arching gracefully above us, where mighty trees interlocked their boughs, the trunks appearing as pillared aisles in a vast cathedral.

From the depot, where, at right angles, the Reading and Columbia, and Pennsylvania Railroads cross each other, a five-minute walk brings one to the village after which the encampment is named. Rising a gentle slope, we descend on the other side, and find a substantial fence with strong gates for ingress and egress. Inside, we pass through a grand piece of primitive forest, unoccupied except by baggage depot, dormitories, and a boarding tent

2

or two, and crossing a small bridge, we are soon within a circle composed of
family tents, tasteful cottages, and the auditorium gradually rising from an
octagon preaching stand. The ground we suppose to be capable of seating
two or three thousand hearers. The circle itself will accommodate five or
six thousand people. On the outskirts of the camp three boarding estab-
lishments were organized for useful purposes, and

THE RESTAURANT,

a large two-story building, L shaped, and temporarily furnished, gave promise
of unusual comfort in this department. It was under the control of Mr. G.
W. Wanamaker, the popular caterer, of Philadelphia, and superintended by
Mr. Jas. McCormick in the financial, and Mr. Sooy in the culinary responsibilities.

THE NATIONAL ASSOCIATION

was more largely represented the first day than we have ever known at any
former meeting under their auspices. There were present,

The President, Rev. J. S. Inskip, and Mrs. Inskip, Ocean Grove, N. J.
Rev. Seymour Coleman, Williamsport, Pa.
  " G. Hughes and wife, Woodstown, N. J.
  " W. McDonald and wife, Boston, Mass.
  " Dr. Lowry, wife and son, Cincinnati, Ohio.
  " W. H. Boole and friends, New York City.
  " A. McLean, wife and daughter, Hudson, N. Y.
  " W. T. Harlow, Duxbury, Mass.
  " J. B. Foote, Syracuse, N. Y.
  " Dr. Matlack and wife, Wilmington, Del.
  " Dr. Wm. Nast, wife and son, Cincinnati, Ohio.
  " W. L. Gray, Philadelphia.
Mr. Levi Perry and wife, Baltimore, Md.
  " Wm. T. Perkins, Cincinnati, Ohio, and
  " G. M. Brubaker, Millersburg, Pa.
Subsequently Revs. L. R. Dunn, Elizabeth, N. J., Wm. B. Osborn, Ocean
Grove, N. J., J. E. Searles and wife, Brooklyn, N. Y., and John Bent, Bos-
ton, Mass., arrived and participated in the services. Only Messrs. J. A.
Wood, of Madison, N. Y., and C. Munger, of Alfred, Maine, were absent—
the former through indisposition, and the latter detained by pressing engage-
ments in his home field.

The hours of Wednesday passed rapidly and pleasantly as new arrivals
came in with every train, and extra tiers of tents were put in position by Mr.
Grove and his working force, to accommodate unexpected emergencies. We
have an inclination to attempt some description of the trials incident to the
officers of the local association, who were under fire of cross-questioning from

morning until late at night. Our own headquarters being prominent, and adjoining the "Office," we had occasion to sympathize with them, and share to some extent in their tribulations.

One party arrives and must have a tent of specified size and eligible position, right away.

"Did you order your tent beforehand?"

"No; but we want it now."

"We haven't time to attend to you. Why didn't you let us know?"

"O, come; where's your men? Get me a tent at once."

The "Committee" yield, and are about to erect a tent for the homeless when another exclaims : "I ordered a tent; show me where it is."

"Here, before you go, please help me."

"Where's your Post-office?" inquires a lady who arrived early, is nicely fixed, and now must dispatch a letter containing advice of arrival and first impressions.

"Can I obtain lodgings?" asks a clerical looking person with small valice and linen duster, already weary with waiting for some one to attend to him. "Our lodging-rooms are all full," is the reply ; "but if you have a shawl and pillow, we can fix you." He has neither, and wonders he had not the common sense to bring some indispensables of this kind with him. He is finally taken in by some one, at great inconvenience to them, because he lacked "common sense" to provide for himself.

"When will my baggage arrive?" asks a sister. This inquiry is addressed to the person who does *not* attend to that department. Another's checks are misplaced, and the telegraph is brought into requisition. Two days must elapse before the trunk is discovered a hundred miles away.

Yonder stands a group of friends after a long journey. No provision made because they didn't write, and they didn't write because it was only on the spur of an impulse they decided to come.

The hammer and saw are plied with vigor. A pyramid of bunks, and every article in the furniture emporium, disappear, until not even a bucket or a broom can be procured.

"I can get nobody to attend to me"—murmurs one. "I never met such clever people," observes another. "Why there is Mr. G., he met us with smiles, and staid by us until everything was complete for our comfort."

"What do you charge for board here?" is the cautious inquiry at the large restaurant.

"Whatever you please," is the answer. "Here is our bill of fare." Ample variety ; every taste and temperament suited; a meal for ten cents ; or, if on the epicurian style, you can extend your order and gratify your taste at higher rates.

We might here throw in parenthesis, that the restaurant plan, introduced by Bro. Wanamaker, in city style, proves most satisfactory, to all parties, of any we have ever witnessed.

"Twenty men needed to help us raise the Tabernacle!" is the announcement; and soon the ropes are manned, and more than forty gather to see how it is done, exchanging opinions on the laws of dynamics, but forgetting to put their own shoulder to the work.

Friends who met at Oakington, or Asbury Grove, or Round Lake, meet once more. Their acquaintance was formed under memorable auspices; where praise and prayer may "unite to perfect them in one," and is joyfully renewed here.

Some arrive early, and wonder why others are so hurried, and so late. Ah! these unfortunates are never up to time. It has been a long race, and they are always a little behind. They miss the cars, lose their umbrella, have to borrow a watch key, or get into their trunks by the aid of a hatchet; they belong to the irregulars in the skirmish line of life.

The opening of the exercises is delayed because the Tabernacle must be made all taut, before Mr. Inskip, perspiring at the work, can devote his attention to anything else. It may seem a useless expenditure of time and energy to fit up such enlarged accommodations in case of rain, for no rain cloud is visible, the sky is clear, and the forest shade refreshingly beautiful.

All this may be; but rain may come (as it did in torrents,) and then prudent foresight will reap the reward, and the success of the meeting may depend on this very Tabernacle. So Mr. Inskip holds on until the work is done. Then the evening meal is partaken of with thankful zest, and at 6 P. M. the welcome bell gives out its summons for the opening services.

FIRST RELIGIOUS SERVICE.

WEDNESDAY, JULY 23, 1873.

THE hour was still and sweet. Torrid heat became tempered with the gathering haze of evening, and the western sky, as the sun descended, appeared like a fleece of fine gold. Serenity like a mantle spread over the scene, and no better mood could be imagined for devotion than that in which the people responded to the tones of the bell, and hurried out to meeting.

Bearing camp chairs, or taking the nearest seats to the stand, in which all the ministers present were invited to sit, the worshippers filled the space in front, and the congregation soon extended far out into the auditorium. A volunteer voice started "Rock of Ages," and the chorus was echoed by nearly "a thousand tongues"; other stanzas followed, improving the time, until the President of the National Association came forward, hymn-book in hand, and said, " Let us sing the 290th hymn."

He then read through, and the people sung

> "There is a fountain filled with blood,
> Drawn from Immanuel's veins,
> And sinners plunged beneath that flood
> Lose all their guilty stains."

By frequent use and never failing power and interest, this is well entitled

THE "BATTLE HYMN OF THE NATIONAL ASSOCIATION."

From the well-remembered opening day at Vineland in 1867, we believe every National Camp-meeting has commenced with Cowper's immortal lyric, which tells the whole Gospel—sin and ruin, redemption and salvation, full, present and free, in life, in death, and through the singing ages of eternity—all in five sweet stanzas. How it has leaped from joyful lips, or welled from broken hearts! How the woods have resounded with its pæan of peace, and note of victory! How England's poet of a century ago, in the seat he found in heaven through the cleansing blood of which he sung, and set the world singing, has greeted gathering thousands by the banks of the river, who entered into life, and "washed all their sins away," under its promptings of faith in the "dear, dying Lamb!"

The singing was indescribably grand, and as the last refrain ceased, everybody, near and remote, knelt down in prayer. One minute of silence most profound, and then in simple, measured utterance, Mr. Inskip proceeded to supplicate the throne, as follows:

"O Lord, we are once more sent forth to labor for Thee. The moment is one of peculiar solemnity and interest. All of us who have anything whatever to do with this encampment, feel that we have now come to a crisis, and whatever we have done previously to meet the issues here drawn, there is a conscious trembling to enter upon the chief work before us. The secularities connected with this occasion have been pleasantly adjusted. The people have assembled, and the arrangements are all complete and satisfactory. But, O Lord, we are now entering upon the spiritual responsibilities of the meeting. We pray Thee furnish special help. We have no experience to suggest any mode of procedure toward success—no help in ourselves, no endowment for this hour. We need as never before the baptism of the Holy Spirit, that we may perform Thy will. O that the blessed Holy Ghost would come into this congregation and influence every mind and heart!
[Amen.]

" We pray that our dear brethren of the Local Association may have their largest expectations exceeded here. They have prayed that the arm of the Lord might be made bare on this occasion. Lord bless them! Bless the President of the Association, and all his associates wonderfully. If there are any souls in their families unconverted, O Lord, save every one of them. [Amen.] On their own hearts pour out Thy spirit, so.that in all the trials incident to the management of the meeting, they may have great sweetness of spirit, great peace with God, and great power in prayer. [Amen.]

" Lord bless us, their brethren who have come here at their invitation to promote Thy cause. We must have a powerful baptism to do this work. May our brother, the Presiding Elder, and all the preachers on his district, be greatly refreshed and have revivals all over the district, and may many souls be converted.

" We pray God that all ministers who have, or who may come on this ground, may receive a great blessing, to enable them to labor on successfully in their holy calling.

" We ask, O Lord, that this meeting may be fruitful in good results; in the sanctification of every minister on the ground. Send on this people a Pentecost of power beyond anything that has ever occurred since that day of wonders in Jerusalem! Lord, save more souls here than were converted there! Thou canst do a great work, if we have faith in asking. Thou hast told us to ask largely, and promised to help and bless. We ask in the name of Jesus, for awakening and sanctifying grace!

" Let there be such a condition of things here that every person coming inside the gate may see in us a spirit. that shall constrain them to say, we have been with Jesus.

" Go around this ground, my God, and take possession of all hearts. If any are here to make money, may they get uneasy. Let them feel now the touch of Thy hand. Send on us now a token for good. On the stand here; on thy people, and on unbelievers, let Thy presence be felt.

" Repeat Manheim—that spot of historic renown—and go far beyond it in power. Now, Lord, arise for our help, and stay with us until the close, and we'll give Thee all the glory. We will trust Thee before the work is done, that Thou wilt give the victory. Hear our cry! Answer prayer! Thou art able to do exceeding abundantly above all we can ask or think. Glory, glory, glory to the Lamb!

" Some of our brethren who would have been here, are on the streets of the city of the Great King. One "swept through the gates," and another lately died " clinging to the cross."

" My God! if this is the last camp-meeting we shall attend, let it be the best, and thou shalt have 'all the praise. Amen."

ADDRESS OF REV. C. F. TURNER.

Immediately after prayer, Rev. C. F. Turner, Presiding Elder of Susquehanna district, within the bounds of which the meeting was held, addressing Mr. Inskip, said:

"It is with the greatest degree of pleasure, that I, as a sinner converted by the pardoning grace of God, having no merit of my own, no virtue of which I may boast, but trusting in the blood of the Lamb, do welcome you, Mr. President, and your Association, to our midst, and to the charge of this camp-meeting.

"We have looked forward to this day with prayerful and hopeful interest. For months we have been praying and hoping for a wonderful Pentecostal visitation to attend this meeting. We have from our family altars, in our love-feasts and quarterly meetings, and in our public congregations, looked to the "God of Hosts," for His all powerful sin-killing and sanctifying presence.

"We know that the President of the Local Association has united with us ardently in prayer that God may make this meeting to be attended with a power greater in the Holy Spirit's baptism, at this first introductory assemblage and meeting, than that extraordinary and ever memorable meeting at Manheim, only a few miles distant from this place.

"What reason I have to remember that meeting. There, by the constraining influences of the blessed Holy Spirit, I first, with fear and trembling, publicly confessed to the amazing grace and power of God in my full and complete salvation. How can I forget that season when my soul was flooded with heavenly light, and the cleansing blood was so sweetly felt to wash away all my sins!

"But I confidently expect this meeting will exceed Manheim. We are expecting the greatest displays of divine power we have ever known. We are expecting that sinners shall be brought to God by scores, by hundreds, by thousands.

"Again we extend to you, gentlemen of the National Association, a cordial, heartfelt welcome." [Deep sensation all around.]

ADDRESS OF REV. C. I. THOMPSON.

Rev. C. I. Thompson, President of the Landisville Camp-meeting Association, followed the Presiding Elder in an address of welcome, saying :—

"Twelve months ago, at a meeting on this ground, it was proposed in the Board of Control of the Landisville Camp meeting Association, to extend an invitation to the National Camp-meeting Association to hold a meeting during the season of 1873, at this place. This proposal was unanimously accepted. A dispatch was sent to Brother Inskip to visit the grounds, but the dispatch, it appears, did not reach him.

"The President of this Association was then instructed to write and communicate the wishes of our Association.

"At the fall meeting of the National Association, it was determined to accept our invitation, and through Rev. G. Hughes, Secretary of the National Association, we were formally notified of the fact.

"The reason of the Landisville Association in addressing the National, was the hope that through the influence of the latter, a higher Christian influence might be exerted on the surrounding churches, as well as on all who might attend the meeting.

"We are here to day, and everything is favorable, thank God! We have passed through all our secularities pleasantly. Everything augurs good for the church; our hand and heart is most cordially extended to you, and we pray and hope that your largest expectations may be more than realized.

"Only five years ago we first raised our banners in this community—at our first meeting we had one hundred tents. Next year we invited you to Manheim. We had such a meeting that its influence extended all through the surrounding country. I talked with a gentleman on the ground during that remarkable meeting, which you so well remember. He said his soul was never so filled with awe. He had sensations that day such as he had never realized but once before, and that was when, under the magnificent grandeur of the Yo Semite valley, amid its sublime scenery, he felt like bowing down to the earth in humility before a present God. O that the work here may far exceed, in the display of God's power, and in results, that of its predecessor!

"We bid you God speed in this good work, and extend a most hearty welcome to you, Brother Inskip, and brethren of the National Camp-meeting Association."

Again the congregation responded in terms of intense satisfaction.

THE SCRIPTURE LESSON,

consisting of Isaiah xxxv, was then read by Rev. Wm. McDonald—commencing, "The wilderness and the solitary place shall be glad for them, and the desert shall rejoice and blossom as the rose." After which was sung the hymn—

"I am trusting, Lord, in thee."

ADDRESS OF REV. J S. INSKIP.

Rev. J. S. Inskip, apparently much affected by the hearty and earnest greetings which had been extended, rose and said:—

"If we do not have the best meeting here that we have ever held as yet, it will not be because we have not had the best beginning that we have ever had. In no case have the conditions surrounding us been so good; we have never met in a more beautiful grove; and what is most interesting of all, our welcome has been the heartiest we have ever had. We respond with hearts full of emotion to the Presiding Elder and to the President of the Local Association. I will say to them that we are here to do all we can to bring about the conversion and upbuilding and entire sanctifiation of souls.

"I do not expect to get through this meeting without making mistakes; the best make mistakes, and I shall do so, I have no doubt; but I will tell you what I mean to do; I mean to cover all mistakes with the blood before they come. We do not expect to please everybody with whom we come in contact; you have invited us to conduct this meeting, and we intend to do it in our own way, because we believe it is the best way for us. This much by way of preliminary.

"I wish to offer a few practical suggestions Ordinary success at this meeting would not suit our ideas. A repetition of other meetings would not meet my demands. Manheim was great, but Landisville must be greater. I know that there are five hundred Christian hearts here, that break forth in a hearty "Amen." The spirits of the departed looking down from the battlements of heaven, say, "Amen." Lord God, make Landisville the greatest meeting that has ever been known! [Shouts of "Amen."]

"I want to guard you against expecting victory because you have had a triumph heretofore.

"This is the 16th National Camp-meeting, but I have no confidence in success here because God has owned us all through our work. Nothing inspires me with confidence in success here except faith in God. Do not permit yourselves to be deceived; the devil does not intend to let us have success here any more than at Manheim. How well we remember the conditions that surrounded us there! The air itself seemed to be hot, as if intended to parch up and destroy even our power of utterance. You remember how it continued, until, in the midst of prayer, when a few of us had met in the Association's business tent, God sent deliverence. We gained the fight on our knees.

"Satan intends to intrench himself here, and we intend to rout him in God's name, with God's help, and by God's blessing.

"Now this is the work before us; and I want to know, first of all, who will consecrate himself here, so that for the next ten days he will labor in every proper way, and devote himself to this holy work. I know that you have heretofore consecrated yourselves to be wholly the Lord's, and that he has blessed, and owned, and washed you in the blood of the Lamb.

"At Manheim he sanctified some of you; at Vineland, and—but at this place, here, now, this moment, for this work, the occasion, circumstances, and success of our meeting demand the unequivocal consecration of our hearts to God. Let everybody consider that he came here to get every sinner con-

verted. Let the influence of the blessed Holy Spirit so rest on your consecrated hearts that it will seem as if this whole inclosure was surrounded by
a wall of fire, so that when the sinner enters our gates he may feel that he
is standing on holy ground. I believe that God will save sinners here. I
cannot adjust the theology of the matter, in regard to forefate, or free will,
but he says: "If ye shall ask anything in my name, I will do it." O,
blessèd Lord, I ask in thy name, that sinners by scores and hundreds, yea
thousands, may be converted through the influence of this meeting.

"Do you believe God is able to do this? or do you fall back on contingencies?

"Believe God. Let there be no failure of our faith. As the Lord liveth
if a thousand sinners are not converted, it will not be because of my want of
faith. Lord, let it be according to thy word.

* "Get the world fenced out of this enclosure. What do you say? Have
you come here for a pleasant, social time? If so, I hope the place will
become too hot for you. I advise you to move out by moonlight, unless you
go in with us for a grand, mighty, overwhelming time of God's power.

"How say you, can this be done? Readily, and we can win the fight here
to-night. We can do more to-night than at any time, or all the time of the
meeting. We are to gain the victory to-night. We are to win it now, with
God's help.

"I feel like getting down to the substratum of this matter. I like to go
over the thing once in a while.

"Some speak of leaving the cross and blood behind.* I shall do no such
thing. I feel like asking you to pray for me that I may get in deeper. You
are all in sympathy with this movement. [Cries of "yes, yes, we are."] If
you are a preacher, I want you to get sanctified to night, that you may help
others to-morrow and next day. O brothers, this is the way to help on the
meeting.

"If I were to propound doctrine, you might not agree with me; but get the
Holy Spirit, get the experience, and we will have no controversy. We have
been blamed for making this a specialty; but with God's help, we will make
it more so than ever. [Amen.] We offer no apology to do that for which you
have distinctly invited us here.

"This is not an ordinary camp-meeting. Depend upon it, there is one man
here who will do all he can to make this a successful meeting. All can do
something. Keep up family prayer in your tent or cottage; read your
Bible, especially the Epistle to the Ephesians, and the sixteenth and seven-
teenth chapters of John's Gospel. This will help you individually, and
help to make the occasion a success. Keep up private devotion. At the
hour of one P. M., when the bell rings, let every tent be closed. If you are

---

* Referring to some teachings at the late Union Holiness Convention at Ocean Grove.

out anywhere, keel down and talk alone with God. Let this camp ground be as silent as a sea of glass, and it will be perfectly awful to the careless ones who may be sauntering about. O that God will help us in this! It is not a difficult thing to do. The sisters can stop a moment, if washing dishes, or engaged at anything else, and if you have visitors, get down on your knees, and they will begin to inquire, ' What means this ?' Try it on, and see what the Lord will do for us. Every man and woman may pray at that hour, and if you do, this camp will be a centre of interest. Sinners, seeing a few hundred godly men and women on their knees, saying nothing to any one but God, and your children, too, will be constrained to cry, ' What shall we do ?' O, my God, let this be a Pentecost! Will you try to do it? If you will, give me a token. Now raise your hand.

[Hundreds of hands uplifted.] " Now mark, when the bell gives the signal, you promise that you will get down wherever you are. Would God we Protestants would excel the Roman Catholics in devotion. They will kneel on a public street. Let us be more bold, and richer blessings will flow into our hearts.

" I would not have any of you worn out by ceaseless service, but go to as many as you can; don't dissipate thought in your tents; be steady, serious, and true to this great principle.

" Now, friends, we are in for a fearful, a terrible contest for success and salvation.

" I'd advise you to take as little of this world along with you as possible. Strip for the race. Don't get into debate, or feel yourself called upon to argue. Keep telling your experience—' The blood of Jesus Christ cleanseth us from all sin.' Some may get tired of hearing it, if they don't get in themselves. They will try to decoy you into controversy; but, remember, all arguing is to be done at the stand. We come here not so much to argue as to assert, demonstrate, proclaim, and announce the truth as it is in Jesus.

" No doubt we shall argue a little, but you will be deceived if you have come to hear us attempt to settle people's quibbles. We are to hold up the banner of full salvation, and go down into the pool to be washed and made every whit whole.

' This is not fair,' you say. Yes, it is fair. You get this blessing and we'll take your creed, whatever it may be; that is, we will then find that there is very little difference between us.

"" This experience wonderfully consolidates all differences. Then tell the story! keep telling it. The matter has been discussed in some quarters until men get to the point of discussing with the ' dis' left off! ' The blood cleanseth!' Let this be repeated a thousand times a day, and they will believe it, if we keep on. Good Lord, help us to overcome ' by the blood of the Lamb and the word of our testimony.' But you doubt this. We don't. Bless God, we know it is true. This is the happy way to win the fight. Any of us can be tripped up if we go into the speculative questions. Let us keep to the fundamental idea. They may say we are people of 'one idea.' So we are, but it is a mighty big one. Good Lord, help us. I want now to go down here and wait for the Holy Ghost to come upon me. Do you think the Lord is able and willing to bless us now? Let us prove him. Get down, brethren, all of us. I will; will you?"

Following the leader, all the ministers present left the stand and knelt at the altar of prayer. The people crowded in, and soon hundreds were prostrate before God, pleading the promise, and believing for the power.

The sublime scene was intensified by a suggestion from Mr. Inskip saying, "Now, pray for the ministers here." After a short time he replied, "I feel your prayers; I feel your prayers. Now, let us ministers in turn pray for the people." There was another pause, improved by silent prayer, after which was sung

> "Take my poor heart and let be
> Forever closed to all but thee," &c.

With deep feeling brother Inskip said, "One more verse; one more verse;" and in softly subdued tones were sung the words:—

> "Here at the cross where flows the blood," &c.

At the close of the singing, Dr. Lowry led in prayer, and the people took hold in faith; souls were filled unutterably; but quiet was obtained. "Just wait here," said brother Inskip; "wait, the Lord is going to save the people. Whisper it all around to one another—'Jesus saves me now.' Tell it all over the ground. Separating here for the night, let this be our salutation. Keep it in mind—'Jesus saves me.'"

Notices were then given of the daily order of services, beginning at five A. M. on Thursday morning, and with a hearty doxology the congregation retired to their tents, shaking hands and saying, "Jesus saves me."

We append the arrangement for each day's service:—

Five o'clock A. M., consecration meeting.

Half-past six o'clock A. M., family prayer and breakfast.

Eight o'clock A. M., general love-feast with an invitation to seekers of heart purity.

Ten A. M., sermon at the main stand. (No other exercises allowed during public preaching.)

Half-past twelve o'clock P. M., dinner.

Half-past one P. M., bell tap for private prayer. Tent curtains to be closed, and all conversation hushed.

Half-past one P. M., children's church, tent meetings and social exercises.

At this hour each day the National Committee meet for counsel, prayer and making appointments.

Half-past two o'clock P. M., sermon, followed by exhortation, prayer, and experience. At five, social meetings may be started.

Half-past five o'clock P. M., supper hour, followed by experience meetings in tents and cottages until evening service.

Half-past seven o'clock P. M., until ten P. M., preaching and altar work, which must cease at the moment the bell rings for retiring.

A PENCIL SKETCH OF THE SUNRISE SERVICES.

In the devotion of every hour, and almost of every moment during each succeeding day of a National Camp Meeting, to active religious exercises, a decided advantage is gained and the largest possible results secured. There is no time allowed for either a lazy siesta or the vapid tattle of unoccupied loungers in tents or shady spots where social pleasantries undo all the serious impressions which song and sermon may have produced. From the hour of sunrise until 10 P. M. the camp presents a busy scene.

"With us no melancholy void,
No moment lingers unemployed,
Or unimproved below."

The management is a despotism. Everybody and everything must bow to the control of one master mind. That mind, imbued by a fervor extraordinary and guided by supernatural wisdom and power, holds the congregation in a steady, unrelaxing grasp. To rebel, in any case, is to mar the grand end in view so far as it relates to the individual and universal good to be attained.

In this chapter we merely touch the first service of the day. The bell is vigorously rung at 15 minutes before 5 A. M. If the weary night watchman, about that hour, is not on the alert, a member of the National Association may be seen issuing from his tent and hurrying towards the bell-rope. Another, after a hasty toilet and just from his knees before God, takes his way toward the Tabernacle. He was designated the previous day to take charge of the early service. From all parts of the camp may be seen hurrying toward the same destination, camp-chair in hand and sleep hardly out of their eyes, men and women, whose desire for spiritual enlightment overmasters all other considerations. A few are already there on their knees, having had no chance for private prayer in the crowded company tents; others are reading out of pocket Bibles, or Testaments, "the words of this life."

The leader, reaching his place, starts a hymn—"O for a thousand tongues," &c., or "A charge to keep I have," or some other with which all are supposed to be familiar, and the melody rising, reaches many ears in distant parts of the ground. Before the song is ended the assembly has assumed pretty fair proportion,s and increases in numbers every moment.

"Now we will spend ten minutes in prayer," suggests the leader. "Leave out all but the personal pronouns. Confine your range to the present day, hour, moment, me. Lord, bless me."

One minute will suffice for a brother to say, "O Lord, fill me with Thy holy presence this morning, and create within me a clean heart, for Jesus' sake. Amen." Another will break forth in joyous acknowledgement of peace or power received the day or evening previous. A third cries, "O Jesus, my Saviour, make me every whit whole!" Often two or three start simultaneously, and the preachers, who begin to drop in, join in brief petitions. The tide of earnestness and confidence grows apace. The sun bursts forth and transfigures the kneeling company, until, with a happy song, the scene changes and "a word of exhortation" is given to guide the further devotions. "It will help us to ascertain how many here are clear in their experience of a heart purified by the blood of Christ. Let all such stand up for a moment."

This "standing up a moment" is of itself, to some who obey the suggestion without carping or questioning the brother's right to handle them in that manner, a means of grace, an exercise of faith and an increase of joy and victory. "Now let us see who are earnestly seeking this blessing. If you want to be fully saved now, listen to the Divine word : ' I have heard thee in a time accepted, and in the day of salvation have I succored thee. Now is the accepted time ; behold, now is the day of salvation.' All who want it in God's way and time, now rise up."

To see twenty, thirty, or fifty persons, old and young, preachers, official members, mothers, young men and maidens rise, and note the earnestness of their looks, the tears filling some eyes, and the transition from doubt and unrest to sweet peace, for this often occurs in the very movement, makes a profound impression on all. Conviction widens out among those hitherto reluctant to take any advanced step. Seekers bow at the altar, and again prayer is made, those pleading for a clean heart being urged to utter their petitions audibly.

The speaking then commences with those just blessed, extending to others, and the kindled fire catches all around.

By this time the stand is full and the large tent crowded. A bell is heard, the signal for breakfast ; but unheeded for half an hour more in this communion of saints. Their unrestrained exclamations of praise fill the camp as they continue to speak one to another. Thus every day, of eight or more, successively begins, and souls thoroughly interested in their own and others' salvation are constantly reminded of the psalmist's exclamation, " It is a good thing to give thanks unto the Lord, and to sing praises unto Thy name, O Most High : To show forth Thy loving kindness in the morning, and Thy faithfulness every night." And again, " My heart is fixed, O God, my heart is fixed ; I will sing and give praise. Awake up, my glory ; awake psaltery and harp ; I myself will awake early."

To facilitate the early awakening and a good start in " holy duties " the rule is absolute, requiring all exercises to be suspended and perfect quiet to reign in the camp after ten o'clock at night. It needs repeated admonitions and exhortations from Mr. Inskip to convince the people of the propriety and necessity of sound sleep, and enough of it, for health and vigor. If excited companies retire to their tents and begin to pray and sing, as they are generally prompted to do, until half-a-dozen are so blessed that they must shout, an officer is detailed to stop the untimely disturbance, or the stentorian command rings out from the President, who, instead of retiring himself, makes a patrol of the grounds to see that others are enabled to rest. " *Stop that noise !* ; hold in until morning ; this is the hour for repose ; we must have quiet here, or we cannot sleep !" These tones sonorously reverberate through the entire grove, and silence most profound ensues. " God bless brother Inskip," is the hearty utterance of tired, nervous people, who have been kept awake by noisy neighbors. A good night's rest, therefore, is the preparation for a joyful morning meeting ; and the general sanitary regulations insisted upon during the continuance of the camp conduce very largely to bodily health, mental regularity, and above all, clearness of spiritual perception and fullness of religious peace.

These meetings, arbitrary as are their rules, have become models of management, good order, and the highest social privilege. But obstinate, narrow-minded men find them too exacting, and should either stay away or yield at once, and move with the mighty current as it flows onward from day to day, until, in personal peace with God and all mankind, they are enabled to acquiese joyfully in every measure that contemplates the helping of souls nearer to Jesus, and from the barren heath of verbal criticism they come into possession of the grace of our Lord Jesus Christ, the love of God and the communion of the Holy Ghost.

SECOND DAY.

OUTLINE SKETCH OF THE MORNING SERVICES.

AT 5 o'clock A. M. the battle for the Lord was renewed on this ground consecrated afresh by the deeply interesting services of last evening. Every one of the Lord's hosts seemed to come forth confident of victory. Hence, at this early hour, hundreds were soon hearkening to the voice of their leader, joining him in singing what might well be called the Christian's morning hymn-call to duty and privilege:

> " Arise, my soul arise,
>   Shake off thy guilty fears,
> The bleeding sacrifice
>   In my behalf appears."

With the chorus:

> " Jesus paid it all,
>   All to Him I owe ;
> Sin hath left a crimson stain—
>   He washed me white as snow."

After the prayer by Rev. John Thompson, others quickly followed in strains of pleading earnestness, imploring to be emptied of self and then filled with divine fullness ; to be made willing to be used anywhere and any-how for Jesus ; to have the power to wait for the baptism ; to understand that the short way to Jesus is down through the valley, and there to realize as never before that the blood of Christ washes us from all sin !

When their searching prayers were ended, the congregation sung:

> " Break off the yoke of inbred sin," &c.

A brother said, " I can't have full rest till I am cleansed."

Leader—" Sing that verse over again."

> " Break off the yoke," &c.

Then followed the testimonies and confessions of preachers and laity in such rapid succession that no moment was lost. These experiences were almost entirely comprised in confession of the cleansing power of Jesus' blood, the testimony being clear and unequivocal as to the conscious knowl-edge of the sanctification of the soul from all sin. During the meeting the enthusiasm rose to such a height as to call forth utterances of burning elo-quence and thrilling power. One, testifying, said, " I want the Lord Jesus to glorify himself in me. If God choose to put me in the dust and to keep me there, I will say, Lord Jesus glorify thyself." Another, " I feel great anxiety for this meeting. I want it to be the best meeting that was ever held on this continent; not for myself or the National Association, but for the glory of God."

PRAYER MEETING AT 8 O'CLOCK A. M.

This meeting, like the one above alluded to, was held in front of the public stand. It was in charge of the President of the Association. There was a degree of originality in the method of conducting it which shows the great anxiety of those in the management of these exercises not to have them degenerate into a mere form. Brother Inskip arose and said, when about to open the meeting, "Any one of you having a word from the Lord, give it to us. It may be a precious word; some message sent from God to guide us. I have this word now coming into my soul : 'If ye ask anything in my name I will do it for you.'" A brother in the congregation—" I have this : 'Come unto me and I will give you rest.'" A sister—"Abide in me and I in you; if ye abide in me and my words abide in you, ye shall ask what ye will and it shall be done unto you." Rev. Mr. Foote: "And this is the confidence we have in him, that if we ask *anything* according to his will, he *heareth* us."

Brother Inskip—" Brother Foote, where is that ? Will some one please find it ?" A young brother, standing up, read it, to the comfort of many hearts.

Other passages of Scripture were quoted promptly and clearly, occupying several minutes, when brother Inskip said, " I propose that we go before God, taking any one of these promises on which to make our plea, but believing them all. But first let us put our prayer into a hymn. Singing :

"O for a heart to praise my God,
A heart from sin set free ;
A heart that always feels thy blood
So freely spilt for me."

"Let us sing another verse."

"Refining fire, go through my heart," &c.

Brother Inskip—" Now I want to know how many of you are here whom the Lord has wholly sanctified. Whoever you are, hold up your hand. (Many hands raised.) There are some here that want this perfect cleansing. Hold up your hands. (Several hands upraised) Now let us have this altar clear. Let all who want the blessing, come. Let those who want a special consecration for the work now before us, come. Now I see but two classes before me: those who want to be washed in the blood and cleansed from every sin, and those who want the power to do work for Jesus as they have never done it before. And now, brethren, I want a new order of prayer. I am not particular about any one's leading in prayer ; but if any

3

of you feel like praying, don't use the ' you ' and ' our ' and ' us;' but use the first personal pronoun ' I ' and ' me.' Lord bless me, *me !*"

After spending a few interesting moments in personal prayer, a brother said, " Jesus taught us how to pray at the grave of Lazarus."

Brother Inskip—" Let us have it, brother."

" And Jesus lifted up his eyes and said, ' Father, I thank Thee that Thou hast heard me. And I know that Thou hearest me always ; but because of the people which stand by I said it, that they may believe that Thou hast sent me.' And when he had thus spoken he cried with a loud voice, ' Lazarus, come forth.' "

Several voices—" That's it ; O glory !" Singing on their knees :

> " I am coming Lord, coming now to Thee,
> Wash me, cleanse me in Thy blood,
> That flowed on Calvary."

Brother Inskip—" It seems that there is a voice in my soul saying : ' Tell the people to wait, to wait ; tell them to get down very low ; to go down to the foundation rock, for the stream is coming over us.' " Amid shouts, the song is sung : "O, the blood," &c. " Now pause a moment and reflect ; close your eyes, let everybody else alone, just think about the blood, the blood that cleanseth."

After several minutes of solemn stillness, the song, " O, the blood," was repeated, which being sung, was followed by the experience of several, among whom Rev. Dr. Nast, author of " Nast's Commentary," made an interesting statement :

" I bless the Lord that I have come here ; I look upon these scenes with thrilling joy. More than thirty years ago I was in this part of the country living near this spot. And O, what the Lord has done for me ! I am dead to sin. I am crucified with Christ. I am saved through the blood of the Lamb. I am glad to come here to tell it. I want to tell it to my German brethren who know me here. Glory be to God !"

At the conclusion of these exercises, the bell announced the hour of public preaching, and soon the increasingly large audience were seated under the magnificent forest trees to hear the word of the Lord.

The preacher was a tall, plain, devout man of four score years, who for more than half that period has been an advocate of personal holiness. His manner of preaching is marked by very frequent wanderings—from his text, to the consciences of his hearers. He is noted for terseness, and an exhaustless fund of anecdote, which he uses to rebuke sin, satirize the fashions of a godless world, and illustrate the short way of salvation by simple, present faith. He is widely known and loved as " Father Coleman."

SERMON BY REV. S. COLEMAN, OF WILLIAMSPORT, PA.

THURSDAY, 10 A. M.

" Elect according to the foreknowledge of God the Father through sanctification of the Spirit, unto obedience and sprinkling of the blood of Jesus Christ."—I Peter 1, 2.

This address of the apostle Peter was made to the strangers who dwelt in Pontus, Galatia, and other places. He addressed a people that were scattered abroad because of the persecutions of the day; they were in the midst of great distress, hiding in the dens and caves of the earth, hunted like wild beasts of the forest; but they were the children of God. I thought, perhaps, we would need such an address to us this morning, for though we are not persecuted in the same way, perhaps, yet we have our fiery persecutors around us.

Now we have set before us the amazing plan of God to save the world. They are elect according to the foreknowledge of God through the sanctification of the Spirit. We have here a reference to the condition of man towards God, ruined by sin, and gone far away from him; and of God towards man, who, looking upon him in his wretched and perishing condition, moved towards him in love and mercy. God so loved man that he could not bear to see him lost; he looked about to see how he could save him, and he brought out this most wonderful plan. It was his own contriving, but it was the strangest thing that ever was known; it is the strangest now; it must be the strangest in all time, that he should so contrive, after man's sin, that all the blame should not be laid upon man, but on himself. Instead of the sinner's suffering the penalty, God laid the plan to suffer himself. To do this, he had to come out in a new character, never before revealed to men. He had to have a new name corresponding to that character,—the name of Jehovah; and in the further revelation of himself, the I Am; and still further the name Immanuel—God with us. Oh! the wondrous plan of God; he had it all arranged as to what he would do beforehand. Hence the text says it was done according to the foreknowledge of God. He foresaw that the evil of sin would be remedied by calling to him his elect through the sanctification of the Spirit. God saw the way all though his plan, or he never would have undertaken to do it. It was so stupendous that the suffering of pain, privation and sorrow, was lost sight of, because of the glorious result of saving lost human beings. So of Christ it was said, "Who for the joy that was set before him, endured the cross, despising the shame." Yet he saw the wondrous plan would save man so perfectly that he forgot the cross, and suffering, and shame, in contemplating the finished salvation of his brethren.

A great deal has been said about foreknowledge. We have not time to go through that subject, nor does it materially concern us to take up the question about which so many silly utterances have been made. All that God foreknew, so far as the text is concerned, was that the elect, through the sanctification of the Spirit unto obedience, should be saved. But how can this be done? Now see what his plan is: 1st. It takes hold of man when he is dead in trespasses and in sin. "When we were dead," says the apostle. If there were any who were not dead, the plan will not do for them; but his great love comprehends them that are dead in sin. 2d. His plan was to contrive to communicate himself to them, and this communication is made in the time of saving them from sin. It is by the Spirit, which goes right to the heart, and talks of the great salvation. It is a part of God's programme. Man would never have known that God had elected him but by the Holy Ghost. Now mark the process. The Holy Ghost reproves man for his sins, and fills the heart with trouble on account of the same. He brings them to adopt God's plan of obedience to the truth. They then, by his guidance, forsake all evil ways to get out of trouble; but he shows them the Lord Jesus Christ, and looking through him to the Father, they get out of trouble. When they come into this condition, they think and say they never mean to sin again; they never will get away from the joyful state, they are so jealous on the subject, and happy all the day long. And God, so great in his goodness, continues to shine upon them through their hearts, and while he thus shines upon them, he so reveals matters to them that they see that all is not as they want it. For he shows every thing in them, like the motes that may be seen in the sunbeam, though they cannot be seen where the ray of the sun does not fall. It is in this light they see something wrong, and they have a hard time of it. The difficulty complained of, is that they can't get along right. When they thought all was right, they find it is not so. Like the apostle Paul, they find that when they would do good, evil is present with them, and they are in distress; they delight in the law of the Lord after the inner man; but they still are not right, until looking through the medium of the light they are made to say, "It is no more I, but sin that dwelleth in me." Paul had the idea that God thought as much of the body as of the soul; hence he made provision for the subjugation of the law of the members. He would not have that variance; he would not rest until that matter was disposed of; he was determined to have religion inside as well as outside; unlike many Methodists of the present day, who are satisfied with the outside only.

Great attempts are made to make figs grow on thistles, and grapes on thorns. It won't do; we can't get along in that way. We have come here to get the inside right. Oh! how many Methodists go about the country grumbling and complaining, walking in heaviness and darkness, never daring to say, nor able to say, "My ways please the Lord." So it will be just as long as the religion you have is all outside. Oh, such people! God can't get a recommendation of his plan at all from professors like these; and on this account many get into difficulty, and make it difficult for other men to be religious, who, if they are converted, do not stay converted very long. God has made an arrangement for all to do better than that. Of your ownselves, you can no more live right than a broken watch can keep good time. Do you think God has made such a shiftless work as that by which he would save the soul? I tell you he has not. If you keep crying up failure in this matter, you make the assertion that the blame falls on God.

Now God stands ready to take away the trouble. And he has notified us of it, and urged us to receive the power adequate to remove the difficulty. Will you do it now? I can't grumble about going on foot if my friend offers to take me in his carriage all the way, nor can you grumble about your troubles as you have done, when God offers to take away the whole difficulty. The saints of whom Peter speaks were elected unto obedience and the sprinkling of the blood. As is said in Ezekiel, "Behold I will sprinkle you with clean water ; from all your idols I will cleanse you, and I will take away the evil out of your hearts, and will put my spirit upon you." If God will do that there is no hard work about it. How he will do it I do not know. God has his way of doing it ; he says the Holy Ghost shall come upon thee, and will perfectly cleanse and wash away your impurity. And when you are cleansed, you will be set apart, sanctified for the Master's use.

Now, sisters, you know what I mean. You do not, after having used your dishes, set them away soiled and dirty ; but you see that they are washed, and then set back to be used whenever they are again required.

The Lord hath set apart him that is godly for himself. He washes in the blood of Christ ; cleanses as the sanctuary was cleansed by the blood of sprinkling ; as the temple and the tabernacle were thus purified and made holy, so God, through the blood, keeps us for himself elected unto obedience ; then, indeed, the great election takes place, God saying of the blood-washed soul, " He is mine."

Some talk about election to heaven and eternal life, or to hell and eternal death. Now, as I look at it, these places are appointed and fixed to the two classes, the washed and the unwashed ; how foolish then to talk of election to either of the places. These and such like errors have come from learned men. I do not undervalue education, but men of learning have been the authors of the most tremendous errors that have ever come upon the world. We have more to fear from men of learning than we have from the devil, for the errors are the more damaging, as they, through their learning, are the more influential. The text says nothing about being elected to heaven ; but it speaks of election unto obedience. A great many seem to want to accept of election unto obedience, but they can't ; God has elected them unto obedience through the sanctification. What is needed is here fully made up ; by this we have the witness of the Spirit, so that whatever we are called to pass through, God says, by the Holy Spirit "that's right." And in all our life-work the Lord keeps whispering, "That's right." One of God's elect through the sanctification of the Spirit, is plunged into the depths of poverty ; but the Spirit says, "That's right, my child." If cast down by affliction, we hear the word of the Spirit again, "That's right, my child, that's right." God knows better where to lead us than we do ourselves. If the devil tempts, that's right ; God will make the devil's wrath to praise him. I am surprised that the old fiend has not been disgusted with his success long ago, and quit his business. For, as long as he is tempting the soul that is set apart for God, he is only increasing the glory that awaits the tempted.

It was told of Bishop Whatcoat that the devil tempted him by suggesting to him once, "You have made a miserable failure in preaching." Whatcoat said : "Well, what more could you expect of me ? I'll fail if I can save souls." And when, after that, he was more successful, Satan tempted him to pride by saying, "You have done so well." Whatcoat said, "If so, glory to God ; I want to preach well to save souls for Jesus's sake." If we are God's, the place where he puts us is the best place for us, and then if the devil tries to hurt us, God will make the hurt the best thing that could take place.

We are elected to the sprinkling of the blood of Jesus Christ. You know when Israel was in Egypt, God qualified Moses and Aaron for their work of leading out the hosts of Jacob, by commanding that a lamb should be slain, and the blood be taken, and the lintels of the door, and the posts, should be sprinkled with the blood of the slain lamb.   That night, when the destroying angel went forth, there was life and protection in all houses covered by the blood; but in the houses of the Egyptians there was death.   The text, I think, refers to this.   So those that are sprinkled by the blood of Christ are defended by the blood.   In the calm, serene passages of human life, God says of those under the cover of the blood, "Don't touch him;" if through the fire, or water, or flood, God's eye is over us as he speaks, saying, " Don't touch that child, he is covered with a robe washed in the blood of the Lamb."

Oh Lord! help us to put it on to-day—now; so that the holy law of God, seeing on us the sprinkled blood, says "all right."   When the blood is on us no calamity can befall us; it is all right.   By and by we shall have to die; but what of that, if we have the blood of sprinkling on us.   When Cookman started for the sweep through the gates, what did he see?   The blood!—the blood of the Lamb!   May God help us to be washed to-day!

OBSERVATIONS.

THE venerable man of God, in his usual rapidity of manner, pressed home on the careless conscience the beauty and blessedness of the white-robed righteousness of Messiah.   His closing allusion to one undying name, Cookman, and every reference to that ascended and redeemed ambassador of Jesus, incidentally made in the course of preaching, prayer, or experience, had the effect to stir every heart with emotion, and start the tear of Christian sympathy.   How strange the ways of God!   By what we supposed to be the untimely removal of our brother from his usefulness on earth, God redoubled the power of his influence, and made his death a ministry of glad tidings, that shall roll on with the ages.

The movement, after a few words of exhortation following Father Coleman's sermon, was quite general on the part of those who were earnestly seeking the predestined " sprinkling of the blood of Jesus," to the altar of prayer.

The reactionary forces, so common at ordinary camp-meetings, are hardly perceptible here.   One of the most thrilling meetings, like that just before preaching, is followed by another and still better one.   Dullness and exhaustion are kept at bay by a lively variety in all the services, and an earnestness of spirit which rises above everything formal or frivolous.

We miss at this meeting many of the features which characterized Manheim.   The number of social meetings is greatly diminished.   Mrs. Keene is absent, but laboring for the Master elsewhere.   R. P. Smith is teaching the simple life of faith and love to interested crowds across the Atlantic, where also Dr. Boardman is laboring.   Dr. and Mrs. Palmer are busy as usual, but in a distant field.   The sisters Lois and Cassie Smith, enfeebled in health, are in seclusion, listening to catch the notes of victory from afar ; and we observe as yet no companies or company tents open to social services.   This is not to be deplored, especially during the early period of the meeting. Concentration for purposes of unity in doctrine and the general leading of the Spirit, tends to harmony and power. As the days pass on, we shall doubtless find the work developing, and the usual tendencies of religious sympathy evinced in bringing neighbors and friends of particular localities closer together for mutual help and encouragement. Meanwhile, the supervision of the National Association is exercised over every service, and the watchwords of the camp are : Prompt attendance at every meeting ; ceaseless prayer for the outpouring of the Spirit, and personal faith in Jesus for the glorious manifestation of his saving and sanctifying power.

SERMON BY REV. A. LOWREY, D. D., OF CINCINNATI.

THURSDAY, 2½ P. M.

" Have Faith in God."—Mark 11 : 22.

A superficial acquaintance merely with the New Testament will convince any man of ordinary perception that faith is an important element in the Christian religion.

It is one of its distinctive features, as no other type of religion has ever given so great prominence to faith. The Bible, so far as the Old Testament is concerned, is largely a history of faith. The New Testament is extensively a treatise on faith ; an exposition of the doctrine, duty and results of faith. The scheme of redemption is penetrated in every part by the conditionality of faith. The life of a Christian is a life of faith in opposition to a life of sense and groveling materialism. Faith enters into all the heights and depths and complexities of Christian experience. It is not only instrumental, but substantive. It is essential to the nature, vital to the existence, and indispensable to the growth of spiritual life. It has both invigorating and nutritive properties. By it the texture of the inner man is built up and developed into completeness and maturity.

Allow us to engage your attention with the *nature, origin, object* and *uses* of faith. Faith, as used in the Scriptures, is an equivocal term. With belief as its reigning idea, it has different shades of meaning. In its lowest sense, it implies only a cold intellectual assent to religious truth, independent of good works. For example : " What doth it profit, my brethren, though a man say he hath faith and have not works ? Can faith save him ?" That is, can the mere faith of credence, or the foreboding faith of trembling devils, save a man ?

Faith is sometimes put for the entire code of Gospel precepts, as in the text. A great company of the priests were obedient to the faith ; that is, they submitted to the general requirements of the Gospel. Faith is also used as a symbol of Christianity or title of believers. For instance, " As we have therefore opportunity let us do good unto all, especially unto them who are of the household of faith ; " that is, the family of believers called " the household of faith," are to have the precedence in our charities.   Some degree of discrimination in the bestowment of our benefices seems allowable.

Literally, and according to the meaning of the original word (*pistis*) faith imports persuasion, confidence and trust.   Parkhurst, in defining the Greek term, says : " It generally implies such knowledge of, assent to, and confidence in certain divine truths, especially those of the Gospel, as produce good works." Dr. Dwight says : " The faith of the Gospel is that emotion of the mind which is called trust or confidence exercised towards the moral character of God, and particularly of the Saviour."   We accept their statements as good general definitions.   According to them, the first thing necessary to evangelical faith is religious instruction.   The second is a convinced judgment; the third is a confiding motion of the heart and mind called trust, by which we renounce every other refuge and shut ourselves up to the merits of Christ for salvation.

As Dr. Bunting justly remarks, " It is such a hearty concurrence of the will and affections with the plan af salvation, as implies a renunciation of every other refuge, and an actual trust in the Saviour and personal apprehension of his merits."   Such a belief of the Gospel and such a reliance on the atonement, as leads us to come to Christ, to receive Christ, and to commit the keeping of our souls into his hands in humble confidence of his power and willingness to save.   Mr. Wesley gives a definition, as we might expect, essentially evangelic and spiritual.   He writes, " Christian faith is then not only an assent to the whole Gospel of Christ, but also a full reliance on the blood of Christ ; a trust in the merits of his life, death and resurrection ; a recumbency upon him as our atonement, and our life as given for us and living in us.   It is a sure confidence that a man hath in God, that, through the merits of Christ, his sins are forgiven and he reconciled to the favor of God ; and in consequence hereof a closing with him and cleaving to him as our wisdom, righteousness, sanctification and redemption, or, in one word, our salvation."

Now faith in the sense of trust, which is peculiar to Gospel belief, is necessary to spiritual life.   For many persons have been sufficiently instructed in religion and also convinced of its truths, who remain unhealed of sin.   Perhaps I now address a multitude who believe in the being of God, the inspiration of the Scriptures ; the divinity and Messiahship of Christ ; the necessity and virtue of the atonement ; the possibility and indispensableness of pardon and the new birth ; the gift and offices of the Holy Ghost, as well as to assent to all the minor and relative proportions of Christian belief; and yet, with this large and true faith they remain dead in trespasses and sin.   What is the matter ? Is there no balm in Gilead, is there no physician there ?   Why, then, is not the health of the daughter of my people recovered ?   It is not the want of faith, but the want of that property of faith which alone appropriates—the property of trust—the property of reliance.   It is that desperate self-renunciation, and universal abandonment of every other refuge, which, looking up to Jesus, says :

> " Other refuge have I none,
> Hangs my helpless soul on Thee :
>
> " Could my tears forever flow,
>   Could my zeal no languor know,
> These for sin could not atone,
> Thou must save, and Thou alone :
>
> " In my hands no price I bring,
> Simply to the cross I cling."

Some, however, use another subterfuge in order to quiet the uneasy and painful sensations of the mind, and obscure the fearful events and responsibilities of eternity. They preposterously assert that they do trust in Christ and have, as others, hope of salvation. And yet they never shed a penitential tear, nor breathe a prayer for mercy, nor quit their cherished sins. They may not be steeped in depravity, but the ungodliness to which they are constitutionally prone, they allow, and love and practice.

Now life and death are not more widely separated and incompatible than this faith differs from that of a living Christian or true penitent. It is the faith of presumption, a trust that Christ will save them in their sins without saving them from their sins. It is a conceit, a delusion which seeks to accomplish an absurdity, a moral impossibility. It makes Jesus, not a Saviour from sin, but a mere warrantee against hell and misery, in defiance of sin, and in harmony with sin. This cannot be: "For what communion hath light with darkness and what concord hath Christ with Belial?"

That faith which is connected with salvation lets light in upon the corruptions of the heart, produces penitential tenderness and creates aversion to sin. Then it puts us upon the pursuit of salvation. It feels after saving merits and healing virtues. It looks up to Jesus, takes hold of his promises, leans hard on his atonement, makes fast the fingers of its confidence in the gory wounds of his side, and finally settles down upon the conviction that Christ has become to him wisdom, righteousness, sanctification and redemption. Now faith is to him "the substance of things hoped for, the evidence of things not seen."

2. *The origin of Faith.* There are always two opposite beliefs on this point. Some men have taken the position that faith is an exclusive and arbitrary gift of God. Others, by consequence, have leaned to the opposite extreme, and represented faith as the independent act of man. It will be easy to show that both these propositions involve error, and that the truth lies at the mean distance between these polemic poles. The Scriptures clearly teach that faith is in part the gift of God, and in part the exercise of a free and responsible agent. The power to believe is of God, the appropriation and use of that power is the work of the suppliant, whether penitent sinner or seeker of holiness.

That there is a sense in which faith is the gift of God is sufficiently manifest from the following texts: "Looking unto Jesus the author and finisher of our faith."—Heb. 12 : 2. "And the Apostles said unto the Lord increase our faith."—Luke 17 : 5. These passages evince that God is concerned in the origin, increase and perfecting of our faith. And it is quite evident that without the inspiration of power giving to the mind believing biases, no man would and no man could reverse the unbelieving tendencies of his nature, and have faith in God in the sense of the text. He might have the faith of a deist, which is cold as a moon-beam, and bounded by the icebergs of materialism; but the faith of a Christian, which pulsates with life and love, and mantles itself with the leaves, and flowers, and fruitage of usefulness, he cannot have without divine help inspiring him with Godward inclinations and trustful dispositions. But other considerations clearly show that the exercise of the power to believe is the act of man. And this exercise is not necessitated. Whether we will believe or not, is a contingency that hinges upon our volitions. The first proof of this position is the serious fact that we are made responsible for our faith. To believe is a duty positively commanded of all men. Not to believe is a punishable offence. " He that believeth and is baptized shall be saved, but he that believeth not shall be damned." The acts of God are irresponsible ; but the acts of men are either rewardable or punishable, according to their moral character. Hence as believing is to be rewarded with salvation, and unbelief is punishable with damnation, it must be man's own proper and responsible act. Another evidence is founded upon the conditionality of salvation. According to the Scriptures, faith is the sole condition of salvation. Paul says, " Therefore we conclude that a man is justified by faith without the deeds of the law." Rom., 3 : 28. Now if faith is exclusively the gift of God, then salvation is tendered to us on a condition which God himself performs, or necessitates us to perform. That is, he makes justification conditional and unconditional at the same time, which is a bold absurdity. We reach then this conclusion that faith is a joint work. The power to believe is given to us of God, the employment of that power, styled belief, is required of us on the part of God. And while God freely inspires the power; yet he will no more believe for us than he will repent or pray for us.

And having bestowed the ability he will not hold any man guiltless; nor suffer him to go unpunished who lives or dies in unbelief. And the assumption is not improbable that we all have vastly more power to believe than we use. It is, with us, a buried talent—a wasted force. In the case of infidels, it is a misapplied and perverted force. But should there be a lack of power it may be supplemented at any time by an appeal to God. Lord, I believe ; help thou my unbelief. It is at this point that the utility of prayer comes in and co-ordinates with faith. Prayer recuperates the wasted energies, and replenishes the fires of unbelief. We must recollect, however, that prayer for more power to believe is but solemn mockery if we do not use what we have. God helps those who help themselves. It was only when the handful of meal in the barrel and the little oil in the cruse were freely used according to the Lord's direction, that he pledged himself to the poor widow of tried faith, saying, " The barrel of meal shall not waste, neither shall the cruse of oil fail, until the day that the Lord sendeth rain upon the earth." The power of belief must be stretched to its utmost tension before he will increase it.

3. *The object of Faith.* God is presented in the text as the object of faith. In his all-comprising fullness and supremacy he is set before us to challenge faith. It is in his being, unity, spirituality, natural and moral attributes, and especially in his redemptive work, that we are invited and required to focalize trust. God here represents every star of hope, every gleam of light, every healing virtue, every festive joy, every beatific prospect. Faith in God comprises so many points that we cannot notice them in detail. We must confine ourselves to those truths which more especially enter into evangelical faith.

At bottom and fundamentally saving faith in God implies trust in the sacrificial and propitiatory offering of Christ. We cannot separate between God and His Son, nor can we ignore the atonement, and exercise a life-restoring faith in God directly and immediately. God does not, and cannot, allow himself to be approached by the sinner in his own name and proper person. To do so would involve connivance at sin, and introduce anarchy into the moral government of God. The emphatic words of Christ are these : " I am the way, and the truth, and the life ; no man cometh unto the Father but by me." (John 14 : 7.) A mediator must come between us and God ; not as a new channel of communication, but as an intercessor, proxy and substitute—not pleading for pardon on the basis of unsatisfied clemency ; but bearing in his hands a full and satisfactory indemnity for the impairment done to the holy order of the universe, by human sin.

Nor was the sacrifice of Christ a mere ceremonial propriety. It was a stern measure, growing out of the desperate exigencies of our case. There was an irreconcilable clash between human crime and the holiness of heaven, which could only be adjusted by satisfaction. Wherefore it is of necessity that this man have somewhat to offer. It was not only an advocate, with eloquent voice and powers of persuasion that we needed, but a priest as well, to offer gifts and sacrifices—a priest with crimson temple and gory side, and hands all dripping with atoning blood. Even the power of Christ to save is confined within the limit of his mediation and sacrifice " Wherefore he is able also to save them to the uttermost that come unto God by him, seeing he ever liveth to make intercession for them." (Hebrews 7 : 25.)

Indeed, all the possibilities, and encouraging certainties of salvation spring out of the blood of expiation. In this blood the faith of Paul waxes strong by contrast. " For if the blood of bulls, and of goats, and the ashes of a heifer, sprinkling the unclean, sanctifieth to the purifying of the flesh, how much more shall the blood of Christ, who through the eternal Spirit, offered himself without spot to God, purge your conscience from dead works to serve the living God?" There is to be an eternal recognition of the blood, as the procuring cause of holiness. Those who have gone to heaven, we are told, washed their robes, and made them white in the blood of the Lamb. Those who sing in heaven, adopt the chorus, " Unto him that loved us, and washed us from our sins in his own blood." It is only when we take fast hold upon the atonement that we get down among the primary rocks of our faith.

> " Rock of ages, cleft for me,
> Let me hide myself in thee ;
> Let the water and the blood,
> From thy wounded side which flow'd,
> Be of sin the perfect cure—
> Save from wrath and make me pure."

Faith in God implies faith in his promises and covenant engagements. God has not only provided saving merits, and healing virtues, and cleansing fountains ; but he has pledged himself to appropriate these efficacies on the most easy and practical conditions. These unmerited promises are so many, and various, and sweet, that they are called exceeding great and precious. In the same connection it is declared that they are given to us for the express purpose that by them we might be partakers of the divine nature, having escaped the corruption that is in the world through lust. The Lord has entered into a solemn contract with the sinning race—a contract to save us fully and forever through Christ ; and now he condescends to make use of means to inspire confidence and hope in the fulfillment of his testamental engagement. He has required its continual re-assertion from the pulpit. He has ratified it with two sacraments, and finally confirmed it by an oath " that by two immutable things in which it is impossible for God to lie, we might have strong consolation who have fled for refuge to lay hold on the hope set before us." (Heb. 6 : 18.) He has even put his fidelity and justice at stake to assure us that there shall be no failure in the fulfillment of his self-assured obligations. Therefore it is said, " If we confess our sins, he is faithful and just to forgive us our sins, and to cleanse us from all unrighteousness." Here the Lord directly commits himself to work pardon and holiness on the sole condition of what is comprehended in the confession of sin. He invites us to put him to the test, and allows us to conclude, if he fails to the extent of one jot or tittle, that his fidelity and justice shall stand forever impeached.

Such promises, underlaid by the atonement, meet us everywhere, and challenge our faith. If we are not fully saved, then the sin must lie at our door, and the failure must be charged up to our own account. Indeed, when we look at the ground and facilities of faith from this stand-point, we cannot be surprised that unbelief has been ranked among the hell-deserving crimes.

But what is it to believe in the promises of God? Is it merely to credit the truth and sincerity of God? Is it the limit of faith to rely even confidently on the future indefinite verification of the utterances of God? If this is all, then impenitent sinners may be true believers. It is not enough to believe God is able and willing to save. Nor is it enough to believe that he is able and willing to save to the uttermost, and to save us now. It is not impossible for a well instructed, clever sinner to believe all this. We must advance a step further and include in our trust the promptitude and actual saving work of God. We must think of him as never allowing a promise to go to protest, as never forgetting the date of its maturity, as never asking an extension of time. We must think of believing and receiving as coetaneous and inseparable. If I put myself under the treatment of Jesus, according to his directions, for a perfect cure, would it not be a reflection upon Christ, not to allow that he heals. Would it not be an assumption that we may perform our part of a most sacred compact; but, alas! Christ may fail to perform his? If, according to my deepest consciousness, I give up all sin, consecrate myself wholly to Christ, trust solely in the merits of his life and death, take his word as the rule of my faith, and practice, and standard of my character, and rectitude and invite the Spirit to focalize all his offices, all his light and fire upon my soul and life—if, in short, I sink all my ambitions and hopes, and pleasures, and death, and destiny in Christ, am I at liberty to question that I am received and saved? Perhaps it will be said you may do all this very sincerely, but through ignorance fail to accomplish your purpose. Be it so. Is Christ so hard a Master that he will take advantage of my ignorance, and hold me off in a frigid disfellowship and reeking corruption? Because I cannot go into a psychological analysis of mind, and moral siftings of my affections and feelings with infinite exactitude—will he withhold the cup of salvation or doom me to years of dark uncertainty? Thank God there is no such severe side to Jesus. His words encourage presumption—" Whatsoever things ye desire when ye pray, believe that ye receive them, and ye shall have them." The Lord seems to delight in seeing his children defy improbabilities.\ All the bold and daring instances of faith on record are most commended by the Saviour. The case of the Centurion, whose servant was sick of the palsy, was a type of faith most pleasing to Jesus. Christ being solicited said, "I will come and heal him." But the Centurion answered and said, " Lord I am not worthy that thou shouldst come under my roof; but speak the word only and my servant shall be healed. For I am a man under authority having soldiers under me. And I say unto this man go, and he goeth ; and to my servant do this, and he doeth it." When Jesus heard it he marvelled and said—"I have not found so great faith, no not in Israel." Then Jesus said unto the Centurion, "Go thy way, and as thou hast believed, so be it done unto thee." And his servant was healed in the self-same hour. This was a crucial case. The disease was incurable—the subject a mere servant, the suppliant unworthy, the means to be employed was a simple word, in the absence of the subject. The cure, such was the nature of the disease, must be instantaneous and entire, or prove a manifest failure But as the faith of the Centurion measured up to the sublime urgencies of the case, the mighty work of healing was done in the self-same hour. The faith was the exact measure of the cure, and the two acts were inseparable. Jesus spoke, the man was every whit whole.

So it is with us. Faith brings just those blessings in kind and quantity which are made its specific object. If it is pardon it brings pardon and the peace of reconciliation. If it is limited salvation, or change of heart, it brings regeneration. If it is a perfect cure, it brings, under proper conditions, full redemption, a pure heart, entire sanctification.

"*Have faith in God.*" It will cancel your guilt, disburden your soul, put a new song into your mouth, and give you beauty for ashes, the oil of joy for mourning, and the garment of praise for the spirit of heaviness.

"*Have faith in God.*" It will bring the cleansing blood and the quickening spirit into contact with thy heart. It will deliver you from sin, and all that frets, and wastes, and burns, and rankles, and festers, and ulcerates within. It will put your soul to rest in God—a rest that no storm can break. "Though the earth be removed, and the mountains be carried into the midst of the sea, and though the waters roar and be troubled, and the mountains shake with the swellings thereof—yet within is a river, the streams whereof make glad the city of God."

"*Have faith in God.*" It will graft you into Jesus and send back his life-currents into all the avenues, and channels, and capacites of your being. It will give to your practical life, thrift, and bloom, and fruitage, crowned with a large culture of Christ-like development.

"*Have faith in God.*" And it will give you to be rooted and grounded in love,—energizing the forces of your nature with an invincible stability.

"*Have faith in God.*" And it will lift you above the world—above its tumult and strife—above its sordid pursuits and dissipations—above its sins, and sorrows, and debasements, and finally it will send you sweeping through the gates washed in the blood of the Lamb; and then it will set you to singing on and on forever. "Unto him that loved us and washed us from our sins in his own blood. To him be glory and dominion forever."

To an observant mind, the scene during the delivery of Dr. Lowrey's sermon was more than ordinarily impressive. The congregation had greatly increased. Much of the pre-occupation attendant on persons arriving and getting settled on the ground had given place to a full and hearty interest in the religious services. It was evident from the almost breathless attention given to the exposition of the Word, that the subject and its manner of presentation were of an absorbing character. Gleams of intelligent appreciation flashed like sunlight over the faces of the listening throng. Long-standing difficulties, to a clear understanding and personal exercise of faith, suddenly gave way. Into the "open door," which became apparent, eager souls were ready to enter. Self-sufficiency, human contrivance, and all the hindrances to God's effectual influence in saving men, for the moment seemed obliterated. Pride, the last stronghold of the spirit that works disobedience, was prostrate in the dust, and when the proposition was made by Mr. Inskip, who during the day superintended all the public exercises, that those present who would test the value of faith, and prove the wonderful power of God in their present and full salvation, would rise up, the movement was quite general. While hundreds were on their feet, and by this act of prompt obedience, helped into light and liberty, the many who feared to venture or commit themselves, appeared to feel reproved for their timidity.

"Do you now believe?" was asked. Some went so far as to speak out audibly declaring they did. "But what of those who have not risen?" inquired Mr. I. "Let us vary the question. O do not doubt God; do anything rather than doubt his veracity. Now all who *will not doubt* God, rise to your feet." This form of the question brought a number up. "Now a step farther; you declare you will not doubt—will you trust him to save you this moment?"

"Do you believe he is able?"

"Yes"—"I do"—"So do I."

"Very well; is he not willing?"

"Yes."

"Now believe *he doeth it*, and you are saved."

"Let us kneel down. Lord, here we are a believing company. We abandon every subterfuge, and look to thee alone. Save now, we beseech thee. Thou art saving, we are receiving. O yes, we trust"—

> "In the promises I trust,
> Now I feel the blood applied;
> I am prostrate in the dust,
> I with Christ am crucified.
>
> "Here, I give my all to thee,—
> Friends and time and earthly store,
> Soul and body thine to be—
> Wholly thine—forever more.
>
> "I am trusting Lord in thee,
> Dear Lamb of Calvary,
> Only at thy cross I bow,
> Jesus saves, He saves me now.
>
> "Jesus comes, he fills my soul,
> Perfected in love I am;
> I am every whit made whole,
> Glory, glory to the Lamb!"

At this point, the exclamation "glory," was repeated and prolonged; for a new experience had burst in upon believing brethren and sisters, and joy like an ocean began to pervade their minds and hearts. In this spirit the doxology was sung and the services were formally concluded; but for half an hour or more, groups remained about the altar. Here and there the soul-struggle had not subsided. Encouraging promises and cheerful songs were repeated as helps to the doubting, and assurance to penitent sinners, who were forward at every service, that " Now is the day of salvation."

THURSDAY EVENING.

SERMON BY REV. W. L. GRAY, OF PHILADELPHIA.

"And to know the love of Christ."—Eph. 3 : 19.

God is only known in Christ: he is only approachable in Christ; only in Christ is there any possible realization for us that he is our Saviour. The prayer of the Apostle was uttered by the consciousness of the knowledge of this; and this same prayer has been instrumental in guiding souls into the enjoyment of the fullness of God. For this cause, said Paul, in behalf of the Ephesians, " I bow my knees to the Father of our Lord Jesus Christ, of whom the whole family in heaven and earth is named, that he would grant you, according to the riches of his glory, to be strengthened with might by his spirit in the inner man, that Christ may dwell in your hearts by faith, that ye being rooted and grounded in love, may be able to comprehend with all saints what is the breadth and length and depth and height; and to know the love of Christ, which passeth knowledge, that ye might be filled with the fullness of God."

My friends, if I shall not be able to give you much of a sermon, I am able to give you a great text, a text which has been a blessing to so many and may be a blessing to you to-night. I present to you a theme of beauty, the love of Christ. It is a theme that Christian ministers have always delighted to dwell upon; its force and power is exhaustless.

It is wonderful and incomprehensible in its compass. We cannot tell where to fix the bounds of that love; the sublime vision of it is most gloriously displayed in all the realms of light, whither the range of human knowledge may lead us. We do not know whether angels and the heavenly orders have any experience of it or not, but we believe that it is revealed to all intelligence in the universe of God, and that revelation is in accordance with the measure of the requirement of each in his immortal necessities. It may be that the heavenly beings of another nature may not be capable of so understanding and valueing it because of their nature and condition; the manifestation may be less to them; but we do know that he has revealed that love to us, as a love incomprehensible in its depth and boundless in its compass.

It is boundless, in that it is extended to us in all conditions of our being, and comes freely to all the human race; to illustrate the attribute of compassion as existing in the bosom of God, and the relation we sustain to him as creatures bearing in their creation his own image. It is boundless because the subjects of Christ's love experience his grace in an invariable degree, manifested in the processes of the development of the race, amid the failures of individuals, the rejection of his offers of mercy and the aversion of the soul to his gracious work.

The love of Christ is disinterested. I know that some have given expression to the notion that everything that God has done through Christ in the manifestation of his love, and the exercises of his mercy, has connected with it some ulterior purpose that pertains to the relation of other intelligences under God's universal dominion. But I look upon the whole process of the manifestation of divine love as manifesting that the intention of God is to save man, and to show what is the character of the plan of salvation.

The love of Christ is not exhibited to show the God-side of the great scheme of human redemption, but the man-side. God could have manifested his love by the constantantly repeated act of the creation of new worlds and orders of beings, by giving birth to new natures conceivable in the divine mind, and numberless worlds springing into order and being, leaping forth from his all-forming hand, or breathed into being from the word of his mouth; these would show his power and love, but they could not illustrate the love of Christ in dying to save us. Some say that there is such peculiarity in the scheme of human redemption, that it is hard to accept it; that God has made only a partial redemption for his family; that only the human race is included in the divine conception of a provided Saviour, passing by the angels who kept not their first estate, and taking hold of man who too had fallen. I am not prepared to accept that position. I do not know what God has in store for others of his fallen creatures. The Bible was not made for angels but for men. Who knows what may be the divine revelation to others? As it comes to men it tells us this wondrous story of Jesus and his love; a love interposing to save us when we were strangers to his ways, and disobedient to his call.

When we consider the condition of the love of Christ, its manifestations are all full with wonder. Christ's love is love in action, moving the divine heart, and plan, and purpose, to work for our eternal well being. Love in men takes the form in some of its highest moods simply, of deep enjoyment, but love in Christ takes the form of active goodness. Now this is manifested towards a race in which there is no one quality of goodness or qualification for the reciprocal development of this holy passion. There is nothing in us that is lovable, nothing reciprocative of his love. In the view of this fact we hear the Apostle of the Gentiles saying, "For scarcely for a righteous man will one die, yet peradventure for a good man some would even dare to die ; but God commendeth his love toward us in that while we were yet sinners Christ died for us." When we were in active rebellion against the government of God, arraigning the principles of his administration, impugning his actions, despising his mercy, and cherishing in our bosoms and actualizing by our lives, principles in antagonism to his law, authority and love, he loved us with a love that hastened him from his throne over all principalities, potencies and dominions, to die the ignominious death of a felon or malefactor on the cross, for us, and our salvation.

Christ's love is again made known to us when we contrast the state to which we are brought by the influence of his love upon us, with our previous condition. Our affections and consciences have been reached by the power of his love. Those bright divine rays have penetrated the darkness of our state, and shown us our poor defiled hearts ; the rays thereof beaming forth in the morning of our spiritual life, have waked us up from the state of sin, and out of that darkness emerging, we have seen the black cloud dissipated by the brightness of his rising. By the power of that love we are made capable of loving him, and under its exercise we do love him. In its infinitude it has covered all our former loves, all our black lines of gloom, all blurs in our nature, and all deformities of character. In his love they are removed, the darkness and moral corruption ceases, and we live a new and heavenly life.

The manifestation of that love has been so wonderful that man has gained by it, in Christ, all that he has lost in Adam. All powers of loving, serving and delighting in God are restored; and there is no capability of our nature but is secured to us in blessing, abundantly, fully and throughout eternity by the love of Christ. We not only have as much, but we more than gain everything we have lost by the fall, being fully restored to the favor and companionship of God, walking with him and hearing his voice, and asserting under the divine authority our privilege of access to the tree of life. Yes, we are restored to a greater dignity, being constituted heirs of God, and co-heirs with his eternal Son, born into the relation of kings and priests unto God and the Father.

The love of Christ is most plentiful, exhaustless, eternal and unchangeable.— Whatever we may see in man that is subject to change, this we know, the love of Christ never changes. Some men are at first able to make plans that are most extensive, and if carried forward to execution, their operation could bear the marks of durability, but as their work grows on their hands, they either change in this or that, or are so involved themselves that they cannot carry out their original designs; or learning of that which will be better adapted to the end sought, alter the whole scheme in which they were interested at the outset; but there is no change in the love of Jesus; nor in the plan that love devised; nor in the power to bring to its most glorious consummation the plan that love devised. The apostle looked at it in its stupendous proportions, its altitude, depth, length, breadth, and force. The grandeur and sublimity of the thing before him, so enwrapped him within the folds of its own sweet mysteriousness, that he could only say, " to know the love of Christ that passeth knowledge." His difficulty is not remarkable, for the knowledge of a thing as existing and conferring benefits, may be attained, when the depth, height, length, and breadth of the thing itself may not be comprehended or grasped by us. O, that we may know that love, though we may not comprehend what it fully is!

Now we know that there are three media by which love manifests itself: namely, by intuition, to the outward senses, and by experience. Love may exist through one of these, or may come to us through all these media; they are all found in the love of Christ. It addresses itself to the self-consciousness when the revealment of the divine compassion is made, and there is the counter-part already implanted in the consciousness. The receptivity is possessed, and it reflects through and through the soul, so that as soon as the object, Christ, is presented to the subject, man, there is a feeling intuitively arising, which delights in the knowledge of his love. It immediately perceives that the fountain is deep enough and wide enough to supply all the wants of the soul, and it plunges in and is washed and filled, purified and saved. So when the voice speaks to the Christian saying, "Sinners plunged beneath that flood, lose all their guilty stains," the soul cries out, " That means me, it meets my case;' he takes hold by faith, and rejoices with joy unspeakable.

The love of Christ may be exhibited to the senses, by the order, harmony and beauty of the world, which he has made for the purpose of manifesting himself to man, in its grandeur, its magnificence and its perpetuity. So also the Word of God, containing the precious promises and divine precepts, which are designed to make us wise unto salvation. These we can see or hear, or feel until their

4

objective power shall come into the soul, revealing through the senses the amazing love of Christ.   David said, under the benign influences of these manifestations, " O Lord, our Lord, how excellent is thy name in all the earth.   When I consider thy heavens, the moon and stars which thou hast ordained, what is man that thou art mindful of him ;" or again, " the entrance of thy word giveth light ;" " open mine eyes that I may see the beauties of thy law."   It is a medium of value to us that we can see God thus objectively, and love him.   Perchance we do love ; perchance these wonders and delights are a living realization to the soul, that come with force enough to fill it.

A blind preacher standing and declaring the word of life, may be affected by the sympathy of his hearers, and the precious word may be more thrillingly powerful in his heart, because he feels that sympathy ; he may express truly the conviction of his soul because he feels the truth, and under the powerful operation of the blessed spirit he may feel his soul to be full of hope, and may impart of that fullness to others.

But there is still a blessed medium through which this love is communicated ; it is realized in the experience of the believing soul, which actualizes in our hearts all the objects of sense, and verifies the intuitions that seem to have been born within us.   Hence we have the spirit of God witnessing with our spirit, coming to bring to us the report of the work of God in the conversion, adoption, regeneration and sanctification of the believing soul. Here on the heart is left the experience of that love ; but who can tell it, who can justly declare all that God has done for him ?   We may know, therefore, the love of Christ.

When I was a boy, I was watching by the bedside of my precious mother. Her physician, who was a good man, came to her, and seeing her prostrated, weak and wasting away, said, " You are very weak, but Jesus, I trust, is very precious to you, and a very present help in your time of trouble."   After pointing her to the cross, he turned to me, and addressing me by name, told the story of salvation as it was revealed in his own life.   That story won my heart, and presenting myself to God, I found his love shed abroad therein. Glory to God !

We may know the love of Christ in its adaptation to our condition in every possible relation that we may sustain to the whole Christion system. It is the principle by which the soul is purified ; our faith working by love makes the dark and dreary luminous and inviting.   It is this love that is so much to be desired.   God's glory is involved in it, for that glory is more displayed in the salvation of a sinner than in the creation of a world.   God comes nearer to us, we find out more fully what he is, than in the most glorious display to us in any part of his vast works.   He is to us in our salvation what he cannot be to the world in all the acts of his creating energy.

The love of Christ, in the experience of believers, is a love that is capable of measuring up to all their need and all the possibilities of their being.   There is nothing insignificant, nothing little or of little worth in his love to us ; and it is just here that we may stand and appreciate and approve the work of God, for as we fall in with the work of redemption, just in the same way we approach the point of being filled with all the fullness of God.   If we are fully sanctified to God, we shall appreciate what is this fullness, for we must know the love of Christ before we can be filled with all the fullness of God.   If sanctified to him, if his love has complete sway in our hearts, if it reigns there, governing soul, body and spirit, what more can we look for ? Then we can be perfect as our Father in heaven is perfect, ready for any operation of the love of God in its fullness. If I have any idea at all on this subject it this: that the entirely sanctified man is just in the condition in which he may stretch out and expand farther and farther ; then he is ready for depths, lengths and heights.

God granting to us his fullness, by the knowledge of Christ's love, vouchsafes to us the light by which we can walk safely, and discover all things around and in us. Light cheers, clears up our pathway, shows us how to avoid obstructions, gleams into the future, and casts its rays beyond the bounds of our present horizon of vision, so that walking we walk in the light, or standing we stand in the light, or searching for the divine will we search in the light. But you say, can God so light up the mind as to give a perfect knowledge of himself to man so that he may not fall into error and sin ? We answer, Christ is the light that lighteth every man that cometh into the world. If he lighteth up the mind in the darkness of sin, so that the way to the cross is seen, there is no limit to the illumination which he is both able and willing to give to the man that fully relies upon his word and spirit. O my hearers, he fills every thought, and so reigns in his fullness that every thought may begin and move and end in him. He can so revolutionize every human soul, and every power of man, that he shall be all in all. But you say again, this is a high experience—cannot a man be sanctified fully to God if this be his privilege, so as to be occupied in all the powers of his soul and nature with God and things divine ? Yes, blessed be God, he can and ought so to exercise himself in these God-given powers until the soul can say, " Whom have I in heaven but thee; and there is none upon earth that I desire besides thee ?"

Cannot a man possessing this fullness so live that his communion with God will be uninterrupted ? You will not even in this life find yourself in that condition in which you will not encounter difficulties, temptations and trials ; but the man that lives up to his privileges will be saved all the time, and saved in all the possibilities of his nature; so long as you abide in Christ you have a refuge that can never be stormed. The sanctified man holds that position, not once for all, but *moment by moment, moment by moment*, in the exercise of faith in the strength and impregnability of his refuge. O, there is more power in the believer, galvanized into the fullness of God by the love of Christ, than there is in anything else in the universe. And who will not have it; now there is room, always room. If you want to be filled with light and purity, come to this feast. If you want to be filled with all the fullness of God, go down, down, down, until you know the love of Christ " that ye may be filled with all the fullness of God."

To "be filled," was the question of the moment, and after the possibilities and promises bearing on the point had been pressed home, a large number of earnest souls bowed around the altar-place, and while prayer ascended, blessings came down as the dew of heaven, sweetly satisfying their longings, and closing the day's devotions in a baptism of holy love.

THIRD DAY.

" This is the hour for prayer," remarked Bro. Boole, who had charge of the morning exercises " Testimony and exhortation may incidentally be allowed, but prayer is our chief business now. It is the asking ones who get. Let us pray."

No one by name was called on ; but eight or ten persons succeeded each other, asking the Father for Jesus' sake to shed abroad his love in their hearts by the Holy Ghost given unto them.

The range at length becoming too general in its sweep, Mr. B. said : " Look to your own individual heart wants. The best way to convert the world, is to be made right ourselves. Let us confine the range of our petitions to personal blessings, present power, the duties of this day on which we have been spared to enter, and not go over the whole creation in our reach of thought. Let us try it again, all kneeling before God. Pray on."

" Fill this tabernacle with Thy gracious presence, O Jesus," pleaded Bro Foote. " Make the place glorious, and give every one of us a deeper plunge in the open fountain."

" Here," said a stranger, "we now renew our consecration. All we are, all we have, or hope, we give, O Lord, to thee, through Jesus Christ. Amen "

Brother Thompson—" We beseech Thee that the Holy Ghost may rest on all who preach to-day, on all who lead the meetings, and on all who attend them. Let souls who have come here hungering and thirsting after righteousness, be filled. Fill us now. Many long to be sanctified, and came for this purpose. O Jesus, apply thine own blood, and wash out every stain. Convert sinners all around us. Help everybody to improve the time, and may this be one of the sweetest and best days we have ever known."

Brother Boole—" It is intimated that many have come here to be made holy. This is the grand object before us. Two things are necessary in guiding a ship. First, keep the course laid down on the chart ; and, secondly, avoid the rocks and shoals that lie hidden about us. The right course is to seek earnestly for sanctifying power ; but I perceive some are nearing dangerous reefs and rocks. You mean to have a fullness of joy ; but joy is no purity—yet joy comes in with purity. If you are determined to get up an inward commotion somehow, you may think you are fully saved ; but when you go home you will get angry again, and discover that the work is not thoroughly done. A National Camp-meeting is not salvation; Christ is. You may have excitement and a good deal of it; but to be wholly sanctified implies a good deal of sub-soil ploughing—a full surrender of yourself, consecrating all you have, and are, and think here, and also everything at home.

"It is a great thing to be saved. Nobody is great when he comes to the cross; that levels all to one platform. A man must go down, if he would be taken up by Christ. You are all, and here I include myself, the meanest kind of creatures. How honored we are that God touches us at all—that He takes hold of us lovingly to help us—yes, that in our uncleanness, his eyes pity, and that he washes us 'whiter than snow.' O how we ought to jump at the chance!

" 'But it is so hard,' you say, 'to give up everything.' Well, make it easy—*just do it.* What have you, anyhow? To hear people talk about consecrating all, and giving up all to the Lord, reminds me of a poor, old, colored pauper, who had been picked up and placed in a comfortable asylum, where his every need was furnished him by the bounty of charitable friends. He, in giving his experience, talked about what he had to give up! So with the poor paupers in my church in New York. They may have the control of millions, and have what is called a high social position; but after all, they have nothing. It is all the Lord's. The trouble is in self. The clinging is here. Self must be given up entirely. No use to think of advance unless we leave off all our sins. People talk about reputation, and some preachers seem to find this bubble reputation a severe test. God pity our folly! I never had any until Jesus gave me grace. Don't bother yourself about that.

"Now you come to a place where your mind is made up to have this blessing, and you feel you can do nothing. Well, *do nothing.* It is God that worketh in you, to will and to do of his own good pleasure. Let him give you power. A man is sanctified by the Holy Ghost, and the witness will be given. You can't get along without the witness. You must trust; but trusting isn't salvation. Something comes of our trusting and we know it. Believe then, once for all. A business man having plenty of money in bank and wishing to draw a needed amount, will make one check and sign it—not several. You need not repeat the act of believing—believe now. Emotion? No emotion is necessary here. It is faith in God—naked faith. I do not say 'dare to believe.' There is no *daring* in the case of believing a truth— all safe here. You need not go out of this meeting without the Holy Ghost. God will give it, and in half an hour every one of you desiring it, while ye pray, shall receive it.

"If not, there is a forbidden something in the way. The price is not paid. God deals in a business-like way. Now take the blood of Christ; let it cover you all over, and the answer comes into your soul, 'It is done.' Oh. this general weakness among us, in our churches, and in our endeavors—all is by reason of the lack of the Holy Ghost. Our difficulties would all vanish if we were clear and honest in submitting to God. Then how easy the work might go forward. Let us banish these misgivings by a clean sweep just now. You have your check. Go to the bank and draw what you need. Take your time at the preparation. Be deliberate, careful, thorough, but when prepared, then it is short work.

"It is just as easy to cast the whole cargo overboard at once as to be dragging out a part of it to-day and a little more to-morrow. Do the thing fully, and the Holy Ghost will wonderfully fill the cleansed temple of your heart.

"Now go on, if you have anything to say."

A Baptist minister—"Light has come to me through our dear brother's earnest exhortation. My views have been confused about this matter of consecration and faith. I now see clearly how it is. We are redeemed by promise and power. We come by promise and trust for power, and both are backed by Almightiness. O, thank God for such a Gospel, and such a way of deliverance from sin and pollution, as is plainly revealed here!"

A sister had espoused Jesus amid persecution, but God made her strong to endure the cross. Her attention was directed to heart-purity as a privilege, by reading some old numbers of the *Guide to Holiness* which she found in a garret. There alone she sought, and God gave her the blessing. By timidity in regard to confessing what had been done for her, darkness came, and the evidence faded away. In great heaviness she passed through her household duties, until one day she knelt down behind the stove and cried out for a restoration of the power. The Spirit came into her heart and filled her again with perfect love. She went out to class and confessed to the glory of God, and the baptism came on all present. She was taken sick and had been an invalid seven years. Through all, God had sustained her, and enabled her to testify of this grace. They thought her entire sanctification was only a preparation for approaching death; but the Lord had restored her, to show that it was for living as well as dying. The word of her testimony had been blessed. Seven girls who had lived in her family, and three young men had been converted. During the past fall and winter God had answered her prayers in the salvation of over one hundred precious souls.

"One word will express my state just now—saved."

"I came, as Bro. Boole said, feeling I was a poor pauper. Christ accepted me and clothed me in his righteousness. I have discovered that the way to live this sanctification is to let self move out, and Jesus come in. With him in my heart I have every want more than supplied. 'I live, yet not I, but Christ liveth in me.' Bless his name!"

" The thought flashed on me with peculiar force a moment since—'Jesus loves even me.' The brother (Boole) touched on some things this morning, which afford me great help. The difference between faith and knowledge in this matter of salvation is, to use the 'check' illustration—with faith we present the check, and when we get the 'greenbacks,' faith yields to knowledge. Jesus lets me fill out the check. He is cashier and proprietor, and his name is signed to it, and good for any amount. I believe this. He saved me, a poor sailor—dirty and dissipated as I was. I couldn't then read my own name; but he took me up where I have learned some sweet lessons. Every day I only have to hand out the faith check and receive the blessings. I say to all here, give up, and you will get Jesus. Some bones will be broken, but no matter. Lord, kill and make alive!"

" Self is all on the altar; I know it is. Now I take up my cross to follow Jesus."

" I have a calm, sweet assurance that the blood cleanses me from all sin."

Mr. Boole—" There may be some here who have received the blessing since they came on the ground. We give way to them a little. The short way to receiving is faith, the safe way of continuance is confession. It is easier to *keep out* condemnation, than to *get clear* of it. Excuse me. *I* do not call it a cross to tell the world Jesus saves me."

This brought to their feet several persons; some of whom, it appeared, had been blessed at the first service ; others on the previous day and evening; but all timid about acknowledging the work. One had been troubled about emotion, but now saw the snare of the tempter, who suggested—" you do not feel thus and so, and you had better wait until you reach home before .you profess to 'have been sanctified."

" For two years," said a sister, " I have been enabled to witness a good profession at home, through the keeping power of Christ."

Mr. Boole—" I am glad that sister referred to her religion at home. It is but a poor degree of justification that will not enable us to live right at home. The family circle is the hardest place and the best place to live it. But don't get confused about the question before us. Get all devil-work out of the heart, and see how quickly you can appropriate this great gospel privilege. It helped my own faith, and it may help yours, so I will relate a little incident :

" A Baptist lady, who had long hesitated to trust God for the full measure of the sanctifying spirit, was asked by her little boy one day for something to eat. She promised it, but continued at her employment and forgot the matter for a time. The little fellow seemed also to forget, as he continued intent upon his play with toys upon the carpet. After awhile she thought of his request, and hastily procured and handed him the cake. He took it, looking up innocently into her face, and saying, ' I knew you would, mother.' This to her was a timely lesson. She felt reproved before God that she could not trust his word, and just then looking up received the full ness of his love. Go and do likewise. Your God is more willing to bless than you can be to receive."

The "little incident" made tears come freely, and won many reluctant souls to an immediate act of trust, which had its effect, as instanced in the genuine earnestness with which the doxology was then sung:

"Praise God from whom all blessings flow," &c.

THE EIGHT O'CLOCK PRAYER-MEETING.

Soon after breakfast several persons were engaged in tacking up the chart with Scripture mottoes, upon the rear of the pulpit.

When the bell had summoned the congregation for morning prayers, Rev. J. S. Inskip gave an interesting account of the chart before us. He said, in order to meet the expenses of the cost of the "Tabernacle," he had written to a large number of persons of all denominations, soliciting donations and requesting also that they should send him a verse of Holy Scripture that most clearly expressed their experience, and that gave them most comfort at the time of writing. Out of the very many responses the passages printed on the chart were taken.

After the description of the chart and the recounting of the history of its origin, the congregation joined in singing, Bro. Inskip then said— " Let me suggest before you go to prayer that you select some promise on that canvas; but don't look to the chart for anything you want. Look to God. O Lord, write thy promises on our hearts to-day!" The first prayer was made by Bro. Perkins. Many hearts were thrilled as he said: "This is a very needy time with us. An hour ago thou didst bless us at the meetiug; we want more power—we come to thee to be supplied. It is not wrong in us to covet earnestly the best gifts of thy grace, and to exercise them to thy glory. May the blessed Holy Spirit select for us that promise that shall fill our hearts with its richness, and while trusting, come and visit us with thy salvation. We come to thee polluted and defiled, to be washed in the blood of Christ. Speak the cleansing word. Make us free from the bondage of sin, fill us with the love of heaven; and bless and sanctify every preacher on the ground, every class-leader on the ground, every steward on the ground, every Sunday-school superintendent on the ground, every member of the Church on the ground. Lord, sanctify the whole Church!"

While these petitions were ascending the "Amens" became more and more hearty until the close: then, in the midst of the enthusiasm, the people still kneeling, Bro. Inskip was heard exclaiming, "Are you trusting the word of promise?"

Brother Perry prayed : "Thou art the source of our strength, O, Jesus! we are looking to thee. Thou art our Saviour, our Redeemer. Thou art our living, loving Benefactor to give good gifts to us. Thou hast never failed us. O, manifest thyself now to us through the Holy Ghost. Thou hast bid us ask of thee. We do ask for the grandest baptism we have ever received. Thou art honored by our confidence, which thou so freely invitest. Lord, help us to tell thee all, to trust thee fully; that, filled with the Holy Spirit, we may realize God is all in all. Amen."

Brother Inskip then introduced an experience meeting, urging the propriety of forgetting self, and acknowledging what the Lord had done for us. His own testimony was, "Saved through the blood of the Lamb."

"This fountain ever springing," said a brother, "is no fancy picture. It is to me a reality. I find it fresh and pure every day, and it seems to get sweeter."

Mr. Inskip—"It is just so with me. It gets better, and makes me better. Glory to God!"

A preacher, converted forty years ago, went to Vineland, and returned with a richer experience. The members of his charge were glad he had launched out into deep water, and could now lead and encourage them in holiness.

Another referred to working power. God had given her one hundred souls last season, and she wanted a deeper baptism for usefulness.

A Presbyterian minister told his joy in knowing Jesus as a full Saviour. "He saves me every moment." This was Rev. Bro. White, who subsequently became "filled with the Spirit," which moved him to prayer for his own congregation, that every member might be sanctified; for the whole denomination, and for all churches, pastors, and people. All knelt while his earnest soul went up to God. He closed by reconsecrating his life to the promotion of holiness, and there were loud responses, and melting emotions.

An official editor of the M. E. Church next arose. He declared himself to be an incontestible monument of the mercy of God, proving that there was no case too hard for Jesus to convert or to sanctify. Unbelief had paralized every fibre of his nature, yet he yearned, O, how constantly, for soul-rest. He described the place and circumstances of his conversion, his call to preach, his early trials, and his conscious need of holiness. This void was now filled. Satan dare not intimate that he was deceived.

Sister Baldwin said these old hymns, "For ever here my rest shall be," &c., taught her the blessed way fifty years ago, and they are just as good to-day.

A Baptist minister gave some counsel, and testified to the possession of perfect love. Others followed, until a call was made for those now seeking full salvation. Forty-six arose. The unconverted, who wanted salvation were next asked to stand up, and, all over the congregation, persons indicated their desire to come to Christ.

Mr. Inskip—"Keep steady. Let me ask, are you in earnest; do you mean to have salvation at any cost, or take it in any way God may determine to bless you? If so, raise your right hand." The sign was given, and further questioning brought out many empahtic and pathetic responses. Embarrassment melted away and the altars were soon filled with praying souls.

"Now be very quiet. Don't speak to one another. Tread softly. Here they come. Let us all go down and join them at the mercy seat. Come on, brethren." Seeing us busy with our pencil, Mr. Inskip shouted, "Come down here, HOME JOURNAL, you need a baptism with the rest of us. Without the Holy Ghost, the HOME JOURNAL isn't worth much. Lord, help here!"

All kneeling, he then recited the hymn, "Wrestling Jacob," some stanzas of which were sung, and before the conclusion, it was given to many to prevail with the angel, for He blessed them there.

SERMON BY REV. WM. McDONALD,

VICE-PRESIDENT OF THE NATIONAL CAMP-MEETING ASSOCIATION.

"Wherefore he is able also to save them to the uttermost, that come unto God by him.—Heb. 7 : 25.

The question is asked, How far can a believer be delivered from the pollution of sin in this life? The text says he can be saved to the uttermost— that is, to the farthest extent, to the most remote point within the limit of human endeavor, so far as the divine ability is concerned; and also so far as the availability of the blood of Christ is concerned. This is confirmed by the Scripture in 1 John. If we confess our sins he is faithful and just to forgive us our sins; and the blood of Jesus Christ his Son cleanseth us from all unrighteousness. Then so far as the divine agency, willingness or power is concerned, there is no difficulty.

The condition upon which this cleansing is secured is that "we confess our sins." Christians claim to believe that they must be saved to the uttermost, and that salvation to the uttermost must be in this life. There must come a time ere the gates of heaven shut us in, when we must be made holy; for nothing that is unholy or unclean can enter there. This is the faith of the universal Church of God.

There are denials which, while the doctrine is admitted, practically vitiate it. Let us look at some of them.

1. There are those who claim to believe the doctrine of heart purity, but deny its immediateness. They say we are not to look for it now; that it is the work of development, of growth, of progress, to be completed at some point between this and the hour of death by a constant accession of spiritual strength, and soul mortifications, but it is not to be expected as an immediate and instantaneous work.

We claim that the work is instantaneous, and that all the blessings of the gospel are, in their very nature, necessarily instantaneous. We all admit the instantaneousness of the blessing of pardon. God does not gradually bestow his pardoning mercy on a repentant sinner. The Scriptures always proclaim the immediateness of every proffered blessing, saying *now* is the day of salvation. We preach to sinners, but we do not offer a gradual release-ment from sin ; we exhort them to believe *now* unto salvation. But if gradualism be God's method, we are compelled to say to Christians groaning for purity of heart—not now ; stop where you are, do not let your desires raise you to a condition of expectancy that God will now save you with his uttermost salvation. But if God can pardon a sinner immediately, forgiving this instant all his transgressions, why is it that he cannot do the other? Cannot the same power that in an instant accomplishes the one, accomplish the other, and that suddenly, with an energy that shall complete the work?

We claim that immediateness is in perfect harmony with the Scriptures. The Saviour says, "What things soever ye desire *when* ye pray believe that ye *receive* them, and ye shall have them," at the very time when ye pray, believe. When? *when* ye pray. If your prayer be for a clean heart, at the time *when ye pray*, believe and ye shall have. The Scriptures do not march us on to wait for any other time than now.

The position of gradualism cannot explain Christian experience. If God does not cleanse now, this moment, from all sin, there is no reason for concluding that he justifies now. But many declare that they have secured both the one and the other instantaneously, while there are no witnesses to be found on the other side of the question. If you deny the immediateness of the divine blessing, you deny the blessing itself, for it is a fact that the economy of God's administration in salvation clearly establishes that—

What is, of purpose, sought gradually in Christian experience, is not found at all; i. e. if we aim at, or intend to receive it gradually. All God's blessings come by faith, Do you know of a single spiritual blessing which is not received instantaneously? Is faith gradual or instantaneous? Is the act of faith by which you touch Jesus, and virtue flows from him to your soul, gradual or instantaneous? According to your faith, so be it to you. If faith be an instantaneous operation, and every one must admit it, according to that faith so shall it be unto you. Believing now, you are pardoned now; believing now, you are purified now. No person ever found entire cleansing who sought it gradually. You as Methodists believe in the teachings of our great founder, Mr. Wesley. Let us hear his testimony. He says :—

" To expect it at death, or some time hence is much the same as not expecting it at all." (*Journal. Sept.*, 1762.)

" I find by long experience, it comes exactly to the same point, to tell men they shall be saved from all sin when they die ; or to tell them it may be a year hence, or a week hence, or any time but now. Our word does not profit, either as to justification, or to sanctification, unless we can bring them to expect the blessing while we speak." (*Works. Vol. VI, p.* 673.)

Mr. Wesley is, therefore, in perfect harmony with my statement. And yet there are ministers, who, claiming to be wiser than Mr. Wesley, whose long experience is here given, constantly talk about what they are pleased to call the " hot-house" process of salvation. Let us give you another quotation from Mr. Wesley ; and mark you, this is uttered after an observation of many years. He says: "In London alone, I found six hundred and fifty-two members of our society, who were exceedingly clear in their experience, and of whose testimony, I could see no reason to doubt. I believe no year has passed since that time wherein God has not wrought the same work in others; but sometimes in one part of England, or Ireland, sometimes in another; as *the wind bloweth where it listeth;* and every one of these (after the most careful inquiry, I have not found one exception, either in Great Britain or Ireland), has declared that his deliverance from sin was *instantaneous,* that the change was wrought in a moment.

" Had half of these, or one third, or one in twenty declared it was *gradually* wrought in *them,* I should have believed this in regard to *them,* and thought that *some* were gradually sanctified and some instantaneously. But as I have not found in so long a space of time a single person speaking thus; as all who believe they are sanctified, declare with one voice that the change was wrought in a moment; I cannot but believe that sanctification is commonly, if not always, an instantaneous work."

A minister in Iowa who related his experience after he had obtained the blessing of holiness, said, " I always believed this doctrine, and preached it to my congregation, but I always reserved an opportunity to give my hearers who made the open profession a slap, because of what I regarded their imperfections." So it is with many who affect to believe with the founder of Methodism in doctrine and experience. It has been said Mr. Wesley taught gradualism in sanctification; but mark you, Mr. Wesley's belief in the possibility of gradual sanctification has not, according to his own confession, a single fact after an experience of forty-five years to prove it. During all that time not a single fact came within the range of his knowledge, so that he concludes that gradualism in entire sanctification is a bare abstract possibility. Scores have taken up the dogma of Wesley's doctrine of gradual sanctification, but do not put the doctrine of *instantaneous* sanctification where Wesley put it, in the fore front, thereby misrepresenting that man of God. Whether Mr. Wesley believed in gradual sanctification or not, you have no facts to sustain you in the position assumed by you as to the work itself.

Let me call attention to another form of denial. *While some persons admit the possibility of obtaining this grace in the present life, they deny that the Spirit witnesses to the work wrought in the soul.* This we claim is to deny the instantaneousness of the work: for how can we know we are from this moment cleansed from all sin, unless there be the testimony of the Spirit to the cleansing by the blood?

If the Spirit be not our witness, we have no witness. It is said, we are to look for the witness in the fruits; but instantaneous fruit-growing is an impossibility. The Bible, it is claimed, does not teach that the Spirit witnesses to the fact of our entire sanctification; but hear what the Scriptures say: " We have not received the spirit of the world; but the Spirit of God, by which we know the things that are freely given us of God."

I can find multitudes who testify that the witness of the Spirit has been given to them, as to the fact of their sanctification, just as definitely and clearly as it was in adoption. This has been the uniform testimony of all who have been sanctified. It is taught as the doctrine of the Church. The testimony is very clear and unequivocal, and we claim that every man who takes the opposite ground is not grounded in Methodist doctrine.

Mr. Wesley, writing to Mrs. Bennes, says: "One of our preachers has lately advocated a *new position* among us, that there is no direct or immediate witness of sanctification, but only a perception or consciousness that we are changed, filled with love, and cleansed from sin. But if I understand you right, you find a direct * * testimony."

This he calls a "*new position, among us.*" Not as *new* now as then, but equally absurd. "*Question,*—How do you know that you are sanctified? saved from all inbred corruption? *Ans.* I can know it in no other way than I know that I am justified. 'Hereby know we that we are of God,' in either sense, 'by the Spirit that he hath given us.'"

Again, while some admit all that is contended for by us, they assert that no public or open confession ought to be made of experience, for the following reasons : First, "We may be mistaken." Is it more likely than in the instance of justification? Do not persons make profession of having attained that state, of whom you are in doubt, and they themselves, afterward, also doubt? Would you insist that persons must not declare that they are justified, because some may be mistaken? Secondly: "It has the appearance of boasting." This is just what the world says of those who profess justification. But is that a valid reason for silence? Third: "It creates caste among us." If this be caste, I go for caste. Is it caste for a man to confess that he is better than he once was? Must we refuse to go forward, fearing if we get ahead of others, we shall create caste? I go for leveling upward, not downward; why not take hold of the best gift and enter into the purest society? Great God, grant that the movement here may annihilate all distinctions, except that between sin and holiness ! Fourthly: "It is discouraging to those who do not profess it." I am sorry for that. If they were deeply earnest about the matter, it would not be the case. If men by our side amass wealth, does that cause you to repine and be discouraged? Do you not rather take fresh courage ? Are you inspired by their successes to labor as you have seen them labor, and to expect the largest success ? Rather than take strength from you, does it not put strength into you? I'll tell you why it is discouraging. It is *because you want to stay where you are.*

The Scriptures enjoin confession. "With the heart man believeth unto righteousness, and with the mouth confession is made unto salvation." These are they that washed their robes in the blood of the Lamb, overcoming by the word of their testimony.

If the blessings of holiness or purity be not confessed, how is it to be known by the world? If full of salvation; if the soul is entirely free from imperfection ; if you are sanctified wholly, it must be confessed. You know when you see a man guilty of a violation of the law of God, that he is not wholly sanctified. But do not imagine that such a condition of things can exist even in a justified state. There ought to be a sinless external life, in the justified as well as in the sanctified ; for no man can break God's law and be justified. But there may be an increased intensity of this spiritual life, in the sanctified; and there is. But mark you, there are men whose external life is no more faultless than that of the sanctified. There is no way of telling of this state but by telling what God has done for them. Let us come back once more to the fathers—we would like to entrench ourselves behind them.

Wesley, writing to Mr. Benson, in 1782, now 70 years of age, says, "I doubt we are not explicit enough in speaking of full sanctification, either in public or private."

In 1787, four years before his death, he writes to Mr. King thus : " It requires a great degree of watchfulness to retain the perfect love of God ; and one great means of retaining it is frankly to declare what God has given you." Vol. 7, p. 13.

Writing to Miss Briggs, he says, " Undoubtedly it would be a cross to declare what God has done for your soul ; nay, and afterwards Satan would accuse you on the account, telling you, you did it out of pride ; yea, and some of your sisters would blame you, and perhaps put the same construction upon it, as many are doing. Nevertheless, if you do it with a single eye, it will be pleasing to God."

" But Mr. Wesley never professed this blessing himself." I can't say he ever did, yet there are a good many things that look like it. Nor do I think the cause itself has suffered in the slightest degree by him not confessing it, if it be so. If, like Bramwell, or Fletcher, or Mrs. Rodgers, or a host of others, he had unequivocally left on record the profession, you might say he was a prejudiced witness—but when we take into account his instructions to others to do it, and his sayings if they did it they would glorify God, it would seem to any mind capable of weighing evidence, that his testimony becomes more important than though he had been a professor of the experience.

1. An uttermost salvation is possible.

He who denies this confronts a great mass of Scriptural evidence in its favor. The commands, the promises, the prayers of God's word meet him on every side, calling him to holiness, to purity, to perfect love, to entire sanctification. God does not mock us with these, but pledges the merit of Jesus' blood for the completeness of the work. Not only does he confront Scriptural authority, but *human experience.* The testimony of the Church, in her brighter examples of holiness, proves that the blood of Jesus Christ cleanseth from all sin. Will we credit or deny the testimony ?

2. An uttermost salvation is attainable now.

The witnesses are here who aver that it can be done. They are multiplying in all parts of the land.

Do you seek uninterrupted communion with God ? then seek an uttermost salvation. Do you seek to be useful to men, and an honor to God ? this is secured by the possession of an uttermost salvation. Do you wish an abundant entrance into the eternal kingdom ? it is given to them whose robes are made white in the blood of the Lamb.

Mr. Inskip, rising at the close of the discourse, and apparently filled with the theme, said :

There are two and a quarter millions of Methodists in our country, every one of whom declares that the mission of Methodism is to spread Scriptural holiness over these lands. It is the only peculiar Methodistic dogma that they teach, and have taught, from the beginning. I aver that the immediate cleansing of the heart from all sin has ever been the doctrine of Methodism, though there are but few that have been lifted into the experience. I know a man who was hostile to this experience, who wrote a book entitled : " METHODISM EXPLAINED AND DEFENDED." He sought to explain and vindicate Methodism by leaving out this peculiar doctrine, or confining it to only two pages, a good portion of which was taken up with criticisms upon professors of holiness. (A voice from the stand : Yes, and that was brother

Inskip himself?) Yes, but glory to God, we stand on another platform to-day!

Baptists are coming to our side, also the Presbyterians and Episcopalians and the other denominations. But we had the field before you, and alas! we have betrayed our trust. True, at all our Conferences, those admitted to membership ought to have been sanctified. In the most solemn manner, questions are asked the young minister, to which an affirmative response is required, and by these he is committed to this all-important theme.

Before a preacher among us can be admitted into full connection he is called before the Conference to answer these questions:

"Are you going on to perfection?" "Do you expect to be made perfect in love in this life?" "Are you groaning after it?" And yet there is a great dereliction of duty in expecting either ministers or members to be made perfect in love in this life. Most of our troubles as a denomination arise from this source. Our difficulties in the Book Concern are attributable to the want of this experience. O Lord, sanctify every minister on this camp ground!

We are desperately in earnest. This is no sham fight. We have drawn the sword and thrown away the scabbard. We intend, by the help of God, to see this thing through. (Great commotion.) This is the old cry that our fathers sounded. If we could get the two and a quarter millions of Methodists into this fountain, and this experience, the Baptists and Presbyterians might look on and see us win the world for Jesus. Our God is marching on. We may have made a good many mistakes, but our hearts are right. Glory to Jesus! Who will come into this blessed experience just now? Give us room here—stand back. Who among you ministers that have not obtained this blessing, will come now—come at once? (Several ministers bow at the altar.) Who among the laity? (They come.) Now, glory to God! I want to get more fully down into deep waters than I have ever gone. Lord help me. Come on, brethren. Now steady. Lord Jesus, save the people!

A deeply impressive season followed, during which several professed to be saved "to the uttermost."

———◆◆———

SERMON BY REV. W. T. HARLOW.

FRIDAY AFTERNOON, 2½ O'CLOCK.

———

"*For all things are for your sakes, that the abundant grace might through the thanksgiving of many, redound to the glory of God.*—2 Cor. 4 : 15.

The original Greek version of this passage is more significant of the fullness of Gospel grace than the English translation. The Apostle seems to labor to express the great idea which is in his mind, reminding one by the number of comparisons used, of that other passage : "Where sin abounded grace did much more abound."

"Thou, O Christ, art all I want;
More than all in Thee I find."

We have in the text,

I. THE ABUNDANCE OF GOSPEL GRACE.

II. THE DIVINE METHOD OF THAT GRACE.

Grace, in general, is any favor bestowed without an equivalent expected in return. In the Gospel scheme of redemption it refers to the divine interposition for the salvation of human kind, with special reference to the provisions made for that salvation. " God so loved the world that he gave his only begotten Son, that whosoever believeth in him should not perish, but have everlasting life."

The abundance af Gospel grace may be seen if we regard—

1. Its source, which is the Divine mind. All the attributes of God stand pledged to insure success to any scheme which his wisdom may devise. When he proposes to make man holy and bring him to a holy heaven, a partner of his throne, infinite power is at hand to carry into effect the gracious purpose.

Human resources sometimes fail when the most beneficent enterprises are undertaken. In a season of drought, not long since, the Cochituate water came near failing the city of Boston. People were alarmed at the prospect of the fountain of their supplies drying up, and the city exposed to the dangers of fire with no possibility of extinguishing it. The city authorities were compelled to forbid the use of water except in limited measure for certain purposes. But there is no danger of a failure in the fountain of divine grace. If the world should make all possible demands upon it, it would still be full. If every one of the thirteen hundred millions of human beings now upon the earth were all together " at the fountain drinking," the river of divine grace would overflow its banks, and with a sea of glory inundate the world.

> "Its streams the whole creation reach,
> So plenteous is the store;
> Enough for all, enough for each,
> Enough for evermore."

2. Look at the particular provisions made for the salvation of the race.

The *Atonement* is the great provision on which all the others rest. See its *amplitude*—" He tasted death for every man." Notice its fullness—" The blood of Jesus Christ his Son cleanseth us from all sin."

The Holy Ghost is abundant for all purposes for which he comes into the world. He " reproves the world of sin, of righteousness, and of judgment," and often against the wishes of those whom he thus visits.

It may be remarked here that the work of the Holy Spirit in enlightening the mind is his fundamental work. All his other work of comforting and endowing with power is in exact ratio of our obedience to the light he gives. Persons sometimes complain of their want of comfort and their want of power over self and over the world. The reason in every case is this: they fail to live up to the light of the Spirit. To walk in the light we must walk up to the light, and when we do this all the graces of the Spirit are multiplied within us. There is no deficiency here. The provision is abundant if we will avail ourselves of it.

And so of the Word of God. There are more threatenings here than many are willing to heed; more precepts than most are willing to obey; more promises than most are willing to claim; and more examples of holy living than most are willing to follow.

The same is true of *prayer.* What an abundant provision has been made for frequency of access to the throne of grace—for liberty to bring our largest requests! And so of all other spiritual helps. The grace is abundant. In another place the Apostle says, " All things are yours." But here he virtually says, " Not only are all the appointments and arrangements of the gospel yours, but all were appointed and arranged for your sakes."

3. The grace provided is abundant to meet all the necessities of the soul. Let us look for awhile at these necessities. What are they?

First. We are *guilty* and need *pardon.* Abundant provision is made to meet this necessity.

The gospel offers pardon to all.

The gospel offers a full pardon to all.

The gospel offers a full pardon to the worst of sinners.

Second. We are *depraved*, and therefore need *purity.* Entire holiness is the normal condition of the human soul, and no one can be at perfect rest without it. To this condition of entire holiness all the provisions of the gospel point. It would be an imperfect gospel were not this the case. This being the case the gospel would be a failure did it not secure entire conformity to the will of God. But provision has been made abundant for this end.

The gospel abundantly provides for the purity of all, and

The gospel abundantly provides for the purity of all in the present life.

II. *The Divine method of that grace.*

The representation which God gives of himself is that " He is a jealous God," and he " will not give his glory to another." " For of him and through him and to him are all things : to whom be glory forever." " The heavens declare the glory of God, and the firmament showeth his handiwork." The sun, moon and stars fulfill the end for which they were made, and they glorify God. And so of the flowers that bloom at our feet, and the ten thousand forms of the beautiful that meet our eyes in every direction. They speak the skill, the wisdom, or power of their Creator, and thus declare his glory.

The same was true of rational beings so long as they continued to meet the end of their creation. They exhibited the skill and wisdom of the Divine Being more perfectly than irrational existences could do, because their workmanship was more exquisite. Material forms glorify their Maker; but the praise they offer is the music of the unconscious instrument that is made to play a given number of tunes of limited power and compass. It is well, yea beautiful, as far as it goes, but the music is after all involuntary and automatic. But the glory given to God by intelligent beings is the music of an exquisite instrument endowed with voluntary power to offer praise. The most exquisite workmanship speaks the greater skill of its Author, and the voluntary offering gives to him the greater glory.

But when man sinned the case was different. It was not that of an unconscious instrument getting out of tune, and thus rendered incapable of making good music. It was the case of a conscious instrument refusing to make good music, and by refusing to do so, putting itself out of tune, and rendering itself incapable of answering the end of its being. Oh ! the hour when man sinned, was the hour of the power of darkness. Then came an awful eclipse in the moral heavens. Then was made an infinite chasm between man and God, that created power could never bridge. If God had not been on the throne of the universe, that eclipse would have darkened the world forever, and that chasm

5

would have been forever unbridged. But God was there. His presence had anticipated the event,-and he was ready for the emergency. From all eternity he had determined to thwart the designs of evil, and seize upon man's necessity as his golden opportunity for displaying his greater wisdom and power, and gaining to himself the greater glory. To accomplish this end his own Son must come to this world to suffer and die, and thereby make atonement for sin.

When the fullness of the time had come, the Saviour appeared, heralded by the angels to the shepherds on the plains of Bethlehem. He throttled the serpent sin. He illumined the moral heavens with a new lustre. He bridged the chasm which sin had made, and reconciled man to God.

The star of Bethlehem was brighter than the old luminary. The bridge across the chasm was better and safer than was the connection before the chasm was made. The old instrument that had become impaired, was put in tune so that it was capable of making better music than before. True, a strain of minor appeared in the melody here and there, but the music was all the sweeter and the richer for the change. The vase that had been dashed to pieces was gathered up again, and the broken fragments polished and wrought into a beautiful mosaic, capable of holding and reflecting back the sweetest odors Heaven could bestow. Man's highest bliss was thus secured, and secured, too, on better conditions than before, and the divine glory greatly enhanced by the change that had been made. Such was the divine method of Gospel grace. It kept constantly in view the enhancement of the glory of God.

But it must be particularly observed that, in order to secure this end, the enhancement of God's glory, " the abundant grace," in all its saving power must be a matter of personal experience. It enters, then, into the divine method that "the abundant grace," in all its fullness, shall be first received by the individual; secondly, enjoyed, and thirdly reflected back in songs of thanksgiving to God.

This divine method is fitly brought to view by the apostle Paul in his epistle to the Ephesians 3 : 10.—" To the intent that now, unto the principalities and powers in heavenly places might be known (be made known) by the Church, the manifold wisdom of God." For this cause, viz.: that the church at Ephesus might make angels and archangels acquainted with "the manifold wisdom of God," he offers that wonderful prayer, commencing with the fourteenth verse and ending with that more wonderful doxology at the close of the chapter. He thereby expresses his deep solicitude that the church might express all the " fullness of God," so that every one in heaven might know that Jesus Christ on earth was " mighty to save." For then God would be glorified when they should be made to understand that the gospel was indeed " the power of God unto salvation."

The incense offered in the temple service at Jerusalem was so fragrant that it is said it permeated the temple and all the city, and all the surrounding atmosphere for miles in extent. They who lived at a distance knew by the perfumed air that service was being performed at Jerusalem, that the Shekinah was still within the holy place, and that God had not forgotten his covenant. Even so the thanksgiving of the Church, saved fully, saved joyously, is designed to be a perpetual incense to heaven, by which angels and men shall know that God is true to his word, and that the gospel is no failure. That incense shall yet fill the world. From every hill-top and from every valley shall go up the " song of Moses and the Lamb."

What a motive is here presented for availing ourselves of the proffered benefits of the gospel—God's glory! The motive is as vast as eternity. No higher one could be conceived.

Come, sinner; moved by this highest motive, come to Christ and help swell the song of the redeemed, and thereby enhance the glory of God. Come, Christian, impelled by the same motive, come for all your privilege in Christ. Come and receive " all the fullness of God," and then let your joyful hosannas go up to the heavens in testimony of the great truth that the gospel " saves to the uttermost," that God may be glorified thereby.

Oh! if I had a thousand souls, how would I delight to bring them all to Christ and thus give him an opportunity to glorify himself in their complete salvation! Then would I sing that glorious old doxology of the apostle: " Now unto him that is able to do exceeding abundantly above all that we ask or think, according to the power that worketh in us, unto him be glory in the Church by Christ Jesus, throughout all ages, world without end. Amen."

THE SERMON,

only an outline of which is presented, was followed in the usual way. The minister rising to exhort, has no roundabout course to pursue before he touches the point of direct application. The discourses invariably end with pointed and personal appeals, looking to immediate action. No single word aside from " Jesus," is more potent than " now." To silence all parleying with self, and the seducer of souls, God's great stirring " NOW " is reiterated, until people, made aware of their spiritual deficiencies, and the need of a deeper work to be wrought within them, become afraid to move in any direction except toward the altar. To give suitable impulse to the minds of those who " come forward," a stanza like the following is sung:

" Here at the cross, where flows the blood,
   That bought my guilty soul for God,
Thee my new Master now I call,
   And consecrate to thee my all."

There is a season of silent prayer, only interrupted by the leader's voice suggesting a promise on which to lean. Then, after it is reasonably presumed the truth is apprehended, and the efficacy of the blood applied, the strains of holy song softly swell out again—

" 'Tis done, the great transaction's done,
   I am my Lord's, and He is mine;
He drew me, and I followed on,
   Charmed to confess the voice Divine."

After a moment's pause, that the full force and effect of this " transaction" may be contemplated, in the same measure, the doxology gives to all the intimation that the service is ended.

The afternoon exercises, beginning at half-past two, including sermon, last until 5 P. M. As the congregation begin to disperse, the tones of a cabinet organ are heard in another part of the grounds, and thither go the crowds who wish to acquaint themselves with new tunes which have taken hold of the popular ear and heart. " The Gate Ajar," " Crimson Stream," " Whiter than Snow," and pieces of this character come into demand, and the evening melody is kept up until the bell gives notice of another service.

A FRIDAY MEETING.

To many of the followers of Jesus all over the land, the Philadelphia Friday Meeting is an institution well known through the columns of the METHODIST HOME JOURNAL. This paper conveys to them weekly a pretty full synopsis of its exercises, through which their souls have often been fed and refreshed, as with manna from heaven. At the camp-meeting were assembled a number of those who regularly attend and participate in it, besides many who never had the pleasure of being personally present, yet greatly desired to enjoy this privilege.

On Friday afternoon, therefore, it was proposed to hold a re-union at half-past 'one. The large prayer tent was crowded, and the exercises, in charge of Rev. W. L. Gray, began with a season of prayer, in which five or six brethren and sisters successively led the thoughts of the congregation to the mercy-seat.

After some delightful singing, in which Mrs. Bangs introduced with good judgment the sentiments best suited to the occasion, Sister Boyle gave an account of the wonderfully gracious manner in which God has dealt with her, in the education of her faith to trust implicitly the naked promise, and the conscious salvation which came to her daily by believing.

Mrs. Dr. Gause, also of Philadelphia, expressed her hearty sympathy with the advancing spirituality of the Church, telling her love for Christ, and her desire to work for the saving of souls.

Brother Perkins, of Ohio, said he greatly enjoyed the Friday meeting, although it was ten days, usually, after date, when it came to his home in the West. With congratulation he bid the friends of Philadelphia God speed in holding up the banner of full salvation, and said in Cincinnati they were following the good example of the City of Brotherly Love, in speaking often one to another of Jesus and his great salvation.

A preacher of the Pittsburgh Conference gave an account of his earlier experience. He was converted, and felt drawn nearer to Christ. The duty and privilege of being wholly sanctified was made plain to him, and he was made a happy partaker of this grace. When he began to profess and preach this special blessing, prudent ones cautioned him about the consequences ; told him the Church could not bear that kind of thing, and to accommodate sensitive people, he was ashamed to own, he had compromised with the enemy by rounding off the corners of this distinctive doctrine. As a consequence, he lost the evidence and power. At Manheim he was brought to feel and see what was wanted. He consecrated himself anew, and went home determined to talk and preach holiness. The Lord had signally blessed him in his soul, and attended the word of his testimony. He had been sweetly kept, and was rejoicing in a present and complete Saviour.

Brother Dunham, an aged standard-bearer in the ranks of the redeemed, rose and requested the meeting to join in singing,

> "Jesus paid it all—all the debt I owe,
> Sin had left a crimson stain—He washed me white as snow."

A stanza or two having been sung, he said the words expressed his experience for fifty years past. He was saved all along. It was something for him to feel that he belonged to a royal family, and that he was heir to a crown of glory. Before Jesus took him in hand, he had been as proud and covetous as the Devil desired, but the cleansing blood had washed it all away; "And now," said he, "I am free in Christ."

Mrs. Dr. Lowery said there was very much in the testimonies given here from day to day that was similar to her own experience. The thought that she could be made entirely pure by the blood of Jesus, and still live, attending to her ordinary duties, was amazing. She hesitated for three days after the work had been wrought, before she could bring herself to confess "the blood cleanseth." She had through all her previous Christian life been convicted for holiness. For twenty-five years she had been tossed about like a weather-beaten bark, when at any moment she might have found rest in Jesus. At the first Urbana camp-meeting she became thoroughly awakened to the fact that she had a work to do, and daily she vibrated between the Tabernacle and the stand, listening, learning, and seeking for help. Brother McLean preached a sermon in which he showed her what was in her heart. It was self she was serving. She was full of ambition, and brought herself to the resolution, if some great wave of power should come over her so that she would be laid prostrate, and then filled with the Divine Spirit, she could testify. But she had to step out on the rock. Her prejudice against the terms "cleansing" and "sanctification" had to be yielded up, and the Spirit applied the word to her heart "Now are ye clean." She then committed herself to this glorious doctrine, and went to Sea Cliff as a hungry, starving soul, wanting to be instructed; and there she *was* instructed in the deep things of God. She went home happy, and ever since her path has been all clear, and is shining brighter and brighter.

A brother said he had come to the meeting to hear and see something new; but this theme was running all through his Bible and Hymn-book. He wondered the preachers did not give it prominence, and urge the people up to their glorious privilege. He was going on to state his intention when he returned home to engage with all his heart in seeking this great blessing——.

Brother Gray—"No, brother; don't wait until you go home. Here, and now, you may have it. Will you accept it?"

The brother—"I will; I do accept it. (Great emotion.) Bless God! O, I believe he can, he will, he does save me fully."

Brother Gray—"Then hold on, just there. You will receive the witness. Brethren sing a verse."

> "O that my load of sin were gone," &c.

" Sing one more verse ; it may help several souls into the pool just now."

> " I would, but thou must give the power,
> My heart from every sin release ;
> Bring near, bring near the joyful hour,
> And fill me with thy perfect peace."

After the stir had subsided a little, a sister told what grace had done in its influence on her temper, and how she loved to speak, and work, and would even forsake all, to follow Jesus.

Referring to the last speaker, another sister said, " Yes, she is willing to confess Christ anywhere, and so earnest is she to win souls, that they must either run from her, or yield, and come to Jesus."

Still another from the same locality, testified that the zeal spoken of helped to get her converted, but she never did much until she sought and obtained a clean heart.   Then she had power to talk with her dear husband about his soul, and led him also into the fountain that washes " whiter than snow."

A Philadelphia minister said—" I have been listening with great interest to what has been said here, and feel convinced just now that I too should say something for the Master.   I have to leave the ground this evening.   Since I became a Methodist, I never had any doubts about the doctrine of sanctification. That was twenty years ago.   I have been a preacher eighteen years.   I am one of those who think everybody ought to do just as I want them ; and if they come short, it disturbs my equilibrium.   I have been kneeling among those that were seeking a heart filled with the love of God.   I had a notion that if the Lord would knock me down by his power, and roll me about, it would be good for me.   But some of my notions have been modified.   The National Committee have been taken out of my way, and several other things.   The greatest thing in my way, however, is—here he pronounced his own name—but self is all on the altar, and I shall go home a better man than I came."

A brother from Massachusetts expressed his joy in being for once in his life in the Friday meeting.   Brother Foote was of the same mind, and exclaimed " Glory be to Jesus !"   Sister Baldwin talked sweetly of resting at the cross, and Amanda Smith sang—

> "O 'twas love, 'twas wondrous love,
> The love of God to me ;
> It brought my Saviour from above
> To die on Calvary."

" Glory be to God ! I am in this blood-washed army.   Hallelujah !"

THE PREACHERS' MEETING,

at 6 P. M., on Friday, was opened in the most informal manner.   " Let us," said the leader, " pray personally—Lord bless *me*—cleanse *me*—help *me* to preach and live true holiness."

"If there are any dear brethren here seeking purity of heart, let them now audibly pray, telling into the listening ear of a present Jesus their wants."

"O, Jesus," said a preacher, "thou art acquainted with my leanness and weakness. How little I have done for thee; how dull and formal all my services; I must have power. I must die unto sin and self. I am lost, if thou wilt not here have mercy, and make me all right. Spirit of burning, come!"

Here a voice full of pathos and holy confidence sang—

> "In the promises I trust,
> Now I feel the blood applied;
> I am prostrate in the dust,
> I with Christ, am crucified."

Then the chorus was taken up—

> "I am trusting Lord in thee," &c.

Dr. Lowrey here intimated that a few passages of Scripture might be quoted, and gave one, expressive of his own present relation to Christ. Others followed, and the range of texts rapidly announced, were all full of comfort.

"I would like to know how many here are ministers of the Gospel. Let them rise." Over fifty men stood up.

"Now," he continued, "I should like to know how many have experienced the purification promised the sons of Levi. Will you rise?"

Only a small proportion of the number answered.

"Please, brethren, indulge me a little further. How many are here expressly to seek it—hungering and thirsting after it, and anxious to have this power, to go in advance of your flocks and lead them up to possess the goodly land. Will you rise?

About a score deliberately rose and stood on their feet.

"Now, let us come forward here and pray together. There is a good deal of talking and theorizing, and we all agree that the blessing may be had instantaneously. Let us ask for it."

Brother Boole—"Out of the number of ministers here who confessedly do not enjoy full salvation, only a few have knelt to seek it. What of the others?"

Dr. Lowrey—"I should suppose all the others have the blessing Surely, if they have not, and are not seeking it—groaning after it, the thought is painful that they remain non-commital."

At this moment there was sad silence for a time, and two or three more came and fell on their knees.

Brother Gray—"We have all been just where these brethren are now. We had to meet the responsibility, and pass through an ordeal of fire. We know how it feels to give up ministerial dignity and cast all at the foot of the cross. We are to seek this, not from personal considerations—but purely, and entirely, to be holy. We pray for power; let us rather ask to be cleansed. Now, Lord, touch these hearts with fire; melt them into tender simplicity."

A preacher—" Pray for me, brethren."

Dr. Lowrey—" Pray for yourself."

Brother Davies then broke out in supplication, followed by Dr. Levy, that the unsanctified might now be baptized with the Holy Ghost.

" Let all kneel," said the leader ; " pray for us ministers."

A brother—" Lord, we have come to a crisis here. Help us to give up all unbelief by believing. May we cease forever *trying*, and just receive the blessing."

The starting of a hymn at length ended what was, to some, an agonizing period of suspense.

A youthful preacher propounded a series of questions, in relation to the possibility of being so saved that all carnal thoughts shall die, and all pride and vanity, ambition, and irritation of temper, shall be taken out of our nature.

The colloquy here became general. Freely questions were asked, and answered by Revs. Boole, John Thompson, Dr. Levy and others.

The latter naively brought up a sentiment in one of Wesley's hymns, which he said used to appear extravagant until he experienced its truth. Now, although a Baptist, he would quote it and emphasize it, to this dear Methodist brother, who seemed to doubt whether such a salvation was possible as is implied in the line :

" Take away our bent to sinning."

The Doctor further remarked that he had succeeded in getting the hymn and the doctrine it teaches into the new Baptist hymn-book, now coming largely into use in that denomination.

The young brother still sought for information He had been converted, and thought he loved God with all his heart. Being put in the ministry and sent to a field of labor, some of his people approached him with the hope that he could lead them on in holiness. He wanted to do so, but the irritation consequent on taking care of his charge, convinced him he must have a deeper work. He talked fluently, and evinced a thorough knowledge of the way of full salvation; but he wanted to be sure that the provision was applicable to his particular case.

Brother Boole abruptly declared that quibbling was offensive to God at this point. If God had promised to do the work, He was responsible for all consequences. He never would or could go back on his word, and anybody who fully trusted that word, would come through all right. He wondered that people professing to want purity, were so slow to move ; they ought to bite like hungry fish.

The sound of the bell for public service at this moment ended this interesting and deeply impressive conversation.

THE SILENT MEETING.

At the hour for evening preaching, the congregation was called together by the usual summons of the bell. Earlier in the evening the question had been asked: "Who is to preach to-night?" and information, derived from authoritative sources, that Rev. Mr. Foote would have charge of the services, obtained general circulation. It was known, therefore, to but few, that the whole order of the meeting had been changed. Previous to attempting a sketch of this extraordinary occasion, it is due to the National Association to record the fact that no part in the service is assigned at any time to the individual members without earnest prayer; and if, after a brother is as-assigned to duty, his colleagues are decidedly impressed that the mind of the Holy Spirit is that a different order of work should be observed, he is ex-pected to cheerfully give place to any suggested change.

Some may regard this as enthusiastic fanaticism, as on the evening we purpose to describe. A member of the congregation did, who, with his wife, had come to the grounds for the purpose of listening to a sermon. When he heard the statement of the President of the Association, he said to his companion: "This is all foolishness; let us go home." But we may not deal with this subject in so light a manner. We remember when the hea-ven-received Cookman was expected to preach at one of the National Camp-meetings on a Sabbath evening, to the immense throng, attracted largely by the expectation of hearing him, that he said his subject was entirely taken from him and he could only deliver an exhortation. We remember the ef-fect of that exhortation, how the outposts of Satan were stormed and carried that very night at Manheim. God does direct His servants in the work to be done; and the success of the kingdom of Christ among men is to be at-tributed to *a fact that is neither promisory nor prophetic, but always oper-ating, viz: "Lo! I am with you alway, even unto the end of the world."*

In opening the meeting on this Friday evening, the President gave exhi-bition of his rare qualities as a leader, or, in military phrase, a general. With a voice that, ringing out clear as the tones of a bell, was distinctly heard throughout the entire enclosure, he uttered the first great sentence of the evening meeting—" Silence !" Within the immediate circle of the tents all was hushed; but those who had not yet taken their place in the worship-ing assembly were still moving about, and the low hum of voices could be distinctly heard. Again: he shouted—" Let every person within the circle of the tents be silent !" Slowly the voices without were subdued to a whis-per, but a low conversation was carried on in the tents. A third time, as if inspired with authority, he said—" I command every person on this ground to be silent, before the Lord!" The effect was magical—a profound stillness reigned over all.

It was a quiet summer evening; scarcely a zephyr stirred the leaves of the forest. The chirping katydid seemed to have suspended his evening love-song to his mate, and all above and around was still. The season so impressed us that we were carried in thought to the apocalyptic vision of the opening of the seals—"And when he had opened the seventh seal, there was silence in heaven about the space of half an hour. And I saw the seven angels which stood before God; and to them were given seven trumpets. And another angel came and stood at the altar, having a golden censer; and there was given him much incense, that he should offer it with the prayers of all saints upon the golden altar, which was upon the throne. And the smoke of the incense, with the prayers of the saints, ascended up before God out of the angel's hands."

In the deep solemnity of the hour, Mr. Inskip, in a subdued voice, said the order of the exercises had been changed by a remarkable chain of circumstances. "In the morning meeting of the Association, Bro. Foote had been detailed for the evening service. It was not in the minds of any of us to change this arrangement; but during the afternoon, several of us were impressed that our dear brother ought not to preach to-night. We bowed together before God in earnest pleading, for we did not know what else to do. While on on our knees, our convictions were increased, and we resolved to find Bro. Foote, and tell him all about it. We found him on his knees, at prayer; we knelt by his side, and one of us then said: 'Dear brother it is our conviction that you ought not to preach; God is going to manage this thing for his own glory, and he don't want our aid." We found that the same weight which had been rolled on us was oppressing him also; for half an hour he had been pleading with God for divine help and direction in the services. We all saw it was of the Lord. This is our situation. We have given the meeting into the hands of the Lord; let Him do as it seemeth to Him best.

"Let us proceed with great caution—waiting solemnly before God. If any of you think you are here to get happy and to shout, I want to tell you, beforehand, that this meeting is not for you. Let everybody remember he is on sacred ground, and in the presence of the great Jehovah; for, if He had put it into the hearts of the ministers to leave this meeting in His hands, He must have some great purpose to serve, and He will be here to work wonders to-night.

"Now, I don't want a word spoken, a hymn sung, or the least noise in any way. If God lets his floods come over your soul, keep it to yourself, if you possibly can. Do not grieve the Spirit. I don't know how God will reveal himself, but one thing I do know, He will come to us with mighty power. O, brothers, let us get down low before Him. I intend to go down deeper to-night than I have ever gone in all my life. This is the turning point in this meeting. God is going to give us the greatest victory we have ever had. I adjure you, in the name of the living God, be careful and prayerful now."

Having uttered these admonitions and precautions, he said : " I want every-body to go out of the altar ; do it quietly ; remove your camp-chairs outside ; be as noiseless as you can ; make no delay, but keep looking up to God in prayer." Quickly, and with great circumspection, these orders were obeyed, and the whole space was left vacant. Then; stepping down from the platform, he said : "I, as President of this Association, want to be endowed with power from on high, so that I may direct these services aright. I want the deepest baptism of my life. Here are ministers who want more of the Holy Ghost, so that they may preach the gospel with fervency and power; then there are people here who know their weaknesses ; let us make a clean breast of it. I want all the members of the Association to come to this altar. (They kneel.) Let all the preachers in the stand bow here before the Lord ; (every one does so.) Steady, brethren. Now let every preacher in the congregation come ; (others come forward.) Now the exhorters ; the class leaders ; the Sunday-school superintendents ; all the members of the churches."

These were represented as the summons was issued to each, until at least five hundred people were prostrate before God. " Now, again I charge you to be very still—be so still that you can hear the one next to you breathe. Lord God, help us!"

This was followed by a long season of deep, silent heart searching; in which every Christian seemed to bow at the cross and wait the will of God.

Everything about the movement was extraordinary. Levity, wherever it prevailed, was utterly banished, and the awful silence produced a degree of seriousness and self examination which led hundreds face to face with the startling inquiry—" Have I any religion? My life is drifting on without solid experience. The mind and spirit of Christ is not in me. I have neither disposition or power to work for God. Lord save me !"

Strangers entering the grounds, as many did after the service commenced, stood amazed for some time surveying the scene—a vast congregation on their knees, and some of the leading ministers full length on the ground with their faces covered, and the stillness of death prevailing; then they too bowed before the Lord.

At last the hour came for preparing to retire ; then the hosts of the Lord being released, shouted the words of victory, the President himself being so full of the Spirit that he could no longer restrain it, shouted—"Glory to the Lamb !"

The pent-up fire now began to blaze around the ground, as various companies sought their tents, saying " Surely the Lord is in this place !"

FOURTH DAY.

THE EARLY MEETING.

THE meetings of the day were inaugurated by the 5 o'clock service at the Tabernacle under the conduct of Rev. Wm. McDonald. The leader said it was his conviction that this must be strictly a prayer-meeting. We had a great battle to fight, and it must be fought on our knees. *Singing* would not secure the victory, and *talking* would not do it. It must be by praying and believing.

After a long season of prayer, opportunity was given for remarks in experience.

Rev. Wm. P. Ray, from East Cambridge, Mass., said he had come to this meeting for no common blessing. Some of the young men from Harvard University had come with him, and they too expected a mighty baptism. They had good things at home, but they had never seen it after this sort before.

Rev. L. R. Dunn felt impressed to say that we need not strive to make God willing to bless. He is infinitely willing. How soon Elijah secured the answer by a prayer that occupied but little less than two minutes, and the fire fell upon the altar and consumed the sacrifice, and even the stones of the altar.

While Bro. Dunn led in prayer the power of God was especially felt, and faith greatly increased. Many souls were drawing near, and claiming the promises, as the leader inquired: "What Scripture have we that we can rest upon as the basis of faith for victory now?"

"What thing soever ye desire when ye pray, believe that ye receive, and ye shall have it."

"This is the confidence that we have in Him, that if we ask anything according to His will, he heareth us, and if we know that He hears us, we know that we have the petitions that we have desired of Him."

Then followed short testimonies:

One said, "This is indeed a mighty meeting to my soul. God has done just what I asked for. I must confess it. After I had been the means of leading many others into this fullness, by some misapprehension I fell into darkness and lost the blessing; but glory to God! it is all right now."

A sister—"I came here for full salvation, and He now saves me fully."

A brother—"The Lord has done a mighty work for me. Refining fire is going through my soul."

Another said—"I thank God I have found what I have been seeking. He fills my soul. Jesus saves me."

After other testimonies, the doxology was sung twice, and while singing, a richer shower of grace fell upon the people, and still others were saved ; one dear brother declared "I am fully saved. Glory ! Glory ! Glory ! " This was a rich and glorious beginning of a blessed and memorable day.

RECITING SCRIPTURE.

The lively exercises of the morning were resumed at 8 A. M., and nothing impressed us more than the singularly well chosen series of texts, for the recitation of which ten minutes were allowed. Bible phraseology is a safe and prominent feature of every service. The Bible is the great standard of appeal, whether the question be one of doctrine, morals or experience.

We can hardly give a verbatim report; but the following will indicate the unity of sentiment prevailing at the moment.

A minister, wishing to confess Christ's mediatorial work and its personal realization and benefits, said : " He was wounded for *my* transgressions : He was bruised for *my* iniquities ; and with *his* stripes *I am healed.*"

" He that cometh to God must believe that he is, and that he is a rewarder of them that diligently seek him."

" Then shall we know, if we follow on to know the Lord. His going forth is prepared as the morning ; and he will come to us as the rain, as the latter and former rain unto the earth."

" He will give grace and glory, and no good thing will he withhold from them that walk uprightly."

" Thou shalt be as a watered garden."

" The Lord is my light, and my salvation; whom shall I fear ?"

" They shall be mine saith the Lord, when I make up my jewels."

" They that wait on the Lord shall renew their strength. They shall mount up with wings as eagles."

" The law of the spirit of life in Christ Jesus hath made me free from the law of sin and death."

" Thou wilt keep him in perfect peace whose mind is stayed on thee."

" Let the words of my mouth, and the meditation of my heart be acceptable in thy sight, O Lord, my strength and my Redeemer."

" To present you holy and unblamable and unreprovable in his sight."

" Truly God is good to Israel, even to such as are of a clean heart."

" He that believeth on the Son of God, hath the witness in himself."

" There is no fear in love."

" Who is like unto thee, O Lord—glorious in holiness, fearful in praises, doing wonders."

" The Lord hath done great things for us whereof we are glad."

" Because the love of God is shed abroad in our hearts by the Holy Ghost given unto us."

" If ye abide in me, and my words abide in you, ye shall ask what ye will, and it shall be done unto you."

" My cup runneth over."

SATURDAY, 10 A. M.

SERMON BY REV. WM. H. BOOLE, OF NEW YORK CITY.

" But ye shall receive power after that the Holy Ghost is come upon you."
Acts 1: 8.

THERE is much in that word "power." Its possession is the condition and assurance of success in any undertaking. The possession, not the promise of it; for though a promise is of value because of the ability and integrity of the promiser, yet it is the fulfillment of it that contains the power of the promise. God's promises are all valuable even as his word only; but chiefly because of what is contained in their fulfillment—the gift of the Holy Ghost.

Power belongeth unto God—all power—man is powerless; and for all the works of mankind, of whatever kind, to which men are called in their present fallen state, our Creator has provided the suitable forces and power.

That " knowledge may increase" in the present advanced stage of Christian civilization, it has become necessary that a man should do as much in ten years as the ancients accomplished in fifty. So God put wisdom in man, and directed him to where lay concealed the reserved resources the Creator had hid in nature's dominion; and steam, air, water, electricity, &c., are brought under contribution to the will of man, to annihilate time by lightning express trains, to break huge masses of stubborn materials, to convey his messages thousands of miles in a moment. These are God's forces, provided by him for man's help. I have seen a plate of solid iron ten inches thick, broken like a pipe stem by the force of a column of water no bigger than your little finger. This is the power of God as displayed in his physical forces. In the legislature of Christian nations there is found the acknowledgment that " power belongeth unto God." If you were to discover a new force in nature, and by its application to novel machinery of your own invention should produce new and marvelous effects, you would be allowed to take out an exclusive right or patent on the machinery, and the application of such newly discovered power; but you could get no patent on the power itself; it is not yours; no, not by discovery; it is the Lord's; he made it, and by an exclusive universal patent he is the sole proprietor of all forces and powers.

There are many powers—powers of different natures, as physical, intellectual, spiritual; and wisdom is manifested in the suitable application of any power to its own proper use or purpose. And to obtain a fair understanding of the real import of our text it is necessary to consider what is the true nature of the work to be done by the power herein promised.

Well, is it not to build pyramids, or drive steamers, or run trains, or work telegraphs. For all these proper things God has provided suitable powers among the forces in nature. This is not, then, a physical power. Neither is it to teach arts or sciences. The nations are not to become learned and cultured in the sciences and arts directly by the dispensation of this promised power.

The Greeks were cultured and refined in much; the musty records of Chinese history show that that people, thousands of years ago, were not devoid of culture of a philosophical and scientific kind; yet these nations were utterly devoid of this promised power. It is not, therefore, an intellectual power.

What is the work to be done by the possession and use of it? In a word, it is the power to save the world of mankind. Nothing new can be added to this stereotyped statement; but we must continue to repeat it until the mighty Holy Ghost is given in full measure to all the Church; and the whole world is saved. This world is a lost world, wrecked and stranded on a lee shore; turned upside down by the wonderful force of that "bad miracle of hell"—sin. The first work of this promised power is to destroy sin. But sin is not located in the mountains, else we could apply the physical forces placed at our command, and beat them small as dust. Neither is it in the body, the flesh of man; else you might by medication and purifying processes abstract and destroy it. Neither is it located in the intellect, though this is impaired by its ravages; so you cannot by much reasoning, and choice and conclusive arguments, reach the seat of the disease. But sin is located in the spiritual nature of man, for, "out of the heart proceed adulteries, fornication, evil thoughts, thefts, blasphemies," &c. If, then, sin is to be destroyed, and mankind cleansed of its pollution and saved from its present and eternal curse by this promised power given by the Holy Ghost, it must be a spiritual power; inward, unseen, but wonderfully felt. There is something more besides the destruction of sin. By this power the kingdom of God is to be builded. But this kingdom is invisible. "The kingdom of God is within you," and this kingdom is established in the regeneration, the transformation, the sanctification, the present glorification of the soul and spirit of man. Thus we reach the conclusion that the power received upon the gift of the Holy Ghost is a vital, spiritual power, which, in its burning energy, purifies and transforms those whom it possesses, and fills them also with a divine anointing, effectual in its manifestation to the regeneration and transforming of many. This is the power of the Holy Ghost in you, and through you, as promised in this text.

It is of interest to note the relation of the little word "but," which begins this text, to this view of the matter. It connects what goes before with what follows, and also introduces a new thought.

The earnest and ambitious inquiry of the disciples was, "Lord wilt thou at this time restore the Kingdom to Israel?" The full proof of his divine Messiahship was now before their eyes, in his healed hands and side; they no longer doubted his ability to establish his promised kingdom at once among his enemies, and by a single word claim and possess the throne of their father David. But their first crude, material idea of the nature of this kingdom remained unchanged by the astounding fact of their Master's resurrection. They believed in the temporal, earthly reign of Christ. Therefore said they, "Wilt thou restore the Kingdom?" By this they meant only the restoration of Israel's ancient magnificence and splendor, as she once shone the "head" and not the "tail" of all nations. In his response, Christ severs the cord of their ambitious expectations, but reveals to their wondering minds the true idea of his Kingdom, and also the responsible relations which they themselves were to sustain to it as its builders and promoters. "It is not for you to know,"

he answers, " the times and the seasons"—the designs of the Father concerning the Kingdom of which you speak, " But ye shall receive power after that
the Holy Ghost is come upon you." The spiritual nature of his Kingdom
now to be set up, he half conceals, half discloses; and turning their minds
from himself, as they said, "Wilt thou restore," etc., he directs their attention
to themselves as the honored, responsible agents in the founding of the coming kingdom of a new and spiritual dispensation.

This is the method of this power; the Holy Ghost dwelling in Christ's
disciples, and acting through these charged batteries upon mankind, when
brought in contact with them, to the awakening and saving of multitudes.
By saved men, are men to be saved.

I will say further, that in this argument the weakness of the instruments
is not to be taken into the account. It is a common objection on the part of
Christians when pressed to seek for the full baptism of the Holy Ghost, as an
endowment for labor—"Oh, I am so weak and of so little ability, the Saviour
can do nothing with me." Consider now to whom he was talking: whom
did he chose? The weakest set of men that ever followed a leader. They
were dull of understanding, mentally not above an average grade, hard of
heart, slow of faith; and altogether they appear before the day of Pentecost
very like children quarreling for an unequal distribution of gifts and honors.
Peter denied his Master with oaths and curses, while John with all the
others forsook him and fled. Christ's selection of these weak things for his
first disciples and ministers is the final answer to all such objections as we have
named. Indeed, it is written: " He hath chosen the weak things of the
earth to confound the things that are mighty." If you say, " I am nothing," God will not be offended, for you and all men are "as nothing before
Him." But why do you hold on so tightly to nothing? Let nothing go for
nothing, and the Lord may then make something for himself out of you.
The slender thread of copper wire which lies under your feet, is a thing without life or sense. There is no power in it. You may lay it on a barrel of
gunpowder, but it does no harm. It can neither talk nor write. But if you
only apply to its end that wondrous invisible force we call the " electric spark,"
instantly it " receives power," and under three thousand miles of unfathomed
ocean it flashes the lightening message to merchant, peer and king, and speaks
forth to the nations the " wonderful works of God." Now bring it in contact
with that mass of twenty-two tons of dead powder lying in the cavity of that
treacherous rock in the harbor of the " Golden Gate " on the California
coast;—that fatal rock on which millions of the commerce of the State has
foundered and gone down, thus retarding and diminishing the prosperity of
the people;—and in an instant, as the fiery spark fills the dead wire and com-
municates with the dead powder, both are kindled in a mighty flame, whose
dreadful force expanding, rends and tears into smallest fragments the solid
granite; the opposing mountain is removed, and the deep waters cover the
place, and wait to bear in safety on their supporting bosom every sail which
has been waiting in the mouth of the golden harbor. Thus the senseless
things of earthly nature, always obedient to the will of their Maker, become
invested with " power from on high " when touched with the finger of their
God. And if you are but a worm, as much a " nothing " as a strand of copper wire, *only be still and let God touch you with his electric spark and you
too shall " receive power*,"—power to burn, to move the mountains, to "speak

forth the wonderful works of God." The Lord God of the promise, send upon us the Holy Ghost !

I would now speak to you of some of the consequences of this baptism. It brings out in marked boldness and relief, the individuality of the receiver. No two human beings are alike in all respects. There is diversity throughout all God's domains, and no where more than in the human family. Each of you are the centre of a circle of influence, and none can be so great, so useful where you are as yourself. Doubtless, each man and woman has received of God a special life mission which is made known to us when we consent to the promised anointing, which alone can qualify us to fulfill our end. And let me say that there is more of any man with God in him, than in the greatest man without God. But it takes this baptism to bring out a man's individuality. Peter becomes *all Peter* in the bold prominence of his peculiar characteristics; and he is not duplicated in any other saint. John is himself, and so is Paul, and so also, the blessed Lord will make *you* all that can be made of you; your work and mission will differ from all others in its special feature; for the Lord has a place for each of you.

The Church is too much like the " milky way " seen in the heavens. You know this is composed of innumerable stars, so insignificant in size as to lose their individuality, so as to appear only as a conglomerate of mere particles, shedding a mild and milky light.

The unanointed masses of our Church are mingled in a vast conglomerate, where individuality is lost, and only a faint and glimmering light is shed along the milky way of his path. The baptism of the Holy Ghost makes a bright particular star of each son and daughter of the Lord.

Again, it annihilates the distinction of self-interest in the man, so that he holds all things in common with Christ. For it is the spirit of Christ in him, who gave himself a ransom for all. Like produces like. The example of Christ leads John to say " We ought to lay down our lives for the brethren." It is, indeed, according to the spirit of this world to adopt the maxim that "Self-preservation is the first law of nature ;" but self-sacrifice is the first law of grace. Man is to deny—not some things—but himself. The true Christian "seeketh not his own." Having under the power of this baptism, merged his being and interests into the spirit and destiny of Christ, this man, this woman, gives all to Christ's cause, as in wisdom he is directed. Brethren, this baptism will fill the missionary treasury, provide generously for the costs of the Church in the great battle for the redemption of the race. Chaplain McCabe declares that these national meetings for the promotion of holiness are the most successful agency in filling the treasury of the Church Extension Society. One man on receiving this baptism gave $50,000, and many others have given their thousands.

Last January, a lady, not a Methodist, who had received the fullness of the Spirit, sent me for the work in Water Street, New York City, among the abandoned classes, $1,000, and wrote : " Perhaps it would interest you to know that the inclosed amount is the price of some jewels of great beauty, which even on my happy bridal day, did not yield me the pleasure they do now, as I put them in the hands of my dear Saviour, for the salvation of my poor sisters." How could any woman do such a thing, voluntarily, and unsolicited by any other person, for the sake of any other than Christ?

6

Another consequence of this baptism is, it makes the receiver willing and fit for the work of his life-mission. The quaint Lorenzo Dow, when asked, "How may a man know when he is in the order of God in what he is doing?" answered, "He will feel in him the spirit of his station." When Isaiah first saw the glory of God he fell down and cried out, "Woe is me! for I am undone; for mine eyes have seen the King, the Lord of glory." But when one of the seraphims flew with a live coal, and laid it on his mouth, and said, "Lo! this hath touched thy lips, and thine iniquity is taken away, and thy sin is purged;" and he heard the voice of the Lord saying, "Whom shall I send, and who will go for us?" immediately he responded, "Here am I; send me." In the same moment the fiery baptism made him fit and willing. So will it also be with you. So will it be with the whole Church of God; when this baptism shall touch their lips and penetrate their hearts; the weak and irresolute Christian, a halting and unpurified Church—all shall feel the spirit of their station and wondrous mission, and they shall leap forward to fill the posts of duty, honor and danger; for "His people shall be willing in the day of His power."

Further, I wish to speak a few words on the necessity of this baptism. We must feel the mighty power of God in ourselves before we can with any considerable degree of faith and confidence expect to see it fall on others. It is our knowledge of the power of God as an experimental fact that increases our faith in expecting it on others. This baptism gives a holy boldness in the proclamation of God's truth, and the testimony of Jesus The testimony is confirmed in us, and we cannot but speak the things which we have heard. And what is a necessity for us at home is a necessity also for laborers abroad. And unless the corps of missionaries on the perilous and rocky fields of heathendom tarry for this full baptism of fire and the Holy Ghost, as their divine equipment, I have but little faith that great or satisfactory results will crown their efforts. In other words, I believe if they all were now so filled, their faith would more easily grapple with the difficulties of their work—the battle sharper and the victories more decisive.

William Taylor is an example in point.

If the entire army of missionaries were to take ship and return home, and hold a National Camp-meeting, to stay until endued with the mighty power of this promise, the world would feel the shock of an earthquake.

I published a little tract called "Wonders of Grace," relating instances I had witnessed of the power of grace in destroying sinful appetites, such as in opium eating, use of tobacco, &c. That in a moment the appetite for any of these was extirpated, and the man felt in his body that he was healed of that plague, and many of these cases continued for years to bear witness in the absence of all desire for them.

A missionary in China to whom a friend had sent a copy of the tract, wrote home to an officer of a mission board, to know whether the statements were really true. "For this," said he, "is a new theory in the Gospel to me, and if it is true, I may give some hope to some sincere Chinamen, whose absorbing passion for opium only prevents them from accepting Christ." Now if that missionary had received this full baptism of power in his own soul before he went out to his work, he would have known that the uttermost salvation of the Gospel contains virtue to do even that much for such as are bound under the power of Satan, however great his power may be.

This baptism is necessary for the whole Church, to create in us all a radicalism with which to successfully attack the fiery, opposing, progressive spirit of the world. The world of carnal men is full of life. "Entire devotion" to pleasure, money getting, honor seeking, dishonest practices, is the motto of this "dead-in-earnest" generation; and if you think the Devil, leading this uncounted host, is to be easily conquered, you will be fatally mistaken. This world is as wicked and radical as hell; an army of dreadful prowess, and flushed with many a victory. Our religion is radical, its spirit uncompromising and aggressive; it brands sin and Satan as usurpers here, and urges a war of extermination against them. Now such a baptism as the text implies only can make us the superiors of this host in zeal, devotion, aggression and victory. "Our weapons are not carnal, but *mighty* to the pulling down of"—what? baby houses? No, of "*strongholds!*" An earnest, wicked man, full of a fiery spirit, sets his eye and mind on a coveted object to be gained, and says, "I'll have it, cost what may," and without turning a corner he goes for it, and the prize is gained. It is for the Church of God to fix her gaze upon a lost world, and straightway, at all hazard and cost, go for the prize.

The uncle of the first Napolean was trying to dissuade him from further efforts at conquest, urging the dangers of failure, the strength of his allied enemies, &c. The believer in destiny caught his uncle by the arm and drawing him to the window (it was night) pointed upward and impulsively said, "Do you see that star?" "No," replied the astonished pleader. "Well, I do," rejoined Napoleon. And if thou, O man of God, art filled with the spirit of Christ, with undimmed vision thou shalt see thy star of destiny, bright and victorious, unseen of the world; and seeing, thy courage shall not fail thee, neither shalt thou be dismayed.

This gift is intended to be a permanent endowment. "He shall abide with you forever." It is not Christ's desire to ever leave a heart when he has once possessed it, and the power of this baptism does not diminish, but increase.

It is possible to fall from the highest degree of grace; nevertheless close investigation would discover that the prime cause of apostacies and declension in religious fervor among Christians, is, so many stopping short in the beginning, satisfied with too meagre a degree of grace; they were not struck through with an electrical baptism, filling their being.

Once more—the baptism of the Holy Ghost is a positive, specific, conscious, instantaneous experience. Here we stand or fall—Methodism stands or falls. Our Church has taught no other doctrine from the beginning; the Scriptures amply sustain the proposition; and the testimony of the host of worthies upon whom the Holy Ghost has fallen, add their willing testimony to the fact. No case of being filled with the Holy Ghost occurs in Scripture, except such as are stated to be of sudden descent.

At Pentecost "suddenly there came a sound. * * And they were all filled," &c. In Acts 4th, it is written again, "They were all filled," while at prayer. In Acts 10 : 24, is written, "While Peter yet spake these words, the Holy Ghost *fell* on all them which heard the Word," and many other passages.

William Bramwell says, "The Lord for whom I waited came suddenly to the temple of my heart," &c. William Carvosso says, "No sooner had I uttered the words, 'I shall have the blessing now,' than refining fire went through my heart," &c. Bishop Hamline says, "*All at once* I felt as though a hand, omnipotent, were laid on my brow. * * * I fell to the floor. * * *

In a few minutes the deep of God's love swallowed me up," &c. Many more could be added to these.

In conclusion, I exhort you, dear brethren, receive the Holy Ghost. Accept the promised power. 'Tis the legacy left to you ; why do ye go without your rightful inheritance? Your God commands you to separate yourselves from all things to receive this anointing. Let all go. No compromising, no parleying. It shall come upon you, it shall cut you loose, every cord, every shore line be severed. Some of you will go to India, others to Africa, some to your counting-houses to transfer your stocks, your ware, your influence over to Christ.

Will you have it—have it *now ?* Who among you, counting the cost will declare, " I will, I *must* have this power !" The pledge of God is in his promise. Take it. " What things soever ye desire when ye pray, believe ye receive them, and ye shall have them."

AFTERNOON WORK.

A heart-searching season followed the morning sermon. The people quietly dispersed to dinner, and the hour for silent prayer was very generally observed in the various tents.

Bro. Thompson's meeting at 1½ P. M., was opened with the precious hymn :

"There is a fountain filled with blood," &c.

Then the whole company bowed in silent prayer, during which the Holy Spirit was manifestly present. Two or three earnest vocal prayers followed ; each one a fervent supplication for a present blessing

Bro. Thompson alluded to the fact that many were there for the first and last time, and asked the question, " Do you now want another baptism ?" He said, " You will find it down in the low vale of humility. Now let us hear from the little ones."

Rev. Selah W. Brown said, " Jesus was giving all the time, and yet never exhausted his resources. It was like Rowland Hill's giving a poor man £200. He first sent £5 in a letter with the words ' more to follow.' The man was overwhelmed with gratitude ; but soon the mail brought another letter with £5 and the words, ' more to follow.' So the letters came for a long time, and it was ever ' more to follow.' So Jesus deals with me ; however rich my previous endowments, I have always ' more to follow.' "

Dr. Nast, said he could speak under the invitation to the little ones. He could feel very little when he contemplated the amazing condescension of Jesus. He felt it to be a great thing to get down, and a great thing to keep down ; and he meant to be as a little child holding on to his Father's hand.

A verse of "Valley of blessing" was sung. A sister quoted Lady Maxwell and Fletcher to the intent that we must be willing to follow the Lamb whithersoever he goeth, not only on Tabor but in Gethsemane.

A brother said—" Eleven years ago I started from Egypt, and this very hour I have entered Canaan."

A Baptist sister said—" I know I am the least of all saints, but Jesus passed by and gave me such a look—O such a look! and then he showed me that I could live by faith."

Bro. Boole spoke of the rain, and the probability that the meeting would be continued for some time; but it was all right, God means something. We are not yet fully prepared for the great battle that is to be fought on this ground. We have not power enough. We must get down on our knees—on our faces. Some of you are not willing to do this. You want the joy, but are not willing to be emptied. God will not permit that thing to be done. Now let us all kneel down and fully consecrate ourselves to God. The stanza—

> " Take my poor heart and let it be
> For ever closed to all but thee," &c.

was sung with great feeling. " Sing it again," said Brother Thompson; and the tide rose still higher. " Sing it over," cried the leader; and during the third singing a wave of divine influence seemed to roll over the whole company. " Hold steady,". cried Brother Boole. " As many as believe God is willing to pour out the Holy Spirit during the next half hour, hold up your hands." A hundred hands were raised. From that moment the cry for the coming Holy Ghost became awfully intense. Many "wept and made supplication;" and in the midst of the Jacob-like wrestling, waves of power rolled over the place, and scores of souls were endowed with the unction of the Holy One; the whole company broke out in the rapturous song—

> " 'Tis the very same power that they had at Pentecost."

SATURDAY AFTERNOON, 2½ P. M.

SERMON BY REV. ALEXANDER McLEAN.

"Not my will, but Thine be done."—Luke 22 : 42.

I REGARD it as more complimentary to the doctrines of our Lord Jesus Christ, advocated here, than to any minister, to see so many people waiting, in the face of a threatening storm, to hear God speak. Let us pray that he may overrule the circumstances surrounding us for our good, and the glory of his own great name.

The words of my text were those of Jesus the Son of God, in that great struggle preceding his betrayal, agony, and crucifixion.

He had gone to an accustomed place of prayer with three of his disciples, on the Mount of Olives. When there he retired a stone's throw apart from them, and engaged in earnest prayer. Returning he found them fast asleep. They may have been listening to his account of coming events. Their sympathy with him led them into deep sorrow, and like little children, they wept themselves to sleep. Again he left them and prayed to his Father, saying : " If it be possible let this cup depart from me ; nevertheless, not my will, but Thine be done."

I need not dwell longer on the strange, sad fact, or raise the inquiry as to how it was that the dear Jesus suffered thus ; nor yet, whether the human or divine nature was most affected ; but rather, let us turn to a few practical thoughts on the will, its submission, entire and complete to the will of God, as instanced in the prayer offered by Jesus for himself.

The will, in its relations to the claims of God upon us, may be classified thus :—

1. The will when in opposition to God : this is the sinner's condition. His own will is of the highest moment.

2. The will when in partial submission to God : this is the condition of the child of God while he is not entirely sanctified.

3. The will when brought into harmony with the will of God : this is realized only in what is known as entire sanctification, or Perfect Love, and there fully.

The will is the mightiest power given to man. The greatest power known to men, devils, angels, or God, is in the will. It is this which subordinates and controls the other parts of man's nature. If you look out upon the great waters, you may with a glance at any vessel, determine what motive power was designed to propel her. From the keel up, everything indicates the motive power. So you may readily see man was built with entire reference to the kingly power of his will. It was bestowed on him that he might exercise it as a free agent, and use it he must and does, in one direction or another. No one who hears me but will bring his power of volition into play either for or against God, in some degree or other, this very day. God grant that it may be for Him, and in the fullest measure. I do not say that the grace of God will not reach other parts of our nature, but it will do this most effectually through the sway of the will. Nor may we by a mere volition will ourselves into the prossession of any grace, but we can determine upon the means and then lay hold upon and steadily employ them. The will, under the Divine assistance, can present the body a living sacrifice, wholly and acceptable unto God, and then we can lay hold of Jesus by faith for the full acceptance of that gift.

1. The will in opposition to God is the condition in which all Christians acknowledge the sinner is found. How dreadful the condition. May God help him to see that all the conflict of the universe has been a conflict of will; that it was this which turned the angels out of heaven, and our first parents out of Eden. Sin is an open, flagrant and persistent rebellion against God, and to Him there must be an unconditional surrender.

2. The will in partial harmony with God, is the condition of the unsanctified believer. This is manifested by the disposition to specify to God the manner in which he shall bless us. That the carnal mind is not wholly removed from us while the will is not wholly subdued to God, may be known by an extreme sensitiveness which is easily wounded. There may be a readiness to criticise, but a hostility to being criticised; a regret to learn the success of a rival, but a pleasure to know the fall of a foe; a faith in man, yet doubting God; a desire of goodness, yet a dread of its consequence; a longing for power, but a listlessness for purity; committed to God, yet living a life of non-committal. The understanding admits to the fullest extent the claims of God; conscience clearly points the path to be pursued; God's word and Spirit say: "Accept it *now*." To this the sinner says: " No, not now." The justified soul says: "I will," and means it, but fails to perform. He feels that his every motive should be what they are not, simply and singly for God's glory. He resolves to have them so, but does not realize his desire.

Oh, how keenly and painfully my own soul has experienced the variations to which I have alluded, while in the unsanctified condition. My will was exerted to its uttermost to abide in Christ, yet without avail. Still I deemed the fault must be in defective willing, and would gird myself for its stronger exercise. Failure followed each newly energized endeavor, until I was constrained to admit that in my will, or in that of the most pertinacious, there was no help. Though I regarded it as ever so mean and unworthy in me not to keep upon the high plane of Christ-like living, where I saw so clearly it was my privilege to remain, yet I did not abide there, if indeed I at all gained those blessed heights. I see the same sad history in your eye. I hear it in the mourning of members of all the denominations who have not yet been delivered from the bondage of sin. I read the sad strains of this experience in the hymns of the churches, and it is everywhere manifest that when we would do good, evil is present with us. The minister, class-leader, deacon, or elder, seeing the young convert running on in his early zeal, admonishes him to carefulness, and seeks to prepare his mind for great revulsions—as though there was no gospel plan for the entire removal of the cause of such revulsions.

Yes, there is a plane of experience, where these perturbations are less frequent, and where, indeed, they do not exist. Luke tells us that while Christ was in the agony of the garden, "There appeared an angel unto him from heaven, strengthening him." So our will must be stengthened from on high.

What may have been impossible by our own will, becomes feasible when assisted of God. Just here men stagger. They see the greatness of the work to be done, but, realizing their own feebleness, they falter, as well they might. Yet, when God enters and re-inforces the will, and energizes the whole soul, how changed everything becomes. God's doing, and our doing are infinitely far apart. It is God who promises, "Then will I sprinkle clean water upon you, and ye shall be clean ; from all your filthiness, and from all your idols will I cleanse you." What signifies our inability, when God declares that he " will" do it for us and in us ?

Self-crucifixion must precede the realization of the fullest harmony between the divine and the human will. Cost what it may, self must go down, all the way down, in every regard where the soul claims a separate interest from Christ. One wish, one will, one way, with Jesus in the lead, must be the soul's unvarying aspiration. John was so far from having a distaste for the fact, that his whole soul was thrilled with joy, when he said of Jesus, " He must increase, but I must decrease." Consent, dear hearer, to die to self. Be not satisfied with a temporary submission. If you would have a thorough work wrought, go down, down into the depths of self-abnegation. As an old sea captain was exhibiting a harpoon several feet in length and of considerable weight, he said, " We do not kill the whale with this ; you might load the whale down with harpoons, and not kill him. We fasten to the whale with this, and when he is well wearied with drawing us through the water, and comes up to breathe, we row close to him, and a strong and expert man in the bow throws a sharp lance, smaller than the harpoon, with all his force right to the spot where he lives. This is the way in which the whale is killed." Self will endure a great deal of harrowing and harpooning, but by an unreserved consecration, and faith in our Lord Jesus Christ, let us strike it where it lives. *Your will*, you will find, is the vital point ; that being in entire submission to God's will, you shall find rest to your soul.

> " Renew my will from day to day,
> Blend it with Thine, and take away
> All that now makes it hard to say,
> 'Thy will be done.' "

A great change in your affections and desires will take place upon the death of self. Why should a woman, dead to sin and self, bedeck herself as though she were alive to human admiration ? Do ear-rings, and a display of jewelry generally, well become the dead ? Shall a dead woman so attest her enslavement to fashion as to still wear her golden manacles ? I cannot understand how self can be fully crucified, while as yet we are so very sensitive to either the praise or censure of men ; or, if we are seeking the honor which comes from men, rather than the honor which comes from God only. If our feelings are wounded so easily by some reflection, remark, or supposed slight, does it not indicate the presence of the self-life ? The foot-ball, though thrown rapidly in one direction, is uninjured, and ready at once for another thrust. Much of our discomfort, and annoyance grows out of our sensitiveness. Be adamant to error and injustice, but clay on the potter's wheel to truth and righteousness.

What restfulness and soul-comfort results from having our will in fullest harmony with the will of God. 'Tis yours, then, to say :

> " Now rest, my long divided heart ;
> Fix'd on this blissful centre-rest ;
> Nor ever from thy Lord depart ;
> With him of every good possessed."

If now you are not in the enjoyment of this grace, resolve to have it. As it is purchased for you, reach forth the hand of faith, and take it as all your own. To-day let this blessed consummation be realized, and then go forward, doing everything in your power to lead others to the cross.

As the preacher intimated on commencing his sermon, a storm was gathering fast, and an admonitory dash of rain at intervals came on the people; but with rapid utterance, lively illustration, and pointed anecdotes, he held the attention until he deemed it prudent to close. The afternoon trains coming in, filled the avenues with new arrivals, and nothing but an all-controlling energy, aided by the Holy Spirit, could have prevented general confusion at the time. Our notes of the discourse were frequently interrupted as we sat in our tent door by the inquiries of strangers, who were looking for lodging, or the localities where their friends might be found. This is our apology for not having a more full and complete report.

Driven at length from the open air by the not unwelcome shower, the Landisville Tabernacle sheltered a large number who resumed the lively exercises which had been suspended for preaching. From testimonies given it became evident that with a large majority of professors, the subjection of the will was the sore point in their unsatisfactory past career. Such a sermon, therefore, was very opportune; squarely up to the alternative were these vacillating minds brought—God's will or mine. If I can ever truly say or sing:

"Now rest my long divided heart," &c.,

it must be by yielding every point, and letting every barrier be swept away by the Divine Spirit. Am I all the Lord's? Can I close my eyes to all possible contingencies of the future, and at the foot of the cross give up forever my own will, preference, and choice, saying, "Thy will be done!" As one after another made the surrender, saying, "I am the Lord's!" bursts of congratulation in holy song rang out, and the kindling fire extended through the increasing storm.

REMARKABLE EXPERIENCE.

A meeting was held at an earlier hour of the afternoon in the grove at the head of the grounds, which claims some notice in the proceedings of the day.

All available places for holding religious services were occupied and crowded.

Rev. John Thompson, Rev. J. W. White, pastor of the Presbyterian Church at Milroy, Pa., Rev. Joseph Barker, Mrs. Amanda Smith and a large company, engaged in prayer, Brother White leading, and the great burden of every soul seemed to be, "Nearer, my God to thee."

Scripture passages were called for, and quoted promiscuously, and with powerful effect. References were made to the preaching of the Word, and the impressions made thereby, through the Holy Spirit, on individual minds.

Sister Smith being urged to take part in the meeting, remarked, " I want to sing, not for the sake of singing; I want to sing for some present good. I want to help somebody. It is faith that brings the blessing, and I like this verse—

> "If He the witness gives
> To loyal hearts and free,
> And every promise is fulfilled,
> 'Tis faith that brings the plea."

"Now, if I can glorify God, I will speak a little. There is one text; I never can understand the whole of it—'Unto me who am less than the least of all saints, is this grace given, that I should preach among the gentiles, the unsearchable riches of Christ.' I am glad the word 'gentiles' is there. I used to be afraid of white people. It will be difficult for me to tell my experience, for when I begin to speak it rushes in on me so mightily. In 1856 I was gloriously justified. I speak of this because some people can never tell when they are justified, and many try to leap over it when they have not a clear evidence of their acceptance with God. I had a hard struggle. I sought the Lord for six weeks, and the enemy said: 'God does his work quick; now you have been so long seeking, you will never be saved, for God will not pay any attention to you; it is no use to try.

" I said I would pray just once more. This was the good Spirit prompting; but Satan said :

" ' No; it is no use.'

" I will !"

" ' It is no use.'

" I'll have religion or die, this afternoon. I went down into the cellar and said : Lord, I have come down here and want to be converted.

"The Devil suggested, 'You have said all that before, and the Lord did not notice you.'

" I came down here, Lord, to be converted, and I will never give it up.

"Then there came on me a mighty baptism, and I said, ' Lord, I do believe !' This is it! Down came the baptism again. So I learned that, as I confessed with the mouth, and believed with the heart, I was saved.

" When I came out of the cellar I looked at myself, and I was astonished. I said : ' I have got all this by believing. I have all the creation in me, and the new creation, at that.' Now I wanted to live a new life, to be a real Christian. I truly enjoyed religion. I never heard of sanctification. It is glorious that we can have the witness of justification, and I thank God I have the witness of entire sanctification. I know that I was entirely sanctified.

"I did not know that anybody was ever ashamed of calling this blessing by its proper name. I sought it definitely, yet I hardly knew what I was seeking. I went to Green Street Church, N. Y., while Mr. Inskip was preaching there one day, and as I listened, I thought some one had been telling him of me. He said : 'Some people want sanctification, but they are troubled how they shall live it, after they have it.'

"I said : That is like me; I have thought just so ; some one has been telling him of me.

"I listened, and Brother Inskip continued :

"You do not fix up any way to breathe when you lie down to sleep ; you just lie down, and you breathe right on. So you need not fix up any way for God to live in you—just let God come in and he will live himself.'

"I said : O blessed God, I believe that is just so. Then he said :

"How long does it take to light up a dark room when you take a lighted taper into it ?' I said : 'Why that is all right. I can see that. Can God give me light in that way ?' and I was blessed already. Then he asked, 'If God can change our vile bodies and make them like unto his glorious body in one moment, then can he save your soul in the twinkling of an eye.'

"I believed this, and immediately the Holy Spirit filled my soul, so that I lost my fear of white folks, and I shouted, Glory to God ! As I shouted, my soul filled up again, and I was greatly blessed.

"I used to wish God had not made me black, and think—if he had only made me white ; but this pride and prejudice was now taken away, and I was glad that God made me as I was. This utmost salvation goes to the very bottom, and covers all cases and all circumstances.

"I was justified by faith, but I thought I must fix myself to get this sanctification ; so I began to fix up on this side, and then it would get all out of fix on the other side. Now I found that I must have this blessing by faith, and so I plunged in, and I was saved. When I shouted, Glory to God ! I was baptized again, and God revealed Jesus to me—my Jesus ! and he took all the prejudice out of me, and I do love white folks, whether they love me or not, and I want them all saved."

At this point, Rev. Joseph Barker rising to speak, was introduced as the man who, until a few years ago was a champion of infidelity and challenged every minister in Philadelphia to debate the existence of God, and the truth of the Bible ; and who held a great discussion with one distinguished divine. He said : "I was indeed an unbeliever ; a desperate case. I fought hard, but I am here to-day to say that I believe in God the Father, and in Jesus Christ. However strong the things that I said before I was converted, they were all vanity and lies. I am happy in God, and he saves me. I cannot give you the substance of my experience, but I will say I have passed from

death unto life; from the power of Satan unto God. Jesus is everywhere
with me. I have not to turn aside to find Jesus. When I am in the cars, I
have only to turn my head aside, and I am alone with God. I cannot tell
when I was justified or sanctified, but I know that I am fully saved. I love
God with all my heart, and my neighbor as myself. I have said many hard
things against the Bible and against God ; but I began to examine everything
in the Gospel that was lovely or beautiful, and I found much more than I
expected. I went through the Old Testament, and then I got into the New,
and that revealed Jesus to me, and the sight of Jesus killed the devil in me.
I saw how he was led as a lamb to the slaughter, and as a sheep before her
shearers is dumb, so he opened not his mouth. I saw them nail him to the
cross on Calvary ; he drew me to himself. He got hold of me and I got hold
of him, and we have grappled and held each other fast ever since. I have
got salvation and I know it.

"Infidelity is an awful calamity and a terrible evil of head and heart. There
is one thing that is worse than infidelity, and that is lukewarmness. God
will take pains to draw an infidel to himself, but he will spew the lukewarm
out of his mouth."

BUSINESS MEN'S MEETING.

It is a pleasing feature in connection with the National Association for the
Promotion of Holiness, that all time and resources are utilized, and, so far as
possible, all phases of human calling are represented in religious service.

While the world at large is finding fault with Christian men, whose business
brings them directly in contact with non-Christian professors, it is a matter of
thanksgiving that our laymen are more and more clearly apprehending the
responsibility of their position. We venture the prediction that the time is not
far distant when every large community, at least, will have organized in its
midst a regular Business Men's Meeting for the purpose of encouraging each
other in their trust in God, and dependence on Him for the safe conduct of their
business. The initial step is already taken, through the National Association.

It was at Urbana, in 1871, as we well remember, this idea took shape. A
New York merchant, Mr. L. A. Battershall, was in attendance at the meeting,
and after carefully noticing the various appliances which had been brought into
requisition, such as special services for children, meetings for young people, for
ladies exclusively, and for pastors, and the wives of ministers—conceived the
thought that a meeting for conference, prayer and experience by men engaged
in active business pursuits, would prove helpful to themselves and largely
promote the welfare of the general Church. He made a beginning, and the
immediate result justified his faith. One year had not rolled round before such

men as Wm. C. DePauw, of Indiana, Levi Perry, of Baltmore, G. M. Brubaker, of Millersburg, Pa., and others long and well-know in the commercial world, East and West, were in active personal sympathy with this specific feature of the " higher life"—the obligations of Christian merchants to consecrate themselves, their faculties for trade, and their gains, to the service of God, and for the advancement of the Redeemer's cause.

At Urbana and Sea Cliff Grove, in 1872, this element of the meetings became one of the most notable and powerful means of success. At Knoxville, Tenn., later in the season, Wm. T Perkins, of Cincinnati, with Bro. Omer Toucey and Col. Robertson, of Indianapolis, led in the movement.

A convention was called, and successfully held in Hartford, Conn., still later at the suggestion of Warren Atwood, Esq., and conducted by Dr. I. M. Ward.

Thus, from what seemed to many but a mere momentary impulse, has grown up a movement, the fruits of which are already ripening in enlarged offerings for purposes of Church Extension and the Missionary Cause, and which is destined to bless in double measure those to whom God is pleased to lend a liberal share of the blessings of his providence.

At Landisville the first meeting was held on Friday, the 25th of July. There were but few in attendance, and it was not of long duration.

The lively exercises in the Board Tent, and an absorbing interest in the National Tabernacle, where the preachers were holding a conference on their knees, attracted most of the floating population of the encampment. Great principles, however, were stated by brethren who spoke. They showed that no business was legitimate for man that did not admit of his taking in God as a principal partner. Every enterprise should be so pure and clean that it could bear to have the name of " Jesus & Co." at its head and front. Then, in both its management and results, He must be consulted, and have His pro-rata of the increase. Avarice was a soul-destroying vice. The love of money, as instanced in hoarding it, was so directly against the spirit of real Christianity, and so subversive of charity, that it must be supplanted by the higher love of doing good. Christian men should not be idle. Every resource of mind and body might be put under tribute; but all for Christ. With Christ, the hum of trade, the rush of machinery, the ring of the anvil, and the circumstances of home, were all helpful to a holy life, and that is the true spring from which flows a happy and useful life.

On the next evening the business men and preachers had a joint meeting in the Tabernacle. It was opened by singing:

" My gracious Master, and my God,
Assist me to proclaim :
To spread thro' all the earth abroad
The honors of thy name."

The leader said—"This meeting is for practical purposes—to show the bearings of religion on business and every day life. I went to one of the National Camp-meetings a moral bankrupt. The latter part of the meeting God gave me a new baptism, and I consecrated to him all my redeemed energies. Since then I have lived in the enjoyment of the blessing. It has been to me songs in the night. It has made my home a paradise. Jesus sits with us at our table, and is with us in our going out and our coming it. This salvation has helped financially, and enabled me to give of my substance willingly to God and his cause. It has wonderfully saved me from evil habits. It had become a passion of my life to smoke, and I could hardly do anything without a cigar in my mouth. As I sat on my neighbor's step with a cigar in my mouth, God spoke to me saying, 'Know ye not that ye are the temple of the the living God, and God liveth in you? He that defileth the temple of God, him will God destroy.' I declared to my neighbor I would touch it no more."

"'I will give you a month,' said he.

"I committed my case to God, and he has so fully saved me, that I no more think of smoking than I do of eating dirt, and I give all the glory to God. I expected to be so nervous that my body would tremble; but I have not had a twinge of nervousness, nor lost a moment's sleep."

Brother Larkin said—"I hardly know when I began to be a Christian. I want to tell you how I got this fullness. I am a Hebrew of the Hebrews. I was early convicted and forgiven. I made blunders and sinned, and the Spirit would reprove, and I repented, and God forgave me. When our people went to Urbana National Camp-meeting, they came home and told us about this full salvation. I got up at once and confessed my faith in it. Satan said: 'How do you know that you have given all to God?' I said: If I have not, I will as soon as I come to it. I was given wholly to God. I am set on wires, and have an awfully nervous system. If you want to find out what are trials, just stand behind my counter. But this grace saves me right through. I thought I had something of this world's good; but since I began to give, God has given me so much more that I am astonished. Yet I mean to keep fully up to my responsibilities, and pour it out as God pours in."

A business man from Williamantic, Ct., said—"I have known what it was to trust God in part, and I know what it is to trust him wholly in my business. I have been shut up in all my plans. I went home and told my wife about it, and then I went and told God. I trusted Him and he gave me a new business that I thought, at first, I was not fit for; but he showed me that I was. I took down my old account book and wrote a vow in it, and gave all for God, and signed my name to it. I called my wife to look at it, and told her that was the way we must go the rest of our lives; and God has prospered me ever since."

Brother Baldwin, of Louisiana, who has given so many thousands of dollars for education and the freedmen, said : " I embraced entire sanctification in 1818. I have had no property of my own ever since. I am only a steward. I have never taken back that consecration. I have never been able to get any useless piece of furniture for my house, or extravagant clothing for my body. I have a pair of shoes that I have worn for three years, and I expect to wear them one year more; and they only cost $1.50. I felt that I ought to do something for the freedmen, and I told the Lord if he would give me twenty thousand dollars, I would go down South and buy a plantation, and build a school for the colored people. In less than ten days I had the money in my hands. I went down South. I bought the plantation. We have a school, and some of the scholars have already gone out to preach. The Lord has gathered about six hundred. I told Bishop Wiley that I thought we should make quite an impression upon the people in the course of twenty years, and perhaps before. We have a steam saw-mill, and I am going to carry down a planing machine. I think I have just as good a right to be fully saved as anybody. We enjoy our work finely. It is good for us to be in the way of duty."

Brother Pfaff, of Cincinnati—" I said a few things in the business meeting yesterday, and my brethren said I must tell my experience here. I have always tried to find out my duty since I was in the Church. In giving away money, my policy was to sow beside all waters. If I had given all to one institution, then it might have failed, and I should have lost the whole. But I give to all causes.

" When a boy I was poor ; yet I supported my mother at the age of ten years. I made up my mind that I would have money of my own or I would die ; that I would have enough to save me from dependence upon others. God blessed me, so I had money enough before I was converted. The day I was thirty-eight years of age I and my wife were converted. If I had not been in the Church I should have been in my grave. I made up my mind to do my every duty. I asked one of the brethren what I ought to give. I soon found out that they made small calculations in religious matters as to money. I knew my temptation, and I made up my mind to make a bee-line for heaven. From my youth I thought that all Methodists were in the way of holiness ; but was surprised to find it was not so. I met a brother on the camp-ground and asked him how much he had given to a certain cause. He said he gave twenty-four hundred dollars in twenty four years. I told him I would give twenty-five hundred dollars to begin with. My brethren told me that I was beside myself in relation to giving money ; that I should learn better as I grew older. I believe we shall be rewarded according to our deeds and the love that prompts. When I see a rich man giving half a dollar and calling it the widow's mite, I think what a shame! God can measure our love; we have no scales that can weigh love. God rewards like a God. The blood of Christ alone can prepare us for heaven; but we are rewarded according to our works."

Thus the speaking proceeded. The theme was new to many who never in their experience had allowed themselves to believe and act as responsible stewards of the manifold gifts of God. We give but a specimen of the exercises held from day to day, with increasing interest.

SERMON BY REV. J. B. FOOTE, SYRACUSE, NEW YORK.

SATURDAY EVENING IN THE TABERNACLE, DURING THE PROGRESS OF A HEAVY RAIN.

What fellowship hath righteousness with unrighteousness? and what communion hath light with darkness?

And what concord hath Christ with Belial? or what part hath he that believeth with an infidel?

And what agreement hath the temple of God with idols? for ye are the temple of the living God; as God hath said, I will dwell in them, and walk in them; and I will be their God, and they shall be my people.

Wherefore come out from among them, and be ye separate, saith the Lord, and touch not the unclean thing; and I will receive you,

And will be a Father unto you, and ye shall be my sons and daughters, saith the Lord Almighty.—2 Cor. 6: 14-18.

Having, therefore, these promises, dearly beloved, let us cleanse ourselves from all filthiness of the flesh and spirit, perfecting holiness in the fear of the Lord.—2 Cor. 7: 1.

THERE are three religious terms in the Bible to which many persons in our churches have a remarkable and unwarrantable aversion. From the word holiness they feel a strange and sensitive shrinking; some fairly hate the word sanctification, and the word perfection is a stumbling-stone and rock of offence. But these are the Bible terms, and occur in some of their forms, not incidentally or seldom, but often, and as the most important word in the sentence. The last mentioned is found nearly one hundred and twenty times; the word sanctify, over a hundred and twenty, and the term holy, over seven hundred. And in most instances these words are applied to human character. This word "cleanse" in our text, is used in some of its forms in a religious sense some eighty times. "Create in me a clean heart." "From all your filthiness and from all your idols will I cleanse you." "The blood of Jesus Christ his Son cleanseth us from all sin." " He is faithful and just to forgive us our sins and to cleanse us from all unrighteousness." " Let us cleanse ourselves from all filthiness of flesh and spirit, perfecting holiness in the fear of the Lord."

The Bible, then, is full of this subject of entire cleansing. And it is a striking fact that frequently a word is added or prefixed, expressing the idea of entireness, or the language is so constructed that the intention to inculcate the idea of full, entire, complete sanctification is manifest, e. g. " Sanctify you *wholly*," " that ye may be perfect and *entire, wanting nothing*." " There is no fear in *love, but perfect love casteth* out fear." In 1 Cor. 13th, the word charity is used alone—but perfect love is manifestly intended.

I am correct, then, in saying the Bible is full of the subject of *entire* cleansing, and in reference to it I purpose to present a few propositions deducible from our text. And O that the Holy Ghost may use his own truth here and now for the full salvation of some who listen. And I grow more and more encouraged to look for immediate results. Two or three weeks ago Bishop Peck made a formal address at our Syracuse Tuesday Meeting. He spoke of the experience and its propagation. After remarking upon the duty of preaching the doctrine whether the experience is enjoyed or not, as the Bible is the standard, and not our experience, he said he rejoiced in the increase of the experience, and believed the day is already dawning when our ministry will so understand and enjoy it that they will be able to so present it that our people will enter into it while it is being presented.

The day has dawned, thank God ; and I verily believe that now, while the rain is falling in such torrents on this canvas, God will sprinkle some hearts here with clean water, and they shall be made clean.

I.—*This Bible suggestion of entire cleansing is made to persons already converted.* I think this is always the case, at least I do not call to mind any exception. There may be, but I think whenever the suggestion is made it will appear either in some expressed term in the passage or by fair implication that the suggestion belongs to those who are reckoned as the people of God. The text is addressed to those " dearly beloved." The beginning of this paragraph speaks of " ye" and " unbelievers"—two classes, unbelievers spoken of and believers addressed. And is it not the case that all of the Epistles are addressed to the Church of God, " to the saints and faithful brethren," and not one of them to the general mass of unconverted persons ? The apostle explains this. He declares plainly that the ministry is instituted for " the perfecting of the saints," " till we all come in the unity of the faith and of the knowledge of the Son of God unto a perfect man, unto the measure of the stature of the fullness of Christ." God's plan is, first, for everybody to be converted, and secondly in childhood, and at home, through the prayers and faith of Christian parents ; and then the Church organization and the institution of the ministry are to take these young converts and lead them on to perfection. And here is another remarkable quotation. "All Scripture is given by inspiration of God, and is profitable for doctrine, etc., that the *man of God* may be perfect, thoroughly furnished unto all good works."

Hence the propriety of special efforts to promote holiness. In fact every meeting in the church ought to promote holiness; but as the insiduous spirit of the world keeps this object out so largely from our regular meetings, the providence of God has started these National Camp-meetings and other meet-

7

ings for this special object. Bishop Haven, in his introduction to Brother Hughes' book, "Days of Power," puts it in this wise :

"The gatherings which this book commemmorate have a churchly specialty. They are designed to summon the Church herself to a re-consecration. They say to her, as Christ said to his disciples, 'Come ye yourselves apart into a desert place, and rest awhile.' The world may follow, as it followed Christ and his disciples when he issued that order ; if it follows, it may also be fed, as were they, with miraculous food ; but the primal object is not the feeding of the multitudes, but the replenishing of the Church with grace. She needs such replenishment frequently.

" The Church has fallen again and again in her past long history ; so will she fall again and again, unless divine power continually inspires, upraises, sanctifies.

" To this end these forest meetings have been held. They have united and uplifted the Church ; they have recalled the wandering, and awakened the slumbering Christian. They have set many a saintly one in more saintliness, and drawn many a worldly one from fatal surroundings."

II.—I pass to a second remark, which is *that holiness in principle and fact is predicable of all truly converted persons.* Look closely at the text. It says: " Let us cleanse ourselves, perfecting holiness,"—completing, finishing the holiness already possessed in an imperfect and mixed state. I claim that every justified person has a kind and degree of holiness. His business is to perfect it by eliminating from the mixture the elements which do not belong to it—which antagonize the elements of holiness planted in regeneration. Some cry out against professing holiness, but they certainly should not unless they give up professing religion. And not only have all true Christians this internal principle ; but they are under obligations to *live a holy life.* The idea that the entirely sanctified are under higher obligations to live a holy life than those sanctified but in part, or which is similar, that the latter can indulge in derelictions and be excusable, though the former would be held responsible in such case, is one of the most preposterous and absurd notions imaginable. No. Not any person can retain justification in the commission of a known sin. " Whosoever is born of God doth not commit sin." It is a great misfortune that we have in the Church such a low standard of piety in relation to the state of justification. We seek to elevate it.

III.—In this connection we state another proposition, *that a justified relation may exist without entire holiness,* and while yet some sinfulness—"filthiness of the flesh and spirit"—remains in the heart. The persons addressed are manifestly in the relations of Christians. But all sin has not been cleansed away. Such is the lesson also from I John 3: 3, " Every man that hath this hope in him purifieth himself." What hope ! the hope of a child of God, the hope of seeing Jesus as he is, and it is a hope *in him,* which form of expression indicates the hope to be an element of Christian experience, and correlates the verse with " Which is Christ *in you,* the hope of glory." The teaching, then, is that one may be a child of God and have in his experience a hope of heaven and not be in the possession of purity of heart, though it should be added he will desire to be pure, and as a matter of fact, also, his continued justified relation is conditional on his seeking to become so.

IV.—A further point this text makes for us is, *that perfected holiness implies the entire cleansing of the heart from sin.* I do not say it embraces nothing more—it does. It is the full, gracious endowment of perfect love. But the point clearly set forth here is, that holiness becomes perfect when the remaining inbred sin of the heart is eliminated. Before, there was a mixedness; now, simplicity. Before, there was love, but also the germs of hate; now, the heart is all love. Before, humility was in the character, with some pride; now, the plague of pride has been cured. Before, a peevish, fretful spirit dwelt in the heart; now, patience has her perfect work. Before, there would spring up at times a spirit of retaliation; now, a pure sweet forgiving spirit is felt, excluding all revenge and malice.

Entire cleansing, then, is an elimination, as bad humors in the blood are expelled by a medicine, or as dross is separated from the gold by the fire. It is an eradication; the removal of the roots of bitterness, of the seeds of sin's disease. It is a crucifixion; the putting to death of the body or the life of sin; and hence is seen its distinct and instantaneous character, and the necessity of looking for it as such. The method of seeking it is not by lopping off a branch here and cutting away an excrescence there. The only successful method is to strike at the root.

But why is not the work complete at the time of conversion? It is a complete regeneration, but not a complete cleansing. But why does not God make it so? If I cannot tell, we still have the universal fact and the teachings of Scripture. But this may be said; the soul seeking conversion does not desire entire cleansing from inbred sin; it desires pardon and hope of heaven; and the word of promise is, "Whatsoever things ye *desire* when ye pray, believe that ye receive them and ye shall have them."

Nor does purity exclude or preclude maturity. On the contrary, growth will be more rapid, regular and symmetrical after entire cleansing than before, just as the plants in your garden will have a better growth after the removal of the weeds. Do you ask how there can be growth after the holiness is perfected? Can anything be greater than perfection? The answer is easy. A circle of six inches diameter is a perfect circle—but so is one of much greater size. A perfect tree, a perfect lamb, a perfect child are susceptible of growth. Christian perfection is one of quality. The heart may be pure and filled, but it is susceptible of indefinite expansion, and so may contain a greater amount. Moreover, religion is susceptible of great condensation; so that a larger quantity can be contained in the same space. A room is full of light at sunrise, but contains much more at mid-day. The space in an air-condenser is filled with air, but turn the crank a little and it contains a much larger amount. A room is full of heat, but open the register wider or give the furnace more fuel and more draft and you get much more heat.

V.—But what is the *basis* of this *suggestion* of *entire cleansing?* We have it presented here in three particulars.

1. In the radical and irreconcilable antagonism between sin and holiness, "What fellowship hath righteousness with unrighteousness?" etc. If these opposites exist in the heart, as they do in the partially sanctified state, it is manifestly a temporary condition. One or the other must sooner or later be expelled. The world will conquer the Church unless the Church heed this suggestion and cleanse herself. The force of this argument at the present day is

tremendous. As Bishop Haven says in the article before referred to, "The world is too much with us. It pushes its corrupting influence upon the Church. It makes her greedy as itself of pleasure, honor, wealth. It thrusts her baubles upon the forms and faces of her maidens, and makes them more anxious for outward than for inward adorning. It makes her youths lovers of pleasure rather than lovers of God. It heats her men of position and power with lusts of the flesh, lust for fame, lust for gold; everything but a burning passion for Christ and souls." O for an inundating wave of cleansing power to roll over all the churches of the land!

2. In the statement of the divine indwelling, "Ye are the temple of the living God," "I will dwell in them," etc., God comes to the human heart, not as a visitor or transient guest, but to make it his permanent residence. "We will make our abode with him." Hence the place must be made entirely holy. "What!" exclaimed a young man, "am I a temple of God?—my soul to be a home for Jesus? Then what can I do to make it agreeable to him? I certainly want everything fitted to his taste, and my tastes in all respects conformed to his." Sensible young man. Legitimate conclusion. Let us cleanse ourselves.

3. In the special promise, "I will receive you." "Come out and touch not the unclean, and I will receive you." From such a basis—the basis of God's eternal, immutable promise, simply as an argument, how irresistible the conclusion. Then let us cleanse ourselves. O the exceeding great and precious promises implied in God's infinite abhorrence of sin—in the great truth of his personal indwelling, and given in a thousand special statements! "I will receive you," "I will save you from all your uncleanliness," etc. Having these promises—what to do with them? Why—use them in cleansing. The promises are our instruments or means of cleansing. We cleanse our hands and face with soap and water. We cleanse our souls by means of the promises. But how am I to use the promises? *By believing them.* The first thing to do with the promises is to believe them—and the next, and the next; and so using them we shall surely realize their fulfillment in our complete purification.

> "I cannot wash my heart
> *But by believing thee,*
> And waiting for thy blood to impart
> The spotless purity.

> "Come then, for Jesus' sake,
> And bid my heart be clean,
> An end of all my troubles make,
> An end of all my sin."

FIFTH DAY.

SABBATH MORNING.

Dr. Lowrey conducted the services at 5 A. M., which were of a deeply interesting character. Passages of Scripture were quoted after the opening hymn and prayer, and such was the beauty, appropriateness, and power of these promiscuous texts, that the people were filled with light and joy, as they participated or listened.

Then followed experience. A sister from Connecticut praised God for the living Word. It showed her the possibility of a present and full salvation ; and believing, she was saved.

A Massachusetts brother also proved its power to sanctify. " Now are ye clean through the word," &c. His heart's desire and prayer to God this morning was expressed in the stanza :

> " Come and possess me whole
> Nor hence again remove :
> Settle and fix my wavering soul
> With all thy weight of love."

" That," said the leader, " is a good prayer for every one here. If we prevail it must be by believing prayer. Now let us again approach the mercy-seat."

After several had prayed, and the general earnestness had been indicated by hearty responses from all parts of the congregation, the entire assembly united in repeating the Lord's prayer, and we never before heard it so impressively uttered.

The Doctor suggested that speaking should be brief and pointed: Some brethren and sisters, he remarked, being full, will speak always, and speak long ; but let us be considerate to others, and put what we have to say in the smallest possible compass of words.

" I know," exclaimed Brother Barker, " that I am a new creature in Christ Jesus, when I contrast my present condition with what I was twenty years ago. I never was a beast, but I came very near being a demon. This morning my heart is full of love to God, and good will to men.

> " My soul's full of glory, inspiring my tongue,
> Could I meet with the angels, I'd sing them a song ;
> I would sing of my Jesus, and tell of his charms,
> And beg them to bear me to His loving arms."

Father Baldwin : " Bless the Lord, O my soul! These last days are my best days. For fifty-five years He has delivered me from the cares of the world, the lust of the eye and the pride of life. I had a good night through the rain ; for God sent it, and my soul rejoices in his salvation."

"I was a very difficult case to manage," said Brother Stockton: "but the Lord understood me from the start, and knows that I love him now with all my ransomed powers. I expect to help sing of His mighty love, through time and all eternity."

"My first concern when I came to this meeting," said a Presbyterian minister, "was to be thoroughly emptied—now I am being gloriously filled. I am down in the fountain, and the tides of salvation are flowing over me."

A brother: "Ever since that memorable Monday night at Manheim, I have tasted the sweetness of this full salvation; and I am saved at home just as much as here."

Thus, for one hour, testimony rapidly flowed in, until the time for closing these morning devotions. In response to the inquiry, "Who here are wholly sanctified?" about one hundred stood up; afterwards fully half that number rose as seekers of the blessing.

———

THE GENERAL LOVE-FEAST.

As the multitude crowded into the Tabernacle, at 8 o'clock A. M., one sentiment seemed to suit every individual present—

> "The peace of Christ makes fresh my heart,
> A fountain ever springing;
> All things are mine, since I am His;
> How can I keep from singing?"

Rev. W. L. Gray conducted the exercises, being sustained by a full corps of ministers on the ground. There was no reliable count kept of the number who witnessed for Christ. As near as we could judge the testimonies exceeded one hundred; not near as many as usual, but impressive and satisfactory; because men and women took time to say something beyond the brief and disconnected sentences which often characterize these occasions, such as "Saved now;" "All for Christ;" "The blood cleanseth," etc.

After a number of preachers had spoken briefly, the people with freedom took up the theme, and it gave great interest to the repetition of experience, as one after another told when, and where they were converted, and the circumstances under which they were wholly sanctified to God; as for instance—

"At Oakington, four years ago, under this same canvas, I was led to make a full consecration; there I received the pledge of 'perfect love.' Ever since I have held up the banner of holiness. Opposition has assailed, temptation beset me, but grace has been sufficient. We have now a regular meeting in my charge, for the promotion of holiness, and the cause is gaining ground."

"Thirteen years ago, the Lord converted me sweetly and clearly. Three years ago he sanctified me, and most wonderfully has he kept me to this day."

"I was brought as a trembling sinner to the mercy seat fifty-six years ago, and found redemption through Christ. I was for long years under conviction for cleansing, and at Oakington through the teaching I there received, I saw it was my privilege to be sanctified wholly. I trusted the blood. The Spirit helped, and the baptism of power came on my soul. O, I have no language to describe it! I am saved this morning."

"I have never been in such a meeting as this: so many saved people here. O, Glory to Jesus! I'm with you in this army of the living God, to go through the war!"

"One year ago at Sea Cliff Camp-meeting, I practically learned that the 'fountain opened for sin and uncleanliness' availed for me, to cleanse from all sin. My pride, myself and all were lost in that tide, and I arose, went forth, and learned to follow Jesus fully. This brought perfect rest."

Dr. Nast, in an emotional way, and in his broken English words declared: "The blood of Jesus Christ, I can testify, cleanseth me—even me—from all sin. It saves me fully; I know no other than a full salvation. I felt the need of it, as soon as I saw my desperate state as a sinner. Persevering in my earnest plea, I found it."

Singing :

"The cleansing stream, I see, I see,
I plunge, and, O, it cleanses me!"

"When quite a child I gave my heart to Jesus, and four years ago I was sanctified throughout soul, body and spirit. I am all the Lord's this morning."

"Nothing but this full salvation could have saved such a drunkard and gambler as I was. What God has done for me is all described in Ezekiel 36, from the twenty-fifth to the twenty-ninth verse. Yes, this fire of the Holy Ghost swept out of me the defilement of rum and tobacco, and purified me inside and outside. Glory to the Lamb!"

Singing :—

"I've washed my garments white
In the blood of the Lamb!
The world is overcome
Through the blood of the Lamb."

"Last fall, the precious HOME JOURNAL brought to my notice the welcome word that a National Camp-meeting was appointed for Landisville. I had a good shout over it. Since that day my thoughts have been turning to this event, and this time. I have been on the ground since Monday, and have not yet had a chance to speak. Twenty-five years of my life have been happily spent in the service of God. At Manheim I first had my attention directed to the 'higher life.' I confess to an awakened prejudice against it; but I could not get rid of the impression that it was my duty to seek holi-

ness. Alone in my room, reading God's word, I'saw the blessing was for me.
One year I was seeking the experience. At the Lebanon Camp-meeting, I
retired one night with prayer that I might wake up sanctified. The first
thought of my waking was—

> " Other refuge have I none,
> Hangs my helpless soul on thee. "

"I went to the meetings during that memorable day, with this verse still
ringing in my ears and soul—' Other refuge have I none," etc. I was on the
point of being blessed, when Satan suggested a difficulty. Looking down
and noticing a spot on my dress, I prayed ' cleanse me from every spot.'
The next moment I was wrapped up in a new emotion. I exclaimed, ' I've
got it, I've got it.' O yes; then I knew the work was done. The leaves
on the trees seemed tinged with gold. Every thing praised God. I went
into the meetings, and was filled with the fullness of God. Soon a voice
whispered to my conscience, ' leave off all your jewelry.' I began to par-
ley, remembering the Presiding Elder wore it; but it had to come off, all
but one little memorial I prized. Finally that was laid aside, and I came
home happy. Satan again suggested,—' better not profess this about home.'
I noticed clinging to my dress a straw from the camp and the spot where I
had been blessed. I took that straw and put it in my Bible, and it is there
yet. I began and have not ceased to profess this blessing. I am honored to
have a meeting in my own house (in Lancaster) for holiness. Oh, how I pray
that this meeting may add to our number."

"I came here from Virginia to regain the power of sanctifying grace. I
first experienced this at Manheim. By inadvertence I lost it, and have been
discouraged and buffeted, until life became unbearable without it. Nine
months ago I prayed on the Blue Ridge that I might be permitted to attend
this meeting. I received an impression that I should ask Father Coleman to
pray with me. Last Friday he did so. I then believed. I found it easy
to believe. I died indeed unto sin. Jesus, the Son of God, did save me.
A definite confession is due here, and I must make it before all the people."

Here it was intimated the people must be short and confine themselves to
present experience, so many wanted to be heard for the name of the Lord
Jesus. A seeker arose and said nothing suited his case at present but the
words—

> " Rock of ages cleft for me,
> Let me hide myself in thee."

A brother from Cincinnati, illustrating the love of God and his compassion for us, referred to a maimed child, or one so sickly and weak as to need
more than others a mother's love and sympathy; so if we are poor and unworthy, God will care for us and come nigh to help and save the weakest here.
The speaking then proceeded—

"At the first Ohio State Camp-meeting Jesus revealed himself to me as a complete Saviour, and I accepted him. He is mine and I am his."

"I am washed in the blood of the Lamb."

"For six years I have been endeavoring to live perfect love at home. All we have and are belongs, and is consecrated to God. Even the chickens are under his care, and belong to him. I remonstrated when they proposed to put a lightning rod on my husband's barn. Why should we do so? It is all the Lord's, and he controls the lightning; if he burns it up, it is all his own."

"I love to tell the story," was now sung with tremendous effect, and wave after wave of emotion rolled over the assembly.

"I was born of a Christian mother, but I was born again of the Holy Ghost, and full salvation is my heartfelt experience this morning."

"Glory to Jesus that I am here; my experience in a word is"—singing:

"Jesus saves, O bliss sublime,
Jesus saves me all the time."

"I am so glad that a Baptist may stand up *here*, and profess this grace. Jesus reigns without a rival in my heart."

A lad hailing from Massachusetts said he and several companions retired to a room, and there determined not to leave until each was wholly sanctified. God took them at their word and fulfilled his own promise. His language was—

"Trusting, trusting every moment,
Feeling now the blood applied:
Lying at the cleansing fountain,
Dwelling at my Saviour's side.

"Long my earnest heart was trying
To enjoy this perfect rest;
But I gave all trying over,—
Simply trusting, I was blest."

A sister from Long Island sang some verses which increased the current of religious sensibility until it became intense.

"I stand all bewildered and wonder,
And gaze on the ocean of love;
And over its waves to my spirit
Comes peace like a heavenly dove,

"The cross now covers my sins,
The past is under the blood,
I am trusting in Jesus for all,
My will is the will of my God.

"I struggled and wrestled to win it,
The blessing that maketh me free;
But when I had ceased from my struggle,
His peace Jesus gave unto me."

The closing verse—"My will is the will of my God," suggested to a brother that this was a great conflict with him, but the point was gained.

"Now," he continued, "my will is the will of my God.   'I am crucified with Christ, nevertheless I live, yet not I, but Christ liveth in me.'   I can say more—the life I now live is by the faith of the Son of God.   Whether I eat or drink, or whatever I do, I do all to the glory of God."

"Three weeks ago, I heard a Presbyterian boy speak of the hope within him, and such was his confidence in the fullness of Christ's power and love to save him in life and death, that I believed it was worth more than A. T. Stewart's property.   I thank God I have the same glorious prospect"

"September 18th, 1845, I was made a partaker, and became a witness for full salvation.   I can assure all here who are desiring this blessing, that God can as easily wash their hearts as to send such a copious rain last night upon the parched earth."

"All is clear with me this morning."   (He had been in perplexity as an inquirer.)   "Not a cloud between me and God.   He led me and I followed. He stirred up my nest.   The thorns pierced me, and I was compelled to fly to the rock.   There I'm resting now.   Lost to self, but cleansed in the fountain."

"I cannot enter into the detail," said Sister Smith, "of when, where and how it was that I was saved, farther than to say I was converted in 1856 and sanctified in 1868, in Green St. M. E. Church when Bro. Inskip was pastor there.   I am a witness that the blood cleanseth.   A verse of Scripture suits my case exactly—'Unto me who am less than the least of all saints is this grace given, that I might preach among the Gentiles the unsearchable riches of Christ.   Hallelujah!"   She then sang—

"The blood, the blood is all my plea,
    Nor should a sinner wonder,
For guilty stain and stinging pain
    Had torn my heart asunder!"

"I rest, I rest supremely blest,
    Without a care to canker;
No gloomy night, my path is light,
    My hope holds like an anchor."

"Seven years ago the Lord taught me this way, and by his mighty power he fully saved me.   I rejoice in his salvation to-day."

"This is the way I long have sought.   I came from Massachusetts, thinking all along my journey, 'Shall I find it here?'   On Thursday I bowed among the seekers, and last night, amid thunder and lightning, and rain, my heart was cleansed by the Holy Ghost, and precious blood of Christ."

"If our fellowship below,
    In Jesus be so sweet."

This sentiment is running through my mind.   I am in the shallows on the edge of the stream.   I want to launch out and float along in the great dee of this salvation."

" At Brandywine Summit some years ago I obtained the blessing of heart purity, but neglected to talk about it to my class, and soon lost the sweetness and light out of my heart. This morning at the early meeting, I pleaded with God to restore it, and while the doxology was being sung my poor soul was again filled. Now I rejoice with exceeding great joy, and you may be sure I'll go home'to tell it. "

" In the language of that sweet hymn, sung by the sister, I feel that I am 'under the blood.' I reached the ground last night in the heavy rain, and went to sleep supperless ; but Jesus was better than supper. He is all in all."

" The Gospel is the power of God unto salvation to every one that believeth. I believe, and am therefore saved."

" That is the way I was saved."

" At the Hamilton (Mass.) Camp-meeting, while Bro. Boole was preaching, the power came upon me, and God has kept me ever since. This was a great event for me."

" In a word, I am entirely, unreservedly and eternally the Lord's."

" At a place called Mt. Tabor, two years ago, I entered in."

"My life flows on in endless song,
   Above earth's lamentation ;
I catch the sweet though far-off hymn
   That hails a new creation.
Through all the tumult and the strife,
   I hear the music ringing ;
It finds an echo in my heart,
   How can I keep from singing.

" I was converted near the spot in England where Bishop Asbury was born. I wandered from the way for five years, and then came back, and Jesus received me. A conviction was given me that I must preach the gospel, and I was told, in answer to a question, that the preparation to preach was a sanctified heart. This I sought, and found it all alone, and it was like a little heaven put into my soul. I was then ready to go and die, if need be, like Cox in Africa. But God sent me to America. The mighty God has been with me. I don't know what is coming. At Round Lake I said I wanted to live long enough to see one hundred thousand souls converted. I think this will prove the greatest meeting ever held. O that sinners might feel the power of conviction ! We must preach hell to them. There is so little said now-a-days about an awful hell, and the world is going there. God help us to feel for them, and preach so as to convict them, and get them saved in Christ."

" I am journeying on the King's highway, and no lion is there, nor any ravenous beast, but the redeemed of the Lord walk there."

"For nearly four years 'the law of the Spirit of life in Christ Jesus, hath made me free from the law of sin and death,' and my confidence is, that 'the Lord shall deliver me from every evil work,' and will preserve me unto his heavenly kingdom, to whom be glory forever and ever—Amen."

"I am redeemed—redeemed." This chorus was sung by a brother, but the shouts became so general that the reporter could not catch his further expressions, except when he fervently closed by saying, "Glory be to the Father, and to the Son, and to the Holy Ghost. As it was in the beginning, is now, and ever shall be, world without end." (Many voices—"Amen !")

A minister referred to his being converted in childhood, and sanctified subsequently. He trembled to think of his past remissness in not holding up a definite testimony. He now felt "free in Christ Jesus."

"The Gate Ajar" was here sung with indescribable enthusiasm.

A brother from the interior of New York said he had the reputation of being the worst boy in his native State; but Christ took him in hand. They said: "He can't be saved," but he was able to glorify the name of Jesus, that his sins were pardoned, and his heart filled with peace. He was now ready for work; would go forth wherever God appointed his lot.

A Wilmington minister said, "I am this morning in heavenly places in Christ Jesus. How can any doubt the power of the blood of Christ to cleanse the soul from all sin? I realize it joyfully in my heart."

"Such a hallowed influence as fills this place, I never felt before. Surely God is here."

I lived thirty-six years in the Church up and down, until five months ago the Lord gave me something that I had never known before. I consecrated everything; and at 3 o'clock in the morning the divine power came and filled me. Now I know the blood cleanseth. It is not a hope so, and no one need tell me this is all nonsense. I know for myself that it is true. I am perfectly satisfied there is no mistake about it. This cleansing was thorough; no taste for tobacco or beer, or any wrong fleshly indulgence left. O I am happy in Jesus, and I want the brethren who are here from our church to get this blessing before they go home, for I am almost alone there on this question. May God bless our church, and bless you all !"

"My testimony here is the same as it was out in Iowa a few days ago. Being made free from sin and become a servant of God, I have fruit unto holiness, and am now waiting for the end, everlasting life."

"I was made a partaker of perfect love, at Manheim, and have never lost it."

"In Western New York I read the good HOME JOURNAL, and through its testimony have been greatly helped and blessed in this way of holiness. I also can say 'fully saved !'"

Brother Dunn—"Where shall my wandering soul begin? It does not seem much to say I am all the Lord's; but it is something to say He is mine. Prom-

inent brethren said they were sorry for me, when it became known I had associated myself with the ' holiness people,' and professed to be sanctified ; but it
has not hurt me in reputation, appointments, or usefulness. I am glad to be
here to-day, a witness to full salvation.

"It is a great thing for me to feel I am all the Lord's. It cost a tremendous
struggle. I had to die to live. For twenty-five years at camp-meetings and
love-feasts (in Rhode Island) I have been able to testify that I am saved."

" I have two testimonies," said Brother Hughes. " One is on my own behalf. 'I am determined to know nothing among men save Jesus Christ and
him crucified.' I hold on to Jesus by simple faith; and he holds on to me
with a divine grasp. The other case is that of a dear afflicted one, who, far
from here, and confined to her bed in constant pain, is yet so interested in this
meeting that her heart follows every service. God bless sister Jennie Smith."
(Those who remember her at Urbana, and all others, felt the impulse to cry
"Amen, Lord sustain and bless her !")

" Still I'm trusting," was sung and Mrs. Inskip took the opportunity to
speak—" I am reminded by Brother Dunn's remarks of a temptation of Satan
which met me, when I wanted to be sanctified. It was suggested ' Now if you
profess this blessing, you will make trouble, and stop up your husband's way.'
Well I must have it, and said, ' Give me Jesus wherever we have to go.' He
came and cleansed my heart, and two weeks afterward he fully saved my dear
husband ; then instead of being sent away from social influences and large
churches, there never was so many calls for us to labor. Bless the Lord ! "

" Yes, sister Inskip, bless the Lord for old Sing Sing Camp-meeting, where
you obtained the blessing. Oh, how many ' Pisgahs,' and ' Tabors,' and ' Elims,'
there are along our journey. I have had some severe troubles, as well as sweet
resting places. I have been a weeping Jeremiah of late, going through the
streets with my heart broken over the perverseness of the people, and some
serious losses, but there is a reason for it all. I soon go to the West to work
for Jesus, and feel that the tempest makes me strong. I ask your prayers."

Here Rev. Wm. C. Stockton sang—

> " I'd rather be the least of them,
> Who are the Lord's alone,
> Than wear a royal diadem,
> And sit upon a throne."

The audience joined in the refrain ; during the singing a holy excitement
swept over the meeting, and while Brother Barker was speaking, the people
praised God, aloud. To this brother the scenes of the Camp-meeting were all
new, and his delight in the sweet Christian fellowship of so many simple hearted
followers of Jesus, was unbounded.

" Ever since I arrived on the ground," said Brother Thompson, " I think I
have been led by the Spirit. I have said but little, but my heart has been full
of unutterable thanksgiving to God. I have some realization of the meaning
of that passage which says: ' In whom ye rejoice, with joy unspeakable, and
full of glory.' I can only say, glory, glory to God, for this salvation." Then
rose in strains of power, and pathos, the song—

> " Glory to the Lamb.
> I've washed my garments white,
> In the blood of the Lamb."

SABBATH MORNING, 10 A. M.

___

SERMON BY REV. J. S. INSKIP, PRESIDENT OF THE NATIONAL CAMP-MEETING ASSOCIATION.

*" And that ye put on the new man, which after God is renewed in righteous-
ness and true holiness."—Eph. 4 : 25.*

The responsibility of the task now before me, I think I fully appreciate.
The subject upon which it is proposed to dwell is attracting the attention of
the people of God everywhere. A profound and wide-spread interest has
been awakened in the mind of the Christian Church upon this all-important
theme. Whatever may be written or said in regard to it, is read and heard
with the most devout consideration and deference. One of the most hopeful
omens of the times is the fact that this topic is before the minds of the great
body of believers unencumbered by controversy. There is an obvious endeavor to preserve the " unity of the Spirit," and harmonize any conflicting
views which may yet remain. I should deem myself most unfortunate, if
anything I may say should at all hinder this. I trust, by the help of the
blessed Spirit, that what I shall say will only stimulate all to press onward in
the " King's highway," and seek that " full conformity to the Divine will,"
which is the real basis of purity, and the true source of happiness.

I. WHAT IS TRUE HOLINESS?

1. As a generic term it includes whatever is connected with the Christian
life and character. Thus interpreted it may be applied to any and all stages
of religious life and development.

2. It is, however, used in a more definite sense than this. Among a large
class the term is synonymous with " purity," " perfection," " sanctification,"
" entire sanctification," " perfect love," and the " higher life," and numerous
others.

3. Which of these terms shall be employed is immaterial in one view,
and yet immensely important in another. If the question be simply one of
terminology, it may perhaps be deemed comparatively unimportant. And
when we propose one of these Scripture terms as more clear and more readily understood than others, this is all right. But when, for any reason whatever, we use the uninspired verbiage of man, rather than the words which
God has chosen, we certainly commit a great error, if not a grave wrong. It
must be admitted that on account of the grievous abuse, and persistent mis-
understanding of these terms, it is sometimes difficult to use them. Yet we
must not abandon them.

4. But what is true holiness? This undoubtedly is the great question.
We should seek to know what it is, as far more essential than the mere words
we may use in speaking of it. The terms we have quoted, we propose to use
indiscriminately. Strictly interpreted there is a shade of difference in their
import ; but as generally used they mean one and the same thing.

5. The nature and true idea of holiness may be gathered from the numerous passages of Scripture in which it is spoken of. The word of God is full of this glorious theme. Dr. Foster has well said : " The doctrine we contend for is not limited to a bare and questionable place, a doubtful and uncertain existence in the holy records, but is repeatedly and abundantly— explicitly and with great clearness—embodied as a cardinal feature throughout the whole system. It breathes in the prophecy—thunders in the law—murmurs in the narrative—whispers in the promises—supplicates in the prayers —sparkles in the poetry—resounds in the songs—speaks in the types—glows in the imagery—voices in the language—and burns in the spirit of the whole scheme, from its Alpha to its Omega—from its beginning to its end. Holiness! Holiness needed! Holiness required! Holiness offered! Holiness attainable! Holiness a present duty—a present privilege—a present enjoyment, is the progress and completeness of its wonderous theme! It is the truth glowing all over—webbing all through revelation; the glorious truth which sparkles, and whispers, and sings, and shouts in all its history, and biography, and poetry, and prophecy, and precept, and promise, and prayer ; the great central truth of the system. The wonder is, that all do not see, that any rise up to question, a truth so conspicuous, so glorious. so full of comfort."

The Scriptures enjoin holiness. A command is equivalent to a promise. As explicitly as words can make it, holiness is presented as our duty. Our Heavenly Father does not command us to do or to be what we cannot. "Thou shalt love the Lord thy God with all thy heart, and with all thy soul, and with all thy mind, and with all thy strength, and thy neighbor as thyself."

" Be ye holy, for I am holy."

" Follow peace with all men, and holiness, without which no man shall see the Lord."

The Scriptures present it before the mind in earnest and pointed exhortation. "Wherefore come out from among them, and be ye separate, saith the Lord, and touch not the unclean thing ; and I will receive you, and be a Father unto you, and ye shall be my sons and daughters, saith the Lord Almighty. Having therefore, these promises, dearly beloved, let us cleanse ourselves from all filthiness of the flesh and spirit, perfecting holiness in the fear of God."

It is also inculcated by the promises. These promises are numerous. We select a few from the great multitudes—"Then will I sprinkle clean water upon you, and ye shall be clean ; from all your filthiness, and from all your idols, will I cleanse you."

" I will give them a heart to know me, that I am the Lord ; and they shall be my people, and I will be their God : for they shall return unto me with their whole heart. After those days, saith the Lord, I will put my law in their inward parts, and write it in their hearts ; and will be their God and they shall be my people."

" Blessed are the pure in heart, for they shall see God."

It is presented likewise as the object of earnest and prayerful desire. " For this cause I bow my knees unto the Father of our Lord Jesus Christ. of whom the whole family in heaven and earth is named, that he would grant you, according to the riches of his glory, to be strengthened with might by his Spirit in the inner man ; that Christ may dwell in your hearts by faith; that ye being rooted and grounded in love, may be able to comprehend with all the saints what is the breadth, and length, and depth, and height ; and to know the love of Christ, which passeth knowledge, that ye might be filled with all the fullness of God.   Now unto him that is able to do exceeding abundantly above all that we ask or think, according to the power that worketh in us, unto him be glory in the Church by Christ Jesus, throughout all ages, world without end.   Amen."

"Now the God of Peace, that brought again from the dead our Lord Jesus, that great Shepherd of the sheep, through the blood of the everlasting covenant, make you perfect in every good work to do his will, working in you that which is pleasing in his sight, through Jesus Christ."

" And the very God of peace sanctify you wholly: and I pray God, your whole spirit, and soul, and body, be preserved blameless unto the coming of our Lord Jesus Christ.   Faithful is he that calleth you, who also will do it."

It is proclaimed in the most explicit announcements of Scripture.   " Blessed be the Lord God of Israel : for he hath raised up a horn of salvation for us, as he spake by the mouth of his holy prophets, that we, being delivered out of the hands of our enemies, might serve him without fear, in holiness and righteousness before him, all the days of our life."

" If we walk in the light, as he is in the light, we have fellowship one with another, and the blood of Jesus Christ his Son cleanseth us from all sin.   If we confess our sins, he is faithful and just to forgive us our sins, and to cleanse us from all unrighteousness."

" But now being made free from sin, and become servants to God, ye have your fruit unto holiness, and the end everlasting life."

" I am crucified with Christ: nevertheless, I live ; yet not I, but Christ liveth in me: and the life which I now live in the flesh, I live by the faith of the Son of God."

"For I am jealous over you with godly jealousy : for I have espoused you to one husband that I may present you as a chaste virgin to Christ."

A multitude of similar passages might be quoted.   These are ample for our purpose.   They clearly inculcate the doctrine under consideration.

6. We must admit some of these quotations are claimed not to contain the ideas we deduce from them.   We have no authorative expounder of the Scriptures.   Yet we are not without a reliable and safe exposition of the word.

7. These passages should be interpreted in view of the teaching and experience of many, and the aspirations of all.   The most devout, and therefore the most reliable expositors of holy writ, have understood the doctrine of purity to be inculcated by these quotations.   Some in whom we all have confidence, declare their experience of this glorious truth.   All Christians desire such a state,—and this desire is *increased* as men *advance* and *improve*. These considerations combined, ought to be of great weight with us.

8. Some of the declarations made by these eminent men to whom we look up for instruction, we may profitably review.

Ignatius, one of the apostolic fathers, in an epistle to the Ephesians, says : '· Nothing is better than peace, whereby all war is destroyed, both of things in heaven and things on earth.   Nothing of this is hid from you, if ye have perfect faith in Jesus Christ, and love, which are the beginning and the end of life ; faith is the beginning, love the end ; and both being joined in one, are of God.   All other things pertaining to perfect holiness follow.   For no man that hath faith sinneth ; and none that hath love hateth any man."

Irenæus, an eminent father of the second century, makes the following pointed observations : " The apostle explaining himself in his first epistle to the Thessalonians, fifth chapter, exhibited the *perfect and spiritual salvation* of man, saying, ' But the God of peace sanctify you perfectly ; that your soul, body, and spirit, may be preserved without fault to the coming of the Lord Jesus Christ.' How then, indeed, did he have the cause in these three, (that is to pray for the entire and perfect preservation of soul, body, and spirit, to the coming of the Lord,) unless he knew the common salvation of these was the renovation of the whole three ? Wherefore he calls those perfect who present the three faultless to the Lord. Therefore those are perfect who have the spirit and perseverance of God, and have preserved their souls and bodies without fault."

Macarius, a member of the celebrated council of Nice, is very clear in his statement of the doctrine. In a treatise upon this subject he says : " What, then, is that ' perfect will of God,' to which the apostle calls and exhorts every one of us to attain ? *It is perfect purity from sin*, freedom from all shameful passions, and the assumption of perfect virtue ; that is, the purification of the heart by the plenary and experimental communion of the perfect and divine Spirit. To those who say it is impossible to attain to perfection, and the final and complete subjugation of the passions, or to acquire a full participation of the good Spirit, we must oppose the testimony of the divine Scriptures ; and prove to them that they are ignorant and speak both falsely and presumptuously."

Numerous other authorities might be cited connecting these times of remote antiquity with the present, and showing that the idea or doctrine has been held in all ages by the Church of Christ. Very frequently there has been great ambiguity, and a great admixture of error, and many views have been advanced which we could not sustain. We quote now a few authorities of modern times.

Luther learned first the doctrine of justification by faith, but for a time sought sanctification by works. As he ascended the holy stairway at Rome the word came to him, which before had struck light into his soul —" *The just shall live by faith.*" The great leading dogma of the Reformation was undoubtedly justification by faith. That point was made very prominent and clear. It remained, however, for the revival of evangelism under those reformers who came after Luther, to bring out the doctrine of Christian purity.

Robert Barclay informs us concerning the views held by the Society of Friends. The testimony of such a quiet and unpretending body of Christians, is of exceeding great value. He says : " In whom this holy and pure birth is fully brought forth, the body of death and sin comes to be crucified and removed, and their hearts united and subjected to the truth, so as not to obey any suggestion or temptation of the evil One, but to be free from actual sinning, and transgressing of the law of God, and in that respect perfect. Yet doth this perfection still admit of growth ; and there remaineth a possibility of sinning, where the mind doth not most diligently and watchfully attend unto the Lord."

Our own denominational testimony has always been very decided and unequivocal. Wesley, Fletcher, Watson, Clark, Bramwell, Asbury, Abbott, Hedding, Hamline, Bangs, Fisk, and Olin, among our honored dead, and Peck, Foster, Wood, McDonald, and Boynton, of living authorities, have all spoken

8

in terms that cannot be easily misunderstood. Their testimony and teaching have been amply confirmed in the life and experience of Hester Ann Rodgers and Mrs. Fletcher, and the world wide spread writings of Mrs. Palmer. This truth indeed is sung in our hymns, recited in our catechisms, and reiterated in our rituals, and illustrated in our biographies, and the only wonder is that any among us ever doubted it.

John Wesley says: "Scriptural holiness is the image of God; the mind that was in Christ; the love of God and man ; lowliness, gentleness, temperance, patience, chastity."

" What, then, is that holiness which is the true wedding garment, the only qualification for glory? ' In Jesus Christ'.(that is according to the Christian institution, whatever be the case of the heathen world) ' neither circumcision availeth anything, nor uncircumcision ; but a new creation ; the renewal of the soul in the image of God wherein it was created. In Jesus Christ neither circumcision availeth anything, nor uncircumcision, but faith that worketh by love. It first, through the energy of God, worketh love to God and all mankind ; and by this love, every holy and heavenly temper. In particular, lowliness, meekness, gentleness, temperance and long suffering. ' It is neither circumcision'—the attending on all the Christian ordinances, ' nor uncircumcision,—the fulfilling of all heathen morality, but keeping the commandments of God—particularly those ' Thou shalt love the Lord thy God with all thy heart, and thy neighbor as thyself.' *In a word, holiness is the having the mind that was in Christ, and the walking as Christ walked.*" This plain statement puts the question of Mr. Wesley's views beyond all reasonable doubt.

Fletcher was equally pointed and explicit. His argument in support of this doctrine has never been equalled—never answered.

Watson, eminent for his theological lore, said : " Regeneration, we have seen, is concomitant with justification, but the apostles in addressing the body of believers in the churches to whom they wrote their epistles, set before them, both in the prayers they offer in their behalf, and in the exhortations they administer, a still higher degree of deliverance from sin, as well as a high growth in Christian virtues. Two passages only need be quoted to prove this : 1 Thes. 5: 23—' And the very God of peace sanctify you wholly : and I pray God your whole spirit, and soul, and body, be preserved blameless unto the coming of our Lord Jesus Christ.' 2 Cor. 7 : 1—' Having these promises, dearly beloved, let us cleanse ourselves from all filthiness of the flesh and spirit, perfecting holiness in the fear of God.' In both these passages, deliverance from sin is the subject spoken of; and the prayer in one instance, and the exhortation in the other, goes to the extent of the entire sanctification of the ' soul ' and ' spirit,' as well as of the ' flesh ' or ' body ' from all sin ; by which can only be meant our complete deliverance from all spiritual pollution, all inward depravation of the heart, as well as that which expressing itself outwardly by the indulgence of the senses, is called filthiness of flesh and spirit."

Dr. Adam Clark once observed: "As to the words which you quote as mine, I totally disclaim them. I never said—I never intended to say them : *I believe justification and sanctification to be widely distinct works.* I have been twenty-three years a traveling preacher, and have been acquainted with some thousands of Christians during that time, who were in different states of grace ; and I never to my knowledge, met with a single instance where God both justified and sanctified at the same time. I have heard of such, but I never saw them, and doubt whether any such ever existed. I have known multitudes who were justified according to the definition which you give of that sacred work; and I have known many who were sanctified in the sense in which you use that word, which I believe to be quite correct. But all these I have found were brought into these different states at separate times; having previously received a deep conviction of the need of pardon, and afterward of holiness of heart. If sanctification be taken in the sense in which it is frequently used in the Old Testament—to separate—to set apart for sacred use—then it implies a state lower than that of justification—such a state as that of a thorough penitent, who, when he is convinced of sin, separates himself from all unrighteousness, and consecrates himself to God. But when I speak of the purification of the heart, or doctrine of Christian perfection, I use sanctification in the sense in which it has generally been understood among the Methodists."

8. Our catechetical and ritualistic teaching is also in the same direction. Of ritualism we are fortunate in having but little. This little, however, bears decisive testimony to the doctrine. In the baptismal service for adults the officiating minister uses this prayer : "O merciful God, grant that all carnal affections may die in these persons, and that all things belonging to the Spirit may live and grow in them. Grant that they may have power and strength to have victory, and triumph against the devil, the world, and the flesh."

In the sacramental service we have the following : "Almighty God, unto whom all hearts are open, all desires known, and from whom no secrets are hid, cleanse the thoughts of our hearts by the inspiration of thy Holy Spirit, that we may perfectly love thee, and worthily magnify thy holy name, through Jesus Christ our Lord."

In admitting any one to the itinerant ministry, we ask the following questions : "Have you faith in Christ ? Are you going on to perfection ? Do you expect to be made perfect in love in this life ? Are you groaning after it." Here is a clear recognition of the doctrine and experience we speak of.

9. Our catechism gives a most explicit statement of this truth. "Question : What are the results of saving faith ? Answer. *Justification, regeneration*, and *sanctification*. Justification is that act of God's free grace in which he pardons our sins, and accepts us as righteous in his sight, for the sake of Christ. Regeneration is the new birth of the soul in the image of Christ, whereby we become the children of God; *and sanctification is that act of divine grace whereby we are made holy*. It is the privilege of every believer to be wholly sanctified, and to love God with all his heart in the present life; but at every stage of Christian experience there is danger of falling from grace, which danger is to be guarded against by watchfulness and prayer and a life of faith in the Son of God."

Again it is asked: "What other term is used to signify the great change which every sinner must experience in order to enter heaven ? Ans. Conversion, which, implying a complete renewal of heart and life, comprehends justification, regeneration and adoption."

"Quest. When is *sanctification begun ?* Ans. In regeneration, by which we receive power to grow in grace and in the knowledge of Christ, and to live in the exercise of inward and outward holiness.

"Quest. *What is entire santification ?* Ans. The state of being entirely cleansed from sin, so as to love God with all our heart, and mind, and soul, and strength, and our neighbor as ourselves.

"Quest. Should Christians, who have attained this high state of grace, pause in their career as though there were no further improvement? Ans. They should still *grow in knowledge and in grace, and improve faster than before.*"

10. It is also announced in our hymns of praise. We may safely assume the orthodoxy of their doctrinal teaching. Most certainly devotional theology is more directly suggested by divine impulse and illumination than mere dogmatism. We have hymns on repentance—on justification—and on sanctification—formerly " full redemption." These hymns have much to do with forming our religious ideas—even more perhaps than our systematic divinity. This is obviously the fact. One said, " I care not who makes the laws, if they permit me to make the songs of the people." This axiom has its application here:

> " Lord I believe a rest remains,
>   To all thy people known ;
> A rest where pure enjoyment reigns,
>   And thou art loved alone."

> " Saviour of the sin-sick soul,
> Give me faith to make me whole ;
> Finish thy great work of grace—
> Cut it short in righteousness.
> Speak the second time—be clean!
> Take away my inbred sin ;
> Every stumbling block remove ;
> Cast it out by perfect love."

> "Oh for a heart to praise my God—
>   A heart from sin set free ;
> A heart that always feels thy blood,
>   So freely spilt for me."

> " Come, O my God, the promise seal,
>   This mountain, sin, remove ;
> Now in my waiting soul reveal
>   The virtue of thy love.
> I want thy life—thy purity—
>   Thy righteousness brought in :
> I ask, desire, and trust in thee,
>   To be redeemed from sin."

11. Our history and biography are full of this glorious truth. Wesley, Fletcher, Clarke, Bramwell, Asbury, Whatcoat, Abbott, and a host of others, have given their testimony, and are held up before us as " epistles" to be " read and known of all men."

II. How may this blessing be obtained?

1. An all-important inquiry. Many err at this point.

2. We must, to start with, assume it is attainable. It will be of no practical benefit to seek it unless we believe it attainable.

3. Next, we must deem it necessary because practicable. Because we may be, therefore we ought to be holy. Being our privilege it also becomes our duty. A low estimate of a state of justification has led many to suppose that whether they will go forward is a matter that may be determined without involving any radical consequences. But if we fail to advance we must retrograde. If we do not obtain more, we lose what we have.

4. We must remember it is God's work in us. It is no ceremonial washing —no mere external change—nor a modification of our habits; but a fundamental —a thorough, radical revolution wrought in us by the cleansing power of the Holy Ghost. *We are saved " by grace."* *Holiness is salvation.* Paul says in 2 Thess. 2: 13—"But we are bound to give thanks always to God for you, brethren beloved of the Lord, because God hath from the beginning chosen you to salvation *through sanctification of the Spirit* and belief of the truth."

Peter in his first Epistle 1st chapter 2d verse, speaks of believers as " Elect according to the foreknowledge of God the Father, *through sanctification of the Spirit.* unto obedience and sprinkling of the blood of Jesus Christ." The Holy Ghost is our sanctifier.

5. It being the work of divine power, it may be accomplished in an instant. How soon and quickly this work may be done, in a large measure, depends on the condition of mind of those who desire it. The question has been often asked, " Is this work gradual or instantaneous?" It has been well answered, *" both."* Yet in seeking after it we must keep it before our minds as that which may come at any moment. *We may look for it every moment.*

John Wesley, referring to this point, says: " Not trusting to the testimony of others, I carefully examined most of these myself'; and every one (after the most careful inquiry, I have not found one exception either in Great Britain or Ireland), has declared that his deliverance from sin *was instantaneous ; that the change was wrought in a moment.* Had half of these, or one-third, or one in twenty declared it was gradually wrought in them, I should have believed this with regard to them, and thought that some were gradually sanctified, and some instantaneously. But as I have not found in so long a space of time a single person speaking thus; as all who believe they are sanctified, declare with one voice, *that the change was wrought in a moment,* I cannot but believe *that santification is commonly, if not always, an instantaneous work."*

Dr. Clarke says: " Every penitent is exhorted to believe on the Lord Jesus, that he may receive remission of sins. He does not, he cannot, understand that the blessing thus promised is not to be received to-day, but at some future time. In like manner, to every believer the new heart and right spirit are offered in the present moment, that they may in that moment be received. For as the work of cleansing and renewing the heart is the work of God, his almighty power can perform it in a moment, in the twinkling of an eye. And as it is our duty to love God with all our heart, and we cannot do this until he cleanse our hearts,—consequently he is ready to do it this moment ; because he wills that we should in this moment love him. Therefore we may justly say, ' Now is the accepted time ; now is the day of salvation.' He who in the beginning caused light in a moment to shine out of darkness, can in a moment shine into our hearts, and give us to see the light of his glory in the face of Jesus Christ. This moment, therefore, we may be emptied of sin, filled with holiness, and become truly happy."

Mr. Fletcher in presenting this point, makes use of the following eloquent and earnest language : " If a momentary display of Christ's bodily glory, could in an instant turn Saul, the blaspheming bloody persecutor, into Paul, the praying gentle apostle ; if a sudden sight of Christ's hands could in a moment root from Thomas' heart that detestable resolution, ' I will not believe,' and produce that deep confession of faith, ' My Lord and my God,' what cannot the display of Christ's spiritual glory operate in a believing soul, to which he manifests himself 'according to that power whereby he is able to subdue all things to himself?' Again, if Christ's body could in an instant become so glorious on the Mount that his very garments partook of the sudden irradiation, became not only free from every spot, but also ' white as the light, shining exceeding white as snow, so as no fuller on the earth could whiten them;' and if our bodies shall be changed, if this corruptible shall put on incorruption, and if this mortal shall put on immortality, 'in a moment, in the twinkling of an eye' why may not our believing souls, when they submit to God's terms, be fully changed, fully turned from the power of Satan unto God? When the Holy Ghost says, ' Now is the day of salvation,' does he exclude salvation from heart iniquity? If Christ now deserves fully the name of Jesus, because he fully saves his people from their sins; and if now the Gospel trumpet sounds, and sinners arise from the dead—*why should we not, upon the performance of the condition, be changed in a moment from indwelling sin to indwelling holiness? Why should we not pass in the twinkling of an eye, or in a short time, from indwelling death to indwelling life ?* "

6. This work God will accomplish for us when we believe. The doctrine of justification by faith has become the prevailing idea of reformed Christianity. Many, however, seem to think we are to be sanctified by growth—development—experience, &c. They forget, however, that as we " put on Christ, so must we walk in him "—and that as the first step was taken in the way, so must all subsequent advance be made. Wesley says: " I have continually testified (for these five and twenty years) in private and in public, that we are sanctified as well as justified by faith; and indeed the one of those great truths does exceedingly illustrate the other. Exactly as we are justified by faith, so we are sanctified by faith. Faith is the condition, and the only condition of sanctification, exactly as it is of justification. "No man is sanctified until he believes; every man, when he believes, is sanctified."

This faith implies implicit confidence in the word of God. It literally takes God at his word—" What things soever ye desire when ye pray, believe that ye receive them, and ye shall have them."

" And this is the confidence that we have in him, that, if we ask anything according to his will, he heareth us: and if we know that he hear us, whatsoever we ask, we know that we have the petitions we desired of him." This is truly great confidence that we know he " heareth us" when we " ask."

7. In exercising this faith we believe God has promised it, that he is able and willing to fulfill his promise, that he is able and willing to do it now, and finally that he does it.

8. To get to this point we must become very candid. The subject is one concerning which we cannot afford to urge captious objections. We must, therefore, as far as possible, avoid all mere theorizing, and abandon ourselves completely to divine guidance and control. Our pride and self-will must be yielded —and in the deepest humiliation before God, we must cry for wisdom and help.

9. We must become docile and childlike. Be willing to learn of any, even the most feeble and unskillful. Some desire the attention and aid of persons who are prominent. But we may learn even of God's little ones—[instance cited here of Bro. Belden and the servant girl.]

10. Let the consecration be perfect. Put all "on the altar." Keep nothing back. Examine carefully and candidly your heart. Thus ascertain whether your consecration is entire. Many wonder why they cannot believe. They may cease to wonder when they learn they have not fully consecrated themselves.

11. Cry day and night for the blessing. Be very much in earnest—face opposition, and welcome odium.

12. Keep looking unto Jesus, and expect the blessing every moment. Don't dwell on your unworthiness and unfaithfulness. This may produce great humiliation, and ultimately despair. But think of Christ's atonement and fullness, and rest there.

The discourse of Bro. Inskip, as given above, when compared with the fervor and liberty which characterized its delivery, will seem but an outline sketch. At every point he pressed home the truth in application, and his disgressions were the really eloquent and effective passages of the sermon. With a voice that reached the ears and stirred the hearts of persons in the remote circles of the audience, and attended by an unction which made the word a "savor of life," eternity alone will reveal the good accomplished. An appeal at the close, for present acceptance of the fullness of Christ, and trust in Him for the immediate accomplishment of the work of entire sanctification, elicited a hearty response from, perhaps, five hundred souls. Others bowed in prayer, and ere long were baptized with the Holy Ghost and fire sent down from heaven. Immediate results are always looked for in these ministrations, and always reached. Persons, while simply listening to the gospel word, as in olden times, believe and are blessed; surrender, and are sanctified; thus attesting the oft-repeated argument that the work is instantaneously wrought, as is the conversion of a soul; and both because it is by simple faith in the Lord Jesus Christ. If the reader will exercise this faith, after the whole theory has been made so clear, God will bless the word, and enable the trusting heart to rejoice in His salvation.

SABBATH AFTERNOON.

Notwithstanding the restriction placed upon Sunday travel, by preventing excursion trains, and the closing of all the modes of access to the encampment, that it might be as quiet and orderly as "the house of God," during the holy hours of the Lord's day a very large accession to the usual congregation was plainly perceptible. People from the adjacent neighborhood, and many who had procured lodging in the village and farm-houses near the ground, on coming to the gates and finding them locked, persevered so far as to get inside at points where pickets had been removed from the fence. There being nothing in the "Rules" which prevented ingress by this means, nobody interfered, as nobody, it was safely presumed, attempted to reach the enclosure, except those very much in earnest to enjoy the meeting. The restive crowd were kept at bay, and the Sabbath services were not only free from interruption, but crowned with the most happy consequences.

THE SKIRMISH LINE.

Immediately after the morning congregation was dismissed, and while the great thrilling truths which had been announced in the sermon were fresh in the general mind, several earnest men were moved to "cry aloud and spare not," wherever they found an unconverted fellow being.

Hearing some lively singing outside the tents, we walked around in that direction, and under a shady oak we found Captain Russell, of New York City, a small Testament in his hand, his hat thrown on the ground, his face beaming with benevolence, and to the listening scores in a circle around him, he was telling the "Old, old, story," of how Jesus came to save sinners; how he himself had been rescued from moral shipwreck; how, among the abandoned in vice and shame, he had witnessed the mighty works of God, transforming them from the sinks of iniquity to a position of respectability and religious peace.

The Captain was in earnest; so were the brethren who stood by him as his body guard—or, as he would call them, his "mates"—Bros. Smith, Gray, Theall, McPherson and others, who generally tent together, and spend the entire season in going from one camp to another to work for Jesus. Every man of them being a "monument of mercy," and saved from the dissipations of an ungodly life, they choose this way to spend their season of recreation, and say it costs them less than when they were the devotees of fashionable folly.

Bro. Gray leads the singing. His register of pieces is peculiar. Throwing his own soul into the words and music, a crowd will gather, hearts will melt, and tears flow, believers shout, sinners fall, and victory crown the day.

Captain Russell did good service on this occasion, by preaching a saving gospel to the "outsiders."

In another place we came upon a preacher named Post, from Central New York, exhorting as for life. His audience consisted of three young men, who looked the picture of embarrassment, and would have fled but that he held them fast, to plead with them to give God their hearts to-day.

Amanda Smith, at another point, was applying the morning sermon to some young people, and telling them, in the language of divine authority, "Now is the accepted time, and behold, now is the day of salvation."

In many of the tents, as the signal for private prayer was given, all knelt in silent meditation for some moments ; then one voice rose in supplication, waxed strong in faith, and naming every individual in the company present, implored a blessing upon each ; then another took up the strain, and a third followed, until every one had a turn at prayer, and every one received " grace to help in time of need."

In these informal prayer-meetings, it was always a wonder to listening ears outside to hear persons of the same family or friendly circle plead for each other, and for themselves. The disposition of the careless to laugh at such disclosures of private sentiment, was soon frozen by a subtle power, which they felt, but could not define, and which sent them away humbled and weeping on account of their own hardness and sinfullness of heart.

A PANIC IN THE TABERNACLE.

While the out-door service was going on, the crash of thunder and a nearing electric cloud surcharged with lightning, drove all who were in the open air into some place of shelter. The large frame tent became densely crowded, and so did the canvas tabernacle where the children's meeting was progressing. Soon the rain descended, and the floods came, and the winds blew, making a scene of wild confusion. Under the pressure a temporary prop gave way in the Tabernacle, and a cry was raised—" The tent is coming down ; run !—run for your lives !" Many started out into the pelting rain ; others sprang to their feet with fearful screams ; an injudicious messenger hastened to the prayer-meeting tent and bawled—" The Tabernacle is falling, save the children !"

For perhaps five or ten minutes it seemed that reason was bewildered in the panic, but faith and self-possession soon rallied, and quiet was restored in both meetings. Mrs. Inskip mastered the whirlwind of excitement in the Tabernacle by a few reassuring words to the children and their friends, and soon had all uniting in a joyful song of salvation. She even turned the fright to good account by persuading people to seek religion and prepare to meet the trials of a day fast rolling on, when the elements shall melt with fervent heat, and the wicked unbelieving shall seek shelter and find no mercy.

A GREAT BAPTISM.

The most sensible manifestation of the Holy Ghost, which some of the preachers and people had ever witnessed or experienced, came upon the waiting company in the " Board Tent," on Sabbath afternoon. Brother Thompson had suggested that the disciples of Jesus here might reach a position of dependence and humble faith, in which " the promise of the Father" would be fullfilled in a most extraordinary manner. " Get down low at His feet," he continued to exhort. " The power is promised ; Jesus is in the midst; God the Father is willing; the Holy Ghost is waiting; it is coming—O Lord, fill us now !"

The people by scores sank to the ground. Some were utterly overpowered with " speechless awe," and others realized the mysterious action of the sacred fire on their inmost nature, purging away the dross, and purifying them, even as gold is refined.

The reporter we sent in to the meeting to take notes, failed to bring us a connected or coherent narrative. His pencil and note book fell among the straw, and soon he was " laid out " himself, with the tide of mighty grace running over him. When we asked for the particulars, Brother Selah W. Brown replied: " Glory to the Lamb !" This is all we gleaned from him ; but from others we learned what we here, without presumption set forth—the occasion was " Pentecost repeated." It may have been on a smaller scale, but it was " The very same fire," and " the very same power Jesus promised should come down."

The rain was so copious that all who were sheltered remained in the meetings, which continued without intermission during the afternoon.

SABBATH EVENING, 7 O'CLOCK.

SERMON BY REV. L. C. MATLACK, D. D., IN THE TABERNCLE.

" *He that cometh to God, must believe that He is, and that He is a Rewarder of them that diligently seek Him.*"—*Heb.* 11 : 6.

The great salvation, of which so much has been so well said, and so sweetly sung, during this meeting, is not the creature of our devotions, but the gift of God. We must not look so much at the meeting of God's people, but we should look more to meeting with God—each soul for itself. There is a possible peril to the interests of pure religion and undefiled before God. It would be involved necessarily, if to any extent, we attach to these means of grace, a creative power. Let us not, therefore, substitute coming to a National Camp-meeting, for the infinitely more important movement of coming to God.

The blessing of " a clean heart " cannot by any possibility result from the aggregation of emotional impulses, which sweep like an ocean tide all around us occasionally. Let that tide rise and swell in mountain waves beneath us. But above its waters we must look aloft constantly. Coming thus to God, floods of harmony, however moving and melting, cannot float our souls into the haven of perfect rest. These both, are aids to the soul. They help us on to God. But they are means only. God himself is the source; the fount of every blessing. The joint support of other souls, who worship God in spirit and in truth, will help us to draw near to God. The melting melody of sweet spiritual singing, will open the mind and liquify the heart preparatory for the admission of a living faith, and the reception of a divine mould of life; yet, the soul must reach beyond and above all its surroundings, and come to God—by direct approach—actual contact—by personal communion—conscious presence. He alone is the Giver of " every good gift and every perfect gift."

From His hand alone we must receive this great salvation. It is emphatically, " The gift of God."

One thought predominates in my mind, as the paramount question for our present consideration; and that is: How may we, at once, get to the Giver? Or, What is necessary, in order to approach Him now, so as to be accepted and sanctified "wholly;" so that our " whole spirit and soul and body may be preserved blameless unto the coming of our Lord Jesus Christ."

To this inquiry, the text gives an explicit answer, which is at once simple and also all-sufficient in its directions and information We must believe,—believe that God is,—that He is a Rewarder—of diligent seekers. And the application of this answer to the question now in our minds, is the legitimate construction of the text, as it stands related to the entire eleventh chapter of Hebrews, of which it is the key.

In this chapter is given a record of pious worthies, who did come to God. They came very near to God; among them were Abel, Enoch, Noah, Abram, Isaac, Jacob, Moses, Samuel, and the prophets. These all received from His hand every thing their faith claimed, and that is assigned as the reason they got what they wanted. "By faith" all these wonders were wrought.

With one, the thing wanted was, a " witness that he was righteous;" with another it was—" testimony that he pleased God." Such witnesses of righteousness are precisely what we would have now. Many of you are longing for the " witness " from the Lord, that " all you do is right, according to his will and word, well pleasing in his sight." And for this we need now to come as this "cloud of witnesses came, by whom we are compassed about." Let us endeavor during this hour of service, to lay aside every weight—every besetment, and press along the very pathway which they trod, looking unto Jesus the author and finisher of our faith. And he himself duplicates the instructions of Paul, with a promise of great scope and power, saying: " What things soever ye desire when ye pray, believe that ye shall receive—and ye shall have."

Thus you have before you the instructions of the divine word. Here is given to you the pathway to heavenly treasures, and the key used by ancient worthies to unlock the magazine of divine supplies. And neither Abel, nor Enoch, nor Abram had any greater work to do than now remains undone all around our pathway in this nineteenth century. Their latest successors on earth, at no time in the world's history were more in need of the utmost God is willing to do in and for his servants, than are we now, who are here to-day.

There are "kingdoms to be subdued," " righteousness to be sought," " promises to be obtained," " armies of aliens" to be " put to flight," many entrenched "strongholds" to be pulled " down," by the help of God. And we must not forget the declaration and promise of Christ, that even his own

great works are to be excelled in the after days. For he said : " He that believeth on me, the works that I do shall he do also ; and greater works than
these shall he do."   These greater works include the vastly extended field of
pious labor, and the multiplied exampe of personal salvation, through the
agencies of truth by human utterance.   Ten thousand times ten thousand,
and thousands of thousands of redeemed spirits, saved by personal human effort instrumentally, are a fulfillment of this declaration from the lips of Christ.
And these greater works we must be prepared to accomplish in the name of
Christ.   Let us therefore come to God.   Let us, my brethren, wake up to
the realities of the stern conflict before us.

We need the divine communing, the filling of love, the baptism of fire,
the whole panoply of God's armor, to fit us for our part in the battle of the
age—under this banner, " Holiness to the Lord "   Perhaps the cry of Job
comes to our lips : " O that I knew where I might find Him !"   Then come
with Job " even to His seat," and order your cause before Him, and fill your
mouth with arguments divinely inspired.   With Job, each of us might say,
" I would know the words which He would answer me, and understand what
He would say unto me !   Will He plead against me with his great power ?
No ! But he would put strength into me ! "   That strength is what we need,
and may have this hour.   O my brethren, let us come to God !

" But will God in every deed dwell with men on the earth ? "   Does he
authorize, encourage, invite any such approach to his presence ?   Hear His
word.   " To this man will I look, even to him that is poor, and of a contrite
heart, and trembleth at my word."   The significance of these words is intensified by the declaration accompanying them, that " The heaven is my throne
and the earth is my footstool : where is the house that ye build unto me ?
And where is the place of my rest ?"   Demonstrating that not in the accom-
modation which houses afford, but in the companionship of man, he delights
and rests.

And therefore it is as Isaiah says, (45: 24 :) " Surely shall one say, in the
Lord have I righteousness and strength. Even to Him shall men come." "For
thus saith the Lord, even them will I bring to my holy mountain, and make
them joyful in my house of prayer."   Come ! Let us up then, toward His
mountain, and find righteousness and strength, and joy in His house of prayer.

Besides these assurances, God is everywhere represented in His word as longing for human love.   His voice of mercy and of love is full of solicitude for
intimacy with man.   God is the infinite lover of the soul.   Although His name
is holy, and He dwells in the high and holy place, yet with him who is of a
contrite and humble spirit, God finds sweeter companionship than even in high
and heavenly courts.   The framework of man, so " fearfully and wonderfully
made," has apartments in it fitted only for and filled fully by the great God.
He made man for himself.   Any other occupant is a usurper.   Any other appropriation of ourselves is an abominable prostitution.   But in order to such
occupancy, we must first come to him, lovingly, longingly, bringing an open
heart as our tribute of devotion.   Then will he fill, replenish and overflow every
believing soul.   Shall we not thus come to him now and here ?

The whole tenor of the divine utterance in the Scripture is as a loving cry
from the heart of God.   These utterances unite in one sweet voice of mercy
and voice of love.   It seems to say : " Love me ! Oh ye sons of men ! Love

me! oh ye daughters of Zion ! I am hungry for your love." "Look up to me." "Look unto me and be ye saved." And yet this almost importunate plea which is repeated age after age, is coldly rejected by the vast majority of men. There are no words more expressive of the sadness of disappointed love, than the words of Jesus. (John 15: 25.) He says : " They hated me without a cause." " Now have they both seen and hated—both me and my Father."

Such is the loving Father and beloved Son to whom we are invited, and to whom coming, as we now approach, we will find precious to us. And we more-over shall thereby be built upon a spiritual house, a holy priesthood, to offer up spiritual sacrifices, acceptable to God by Jesus Christ.

This coming to God will please Him. Such an affirmation is implied in the words joined to the text. " Without faith it is impossible to please God." Enoch did please God, and God told him so—gave him " this testimony," be-fore the translation.

My brethren : we should delight to please Him. And we are no more pleased to be blest of God than is He pleased to be trusted by us with a loving confi-dence. Let us then seek to be gladdened by His favor, and also delight Him with our childlike faith, by coming on the line indicated, as diligent seekers. For even the most delicate relation of husband and wife is sanctioned and sanc-tified by God himself as illustrative of his delight in human love. "As the bridegroom rejoiceth over the bride, so shall thy God rejoice over thee." No other beings have the capacity to afford such delight to the Infinite One.

Jesus assures us that " the true worshiper shall worship the Father, in spirit and in truth. For the Father seeketh such to worship Him." Yes, seeketh such, whose spirit approaches His so near that they realize his presence person-ally manifested. O, yes, it is possible that we may, with favored John, recline our wearied heads upon the dear Redeemer's breast. God's arms of love would compass us. Close up against his bosom we may lie : so close, that the throb-bings of His loving heart shall give perpetual impulse to motive power, which in us shall be exhaustless and eternal.

It was no pain to Jesus, but a pleasure, when his frame thrilled to the touch of the poor woman whose faith brought virtue out of him, to heal her so com-pletely. And so God would be touched by the hand of faith, and realize the joy of giving the Holy Spirit to them that ask Him. The joy which parents feel in giving good gifts to their children, whose eyes sparkle with delight in receiving, is only a faint semblance of the divine joy which, on coming to God, will awaken in Him and in us. Come then ! Come now ! We can, we will, and we do believe, that He is a Rewarder—to them who thus seek Him !

But it may be asked, does human experience in modern times realize the an-cient ideas of divine communion ? Have any in our day been able to approach, or come to God ? O, yes. Human experience does confirm and fulfill the pre-cious promises. Men do get near to God, and even dwell in the secret place of the Most High, and abide under the shadow of the Almighty.

* " Payson, at times almost lost a sense of the external world, in the ineffa-ble thoughts of God's glory, which rolled like a sea of light around him at the throne of grace.

" Cowper, in one of the lucid hours of his religious life, had an experience of God's presence which he enjoyed in prayer, that he thought he should have died with joy, if special strength had not been imparted to bear the disclosure.

---

* Phelp's Still Hour.

" One of the Tennents, on one occasion, when engaged in secret devotion, was so overpowered by the revelation which God opened upon his soul, with augmenting intensity of effulgence as he prayed, that at length he recoiled from the intolerable joy as from a pain, and besought God to withhold from him further manifestations of His glory. He said : ' Shall Thy servant see Thee and live ? '

" Edwards enjoyed sweet hours on the banks of Hudson's river in happy converse with God ; and the inward sense of Christ which came into his heart he says he knew not how to express otherwise than by a calm, sweet abstraction of soul from all the concerns of this world ; and sometimes a kind of vision, of being above in the mountains, far from all mankind, sweetly conversing with Christ, and rapt and swallowed up in God."

These experiences of men, not one of whom were Methodists, do most fully anticipate and sustain the utterances and experience of Wesley, Fletcher, Bramwell, Asbury, Roberts, McKendree, Sharp, and thousands of others who all came to God—came close to Him—and were received.

Brethren, you have had the theory of sanctification ably presented, both as a doctrine, and as an experience. The duty of consecration—the preparatory and essential conditions of heart purity, have been amply and fitly urged on your attention by others. To-night I dwell mainly on a result of it—nearness to God. And I press on your attention those peculiar words of the Saviour about prayer. They have a deep significance. " Pray to thy Father, which is in secret, and thy Father which seeth in secret shall reward thee openly."

This closet intercourse, shut in with God, produces results which are manifested openly, when we come away from the secret place. The glorious light which shone through the skin of Moses' face, did no more plainly show his having been with God in the mountain, than does the light of their good works, and the overflowing love, and increased power of prayerful souls demonstrate that they have been with God in the closet.

Paul speaks of " an inheritance " peculiar to " them that are sanctified."

One peculiar feature of the sanctified ones, who, with God are permitted to enjoy familiar intercourse, is stated thus by a late writer :

" The sanctified one seems to me like a vessel which God takes up to heaven, and fills with his love and power, and then returns to the Church and the world to impart of the fullness of its salvation. It is by such that God has access to those so far away from Him that they do not hear the Spirit's whisperings. Sweet privilege, to be thus taken into the inner chamber of the Beloved ! Blessed interchange of thought, between the soul and the High and Holy One that inhabiteth eternity !"*

These souls become magnetic centres of attraction. Filled with God's gracious power, their light shines, and is seen of men. They radiate pious influences over a vast circumference. Instrumentally they fulfill the Saviour's words, " I, when lifted up, will draw all men unto me." And no lifting up is more effective in drawing men to Jesus than the exhibition of a holy life. Such exhibition you and I desire to make. Therefore we pray for the hyssop-purging and the blood-washing. Hence the cry within so many hearts : " Create in me a clean heart." O that we may come to God and get that

---
* Drops from many Fountains.

precious cleansing at this hour. This will precede and prepare for the close communings with God which our souls were made to enjoy.

Such fellowship divine is not unknown among our own brethren, living as well as dead. Alfred Cookman, of blessed memory, who was so childlike in his friendship, and so pure in heart, said at Des Plaines National Camp-meeting, after a season of prayer: "God was so near to me, so fully revealed, that I almost thought I should have died with awe and love."

The childlike spirit of Cookman is a feature of Christian character only those can have who live near to God. They who come to Him must part with their self-hood, assumption, and pride of manhood, and become as little children. They will abase themselves, however, only to be exalted higher in the scale of spiritual being. Down with self and up with God, above all, over all, blessed for evermore!

Dr. Steele, whose newness of life he characterizes as "One year with the Comforter," was at one time, while engaged with God in pious meditation, visited with such a manifestation of the presence of Jesus, and so filled with love to him, that it seemed as if his enraptured soul would lift his body out of the chair, and float away with it heavenward.

And O, my brethren, I too, understand what it is to be very near to God. Passing down the lower Mississippi, seventy-five miles below New Orleans, in 1870, to a new and untried field of labor, where, as yet no Protestant Church had been organized, God met me on the way. It was night. Alone on the deck, in the darkness, my heart was drawn out sweetly and reverently toward Him. His infinite purity—His condesension—His love to man—His incarnation—the way of life in Jesus Christ—all stood out in such grandeur, and power, and glory, that the bright constellation of heaven paled before the brilliancy and beauty of these diviner things. Waves of joy rolled over my soul, when I bowed in rapturous amazement, and wept from my very excess of delight in these thoughts of God.

Laid low with the yellow fever in 1871, on the border of the grave, yet recovering slowly, I drew near to my God. My relations with Him, my work, my interior life, were all searchingly analyzed. Naked before the All-seeing, and not afraid when God drew near, my soul talked with Him fearlessly. I said: "O God, thou knowest that I love Thee. Search me and try me. If it be not so, reprove me from my presumption. I want no favor, no friendship but thine. Only do Thou allow me to draw nearer to Thee, by transformation of character, so that Thou canst put thy hand on me and say, 'This is my friend!' Then I will forego every other ambition, and become absorbed in Thy love and service." God sweetly assured me of his favor and friendship. Precious confidence of faith! In an ecstacy of delight I was led to say: "Now God and I understand each other!"

Excuse this personal narrative. I return to a direct appeal. "When shall I come and appear before God," in a divinely inspired solicitude? I look out upon a multitude before me, many of whom are leaning that way. You are ready to move in that direction. Some of you are thus near God now. Before you all the pathway is opened up in the words of the text. They are words fitly spoken—like apples of gold in a picture of silver. Here is the mercy-seat on which God waits to greet you. Over the entrance-gate, graven in letters of light, are the instructions of the Master of Ceremonies, for the guidance of all who seek an interview with the Heavenly King, in His courts.

Pause, ere ye enter—read—remember : " He that cometh to God," "must believe "—" that He is "—"that He is a Rewarder "—" of them that diligently seek him !"

You want the pearl of purity ; he has it. He is here to bestow it. Believe this. Approach him as a Rewarder. One " has ascended up on high, led captivity captive, and received gifts for men." The Father distributes them in his name, to those who have faith in his name. Draw near, in full assurance of faith. Come thus to God. Come now.

Remember : the successful seeker must be a diligent seeker. You must not act from an impulse merely, and only for a moment. A spasm or desire will not accomplish the end. Make it a business. Thoroughly examine yourselves, A life-purpose of entire consecration, at the start, will shorten the path wonderfully. An indefinite aim will prolong the search.

But God does not hide himself. He calls to you. He announces where he may be found. Even the way of approach is pointed out. The very conditions of acceptance are proclaimed beforehand. He would not have you miss your way. He watches for your coming. The blessed Holy Ghost is provided to help your infirmities—to strengthen weak hands and confirm feeble knees. This way—this way to the mercy-seat ! God help you to come to him, believingly, hopefully, trustingly, lovingly.

"He that cometh to God, must believe, that he is, and that he is a Rewarder of them that diligently seek him."

REV. WM. McDONALD'S EXHORTATION.

The temperament of some of the brethren would have moved them, at the close of Dr. Matlack's sermon, to take advantage of such a tidal-wave of religious excitement as prevailed, and intensify it into action. But Bro. McDonald in his cool, deliberate way, arose and began to unfold his favorite topics, reason and faith—reason, the ground-work of all religious obligation, and faith the most reasonable thing in the whole universe of mind. He observes numbers of people, professedly seeking heart purity. They seem to be self-desperate ; they are the first to come forward, and the last to leave the altar ; they mean to bear the cross, and " go through." He wants to say to them that all this isn't salvation—it is a rough road, but can never lead them to purity ! There are misapprehensions existing that he would fain remove. At every meeting, so far as we remember, he seized the opportune moment to take the latitude and longitude of spiritual progress. Who can forget, if they were within hearing, that night at Des Plaines, when hundreds of eager souls listened, and followed his every word, even repeating after him, like a Sabbath-school class in concert, the act of surrender, and the exercise of immediate faith, until the ground seemed as if shaken by an earthquake, so manifest was the power of God unto salvation.

Our Iowa brethren will also recall the day he stood one hour answering objections, reconciling discrepancies, explaining the simplicity of the divine arrangement, and placing before every man and woman the alternative, then and there, of sudden rest and full salvation, or continued uncertainty and distress, as they stepped out on the naked promise, or shrank with fear from the step.

His "talk" on Sabbath evening was of a similar character, and for similar ends. Assuming that they wanted deliverance; that the dominion or indwelling of sin was distasteful, yes, hateful, intolerable—and that they really wanted it now, he first stormed the entrenchments of error, and then pointed out the path to the valley of blessing, and through it to the fountain that washes away every stain of sin.

The great object sought, he declared, could not be obtained by feeling. "Feeling is no part of faith. You must cease from your struggling, and quietly cast yourself, all helpless, on Christ. Then, and only then, can the blessing you are seeking be found. You must honor God by believing in him.

"But there is something which precedes believing, and you cannot believe until it is done. It is consecration—not by piecemeal, but entire. The will must be surrendered, and *this takes all.* You must become nothing, and let Christ be all in all. Self-will is incorporated in the veriest trifles sometimes. Each one has his or her idol. You know what it is—this in one person, that in another; and there centres your will.

"A certain lady sought purity. She had a brooch which she greatly valued as a memento from a dear friend. It was strangely suggested that this must be cast aside. For some time she resisted, but the impression grew stronger. At last the golden treasure (which was found to be mostly alloy—'pewter')—was parted with, and with it went the surrender of her will, and the blessing soon came."

Numerous instances were cited, showing the influence of trivial hindrances preventing a full consecration.

"With the surrender of your will," he continued, "goes that which supports it; you must yield your will entirely before you can believe that *God saves you.* The conditions are a perfect consecration—not of your tobacco, or any such trash, but *your will.* Be sure you are sincere at this point. Then you are to honor God by faith; that is, by believing his word—'I will receive you.'

9

" You are to believe he does save you; not because you are struggling, and worrying, and crying—no, this is no part of faith; nor is it incited by these things—they only obstruct faith. Believe he receives you now, because *he has promised to do so.* Suppose a man greatly needing a certain sum of money is presented with a check for the full amount by a friend known to be perfectly able to pay it, and the man on his way to receive the money works himself up to a condition of distress, seeking for evidence that the check he himself believed to be good was good—what would be thought of such inconsistency? Will you thus dishonor God?"

Admonishing all to consider well this matter, he asked an expression, by uplifted hands, attesting whether they surrendered the will, and believed that Jesus saved them now?

" Lord, I believe," was the sentiment, " uttered or unexpressed," of hundreds in that audience. " Now," added the speaker, " let us avoid any mistake here. This consecration and faith is *not the witness.* Tarry a little. Look for the answering fire—the baptism of the Holy Ghost. You have believed. God accepts; you are saved! All this without any feeling— saved by faith. Now look for the ratification of this act; the witness will be given."

All this time mighty prayer had been ascending. Emotion, long pent, swept over every barrier, and the floodgates of glory were opened; the power was like billows rolling in on the shore. The close of the meeting was sublime. The presence of the Lord filled the Tabernacle. Shouts of victory were heard on every side, and the singing of the doxology ended a meeting, the remembrance of which will never fade from the minds of those who participated in it.

SIXTH DAY.

MONDAY MORNING MEETINGS.

Instead of reaction or mental and physical lassitude, after the exhausting labors and holy excitements of the Sabbath, the people were out even more promptly than usual, and at the sunrise services. Many wanted an opportunity to acknowledge the Lord, and to speak of his love, which had been shed abroad anew in their hearts, establishing them in their most holy faith. Others had passed through the day and evening meetings without any sensible manifestation or increase of light and power, and their continued cry was " Bless me, even me, O my Father."

" A crisis is upon us," remarked the leader. "While it is proper that we should praise God for yesterday, we must improve the grace given, and then he will give more grace. Let us spend some time together in prayer for the descent of the Holy Ghost."

Here ensued some moments of wrestling for victory, and pleading the promises of God, which are " yea and amen to every one that believeth."

" We must have mighty power to-day," it was said, " and now the gates are open ; yea the windows of heaven. Lord, pour out such a blessing as there shall not be room to receive it."

Prayer was asked in behalf of a pastor who was taken very sick. This brought out the intelligence that a case of severe illness had been healed during the previous night. Then was sung :

> " I love to tell the story,
> Of unseen things above,
> Of Jesus and His glory,
> Of Jesus and His love," &c.

" Now for experience—short, distinct expression of present feeling or faith."

" Bless the Lord, O my soul, and forget not all his benefits."

" I am helped. Self is cleansed out this morning, and Jesus is all in all."

" I ventured to touch the hem of his garment, and he restored my soul."

" Sixteen years ago I laid my soul at Jesus' feet, but I was lacking an entire consecration. Now I make a full surrender. I have a great work to do at home. Pray that the Lord may help me."

" My soul doth magnify the Lord. I am saved."

"He saves me sweetly.   His love casteth out all fear."

"Yesterday I was filled.   God is still giving, and I am receiving."

"I now trust in the Lord with all my heart, and love him supremely."

"After hesitating about it long, I came to the hard place, and taking hold of his hand he has helped me over.   I reckon myself dead indeed unto sin."

> "I want to be little, more meek and more mild,
> More like my blest Saviour and more like a child ;
> More watchful, more prayerful, more lowly in mind,
> More thankful, more gentle, more humble and kind."

The singing of this by Brother Gray produced—always does—a sensation. It is "multum in parvo," and presents a fine picture of completeness in Christian character.

"Bless God for the victory he has given me.   I am free."

"All clear and bright within, and the Everlasting arms are around me."

"This highway is grand !   O how glad I am, that even late in life, I have entered on it to journey with the sanctified."

"I am still seeking a pure heart." (Voices—"Why don't you believe and receive?")

"I humbly, yet confidently, say: 'The Spirit and blood make my cleansing complete ; and his perfect love casteth out fear.'"

"Like those lightning flashes yesterday, the Lord revealed himself to me when a poor drunkard.   At first it was all terror; then it was all tenderness; now it is all love—love to God and love to man.   Oh, it is good to be here.   I'll tell you the rest when I get to heaven."

> "O the blood, the precious blood,
> That Jesus shed for me :
> Upon the cross, in crimson flood,
> Just now by faith I see."

"For one year and a half I have rested sweetly in Jesus.   No storm can shake my inward calm while to this refuge clinging."

"At Oakington the invitation came to me—'O taste and see that the Lord is good.'   I did; and O how sweet it is to me still."

> "I'm happy, I'm happy, O wondrous account,
> My joys are immortal, I stand on the mount;
> I gaze on my treasure, and long to be there,
> With angels my kindred, and Jesus my dear."

"Just at this moment I know the blood of Jesus cleanseth me."

"It was not to ascend Pisgah I came to this meeting, but to have more of the nature of Christ infused into my soul.   I want the working spirit.   I long to be like Jesus."

"I have found a satisfying portion here.   In early life I gave my heart to Jesus.   When I was convicted for sanctification, I met with peculiar obstructions. For three years I mourned my inward depravity. Sometimes all became as dark as midnight; but He gave me one promise at a time to keep me encouraged in the effort. At times a little light gleaming from the precious cross was more to me than all the world. Then hope began to dawn. Satan tried his arts to deceive me; but Jesus meant to make me wholly his, and I am now all the Lord's. He is filling me up, bless his name!"

"But for the 'Whosoever,' I should have despaired. That kept me from sinking. I rest on the Rock."

"The more I am saved, the more it seems my hunger and thirst increase."

Father Coleman—"That's a good sign, sister. Sick people haven't much appetite. It is the healthy and active who get hungry and must have sustenance. Bless God, there's enough for all."

Many voices—"Amen. Bless the Lord!"

"I magnify the grace of God in every instance where I see the once poor, degraded followers of vice changed, and washed, and lifted up to sit in heavenly places in Christ Jesus."

"Last night Brother McDonald's talk helped me. I never understood the simplicity of faith before. Why, it isn't much, after all, to be saved. I believe, and he saves me. Hallelujah!"

"This faith brings present salvation to me also. Last night I touched Him, and now I'm resting at the cross—washing in the crimson tide."

"Yesterday I was enabled to believe that Christ's blood cleansed me. This morning I have no doubt on the subject. Glory to Jesus!"

"It was painfully discovered to me yesterday, under the Word and by the Spirit, that roots of bitterness were remaining in me. I had often been powerfully blessed, but this took every prop from under me. In my tent I looked over the matter calmly, aad then made a full consecration. I meant it, and He blessed me so that I had to shout his praise. Oh, I know He loves me and saves me this moment."

"I came here all the way from Connecticut, and was happy when I started; became happier as I neared this glorious place; and now it is getting better and better all the time. I shall try to tell them when I go home how the Lord was present in this place."

"I feel ashamed—not of Jesus, but of what I have been, and what I have done and failed in doing. O how recreant I have been in His service; but He pardons my past unfaithfulness."

"Jesus comes—he fills my soul—
Perfected in love I am;
I am every whit made whole,
Glory, glory to the Lamb!"

"I have three little boys here, and I believe they are all convicted; pray that they may every one be converted before we go home." (Sensation.)

Brother Stockton—

> "Oh, if there's only one song I can sing,
> When in his beauty I see the great King,
> This shall my song in eternity be,
> Oh, what a wonder that Jesus loves me.
>
> "I am so glad that Jesus loves me,
> Jesus loves me, Jesus loves me,
> I am so glad that Jesus loves me,
> Jesus loves even me."

"I cant't tell how I am saved. But twenty-five years ago the Lord put in me a desire for purity, and gave me the witness that I was fully sanctified. I have made but poor progress, but have never willingly departed from this new and living way."

"The first camp-meeting I ever attended was Manheim. When I heard about the nature and necessity of this heart cleansing, I was bewildered. I did not know exactly where I stood, but the blessed Spirit never let me rest until I found out my latitude. Now I know that I am saved from the dominion and power and love of sin."

"I was surprised at many things I heard here last night in the sermon and exhortation. The brother said angels wondered at us that we don't believe God. This is strange and sadly true. Ever since that day in the Garden of Eden, it seems we are prone to believe Satan rather than our Heavenly Father. Why is this? Our sin, how deep its stains! O Lord, I believe; help my unbelief!"

"I must get up here in the love of Jesus to say he sought me when a stranger, wandering from his fold. Now I know he saves me. It is not a hope-so, or an inference, but I *know* it."

"I was a poor tavern loafer and drunkard, when a new thought came into my heart to look upward and pray to be saved. I found in reading the blessed Bible there was hope set before me, and I thank God I found it at the cross. I heard nothing said about sanctification; but, while reading the sixth of Romans—'How shall we that are dead to sin live any longer therein?'—I saw God's will. A dead man in his coffin cannot sin, because he cannot feel or think, or speak; so the Christian, dead with Christ, is dead to all the world, and I asked the Lord to separate me entirely from it. He saved me through and through."

"Please, brethren, allow me to say a word. I was raised in this neighborhood, but have been away in the West fifteen years. How glad I am to be here, near the place of my birth, and the equally memorable spot of my second birth. Oh, my heart is affected and full of love by reason of what I see and hear around me. My old friends are here on the way to glory. I, too, have good hope of eternal life, and I expect to meet you all in that beautiful world on high."

Father Baldwin—"Like one of old, I will say this people shall be my people, and their God my God. With them I expect to live and die and be buried, and have a glorious part in the first resurrection."

"Two years ago I was cleansed. I say this to the honor of Jesus, but to my own discredit I must say I failed to live up to the light I had, and fell into great darkness. Yesterday he restored unto me the joy of his salvation, and the light returned. Now, by the help of God, I will confess it everywhere"

"If you do, brother, your path will shine brighter and brighter."

"I was not so particular in coming here to be made happy, as to be made radically right. I ventured last night to step out on the Rock, and all is calm. I rest on the immutable word of God."

"The greatest blessing of my whole life came to me just here last night. It seemed as if I felt the Holy Ghost burning out all dross from my soul."

"The question asked in the Preachers' Meeting on last evening, 'Is your heart pure?' followed me. I had to acknowledge mine was not. I could not doubt but that it might be made pure after all I heard; so I began to cry like David, 'Create within me a clean heart, O God.' Now, I think the work is done, and there is not an impure thought in my heart."

"I was, as some here know, a tremendous sinner, but my case was not beyond the skill of the Great Physician. I am gloriously saved."

"I want to leave my testimony. Six of us came up here from Fall River, Mass., to be baptized afresh. We need this baptism at home, and every one of us has been blessed. I am the happiest of all. We take the first train for home—pray for us."

Another of the Fall River band spoke—the youngest of them. He had been in the fountain—went clear under, and thought *he* was happiest.

Quite a joyful time was had in pledging these dear brethren to be faithful to Christ, and to meet them on the shining shore.

"Since the Lord revealed himself to me as a Saviour from all sin, I have been enabled to acknowledge him in all my ways, and confess this blessing everywhere."

"I was happy all day yesterday, and I know if I keep faith as active to-day I will be just as happy."

"I shall never forget yesterday. My chains fell off, and I was made free n Christ Jesus."

"While the stream was running so deep and free last evening, I trusted, and it cleansed me."

"Four years ago I was converted. Now I feel that I am fully saved."

"How it is that I am here, seems incomprehensible. I wanted to come, but saw no way. I laid the matter before the Lord, and he has brought me here to testify—fully saved."

"Last year I went to Urbana the wretchedest man to be found, and left that place one of the happiest, because I had Jesus in my heart. I came on here to have my strength renewed, and return home a better husband and a better man."

"Jesus is mighty to save; for he saved me, and took out of my nature the craving for tobacco, rum, and all such filthiness of the flesh and spirit."

A brother from Washington, D. C., and about to return, gave his testimony and asked prayer that God might bless that city with a great revival, and fill the new church with which he was connected, (Hamline,) with full salvation and a holy people. "Jesus," said he, "is with us; and we intend to stand up for this great doctrine."

Bro. McLean stated that he had entered into a new and very solemn engagement to be as full of the Holy Ghost and faith as was Stephen of old. He did not aspire to the intellectual rank of Stephen, but his faith. "I am believing to be filled with faith and the Holy Ghost, whatever it may lead me to; and there is a sweetness about the thought of having this endowment, I never knew before. Glory be to the Father, and to the Son, and to the Holy Ghost!"

Rev. Mr. White was daily learning more about this wondrous way of love and liberty. He dated his entire sanctification two years ago; but this meeting would be to him the date of many new sensations of delight. He had not attached much importance to the witness of the Spirit before; now he saw this in a clearer light, and, like Bro. McLean, he was ready for whatever God might appoint, and was being filled with this glorious salvation.

"I came here," said another, "to be filled; not that I was empty before—for I have had a good time all along. There have been periods when the Spirit came in unusual power to my heart. While Dr. Lowrey was preaching the other day, I felt the first ground swell. Then while Bro. Boole showed us how willing God was to make something out of the feeblest, I put myself right into the hands of God to be used for his glory. All is serenely sweet now."

"I feel the better," said a preacher, "for going down there (to the altar) and making a new consecration. My soul is strengthened out of Zion."

A brother rose to ask for help, having to leave the ground this morning. He stated his exercises of mind in entering into covenant the evening before. His difficulties were explained, and, we trust, he went on his way rejoicing.

"Bro. Barker's religion," he said, "was the simplest and sweetest thing in the universe—it was love, only love—all love." The meeting closed by asking and answering questions, and a final doxology.

8 O'CLOCK SERVICES—MONDAY.

As the people resumed the morning meeting in the Tabernacle, there was first a season of deep, earnest pleading with God.

"I know just what I want, and that is just what I am going to ask, and have," said the minister who led the devotions. "Now each for himself and herself—pray."

It is difficult to attempt a descriptive sketch of scenes like this. The obvious duty of every one present is, instead of gazing about, or trying to measure the amount of influence prevailing, to close the eyes and shut out all considerations but one—

"Come Holy Spirit, heavenly Dove,
With all thy quickening powers;
Come shed abroad a Saviour's love,
And that shall kindle ours."

Amanda Smith had the spirit of prayer, and her faith took hold of "the horns of the altar." With singular adaptation she put herself in the place of the humblest, prayed on and up through all intervening experiences until the petition was lost in "realizing light," and turned to thanks and blessing, and honor, and glory, unto "Him who loved us and washed us in his own blood."

"Now we give those who have just been blessed, the first chance to speak."

A sister—"I am just now receiving the things I desired when I prayed. He is saving me."

A brother—"The power is coming on me. I want all I can hold, for I have ways in which to use it at home."

A sister—"I once lost the power and joy because I gave up working for Jesus. Then an uneasy feeling came over me, and the next step was condemnation. I was quite disconsolate. Hearing of this meeting, hope sprang up that I would regain what I lost, and I have. O how gladly will I speak and work for such a Saviour, if spared to reach my home once more." Her home is Harrisburg.

"I don't feel any inclination to doubt God; but somehow I am slow to believe. My prayer is—'Lord increase my faith.'"

"You needn't pray that way, brother," said the leader; "for he won't do it until you put in exercise what faith you have."

MONDAY MORNING.

SERMON BY REV. EDGAR M. LEVY, D. D., OF PHILADELPHIA.

" *And the very God of Peace sanctify you wholly ; and I pray God your whole spirit, and soul, and body, be preserved blameless unto the coming of our Lord Jesus Christ. Faithful is he that calleth you, who also will do it.*" 1 *Thess.* 5 : 23.

The doctrine of justification by faith alone, without the deeds of the law, is a fundamental article of the Christian faith, and occupies, as it ever should do, a prominent place in our pulpit discourses.   Luther did not use extra vagant language when he said, that the manner in which this doctrine was held would ever be the sign of a standing or a falling Church.

Justification by faith lies truly at the foundation of our Christian life.   It is the beginning of all true fellowship with God, and it secures to us all that God has promised to his children.   It lies also at the root of all real honor to Christ's atoning work, of all real abiding peace of conscience, of all real service of God.

But while we regard justification by faith of vital importance, we must not overlook the equally important doctrine of sanctification by faith.   If justification be the root of this heavenly plant—the life of God in the soul—sanctification is the beautiful blossom and the delicious fruit.   Justification is that sovereign act by which God, for the sake of his worthy Son, declares the sinner who believes, absolved from all sin, and entitled to all the righteousness of Christ.   Sanctification is that act of the blessed Spirit by which the believer is made holy.

It is of great importance to distinguish the difference between sanctification and justification.

" Justification," says that eminent man of God, J. Angel James, " is the work of Christ for us—Sanctification is the work of the Spirit in us."

"Sanctification," says Dr. Scott, " is to have soul, body and spirit, every sense, member, organ and faculty, completely purified and devoted to the service of God."

In a measure and to a certain extent, the Christain is sanctified when he is converted.   He is set apart for God.   He is made a new creature in Christ Jesus.   He has divine life created in his soul by the operation of the Holy Ghost.   The two, justification and sanctification, different in their nature, are yet closely united.   He that is justified has new impulses, new tastes, new desires.   Clothed upon with the righteousness of Christ, he has a beauty he never had before.   He no longer "lives unto himself."   "His life is hid with Christ in God."   He now turns away disgusted from those pleasures, objects, associations, in which he once delighted.   He now finds happiness in those acts of worship, and meditation, and prayer, and praise, which he once loathed. With the great apostle he says : "What things were gain to me, those things I counted loss for Christ." "Yea, doubtless, and I count all things but loss for the knowledge of Christ Jesus my Lord."

But this condition of the believer, "accepted in the Beloved," is most generally accompanied with *incompleteness* of sanctification. This is implied in the text. "And the very God of peace sanctify you *wholly*." In another passage the apostle thus writes : "Having therefore, these promises, dearly beloved, let us cleanse ourselves from all filthiness of the flesh and spirit, perfecting holiness in the fear of the Lord." The apostle admits, you perceive, that they were justified and renewed, for he calls them "dearly beloved," unto whom God had given many precious promises, and yet declares that they had need of cleansing from filthiness of the flesh and spirit, and to be made perfect in holiness.

And this is in harmony with the experience of all Christians in all ages of the Church. At the time of conversion, it is very easy for the soul to imagine that sin is not only forgiven, but is entirely destroyed. The change is so great, even as "from death unto life," that the work of moral renovation seems perfect. But very soon the workings of the old man are experienced, and pride, envy, uncharitableness, unbelief, discontent, impatience, sloth and impurity are daily made manifest, bringing us into bondage again to the law of sin and death, and extorting ever and anon the bitter cry—"Oh wretched man that I am, who shall deliver me from the body of this death ?"

The penitent, convicted of his sins, sought pardon from God. The believer, convicted of his guilt, sighs for inward purity. He wants the roots of sin destroyed, not merely to have its branches lopped off; he longs to have the old man slain, not merely wounded. He prays not to have the disease modified, but entirely eradicated—not to gain an advantage occasionally over Satan, but to have him under his feet at all times. The works of the devil he does not wish to have mended, but utterly destroyed. He yearns for perfect love, that he may "serve God without fear in holiness and righteousness all the days of his life."

Now this is what sanctification accomplishes. To the eye of sense it would indeed seem impossible, that hearts so base, so dead, so polluted, wayward, could be purified and sanctified, and "preserved blameless," moment by moment, unto the coming of our Lord Jesus Christ. But "all things are possible with God," and "all things are possible with him that believeth." The apostles would never have prayed for the accomplishment of an impossible thing; neither does God excite a hope which he is not able and ready to fulfill, or create a hunger in the soul which he cannot more than satisfy. As Faber beautifully expressed it—

> "There's not a craving in the mind,
> Thou dost not meet and still;
> There's not a wish the heart can have
> Which Thou dost not fulfill."

Permit me, men and brethren, to speak to you in all simplicity,—

First, of the Author of sanctification.

Secondly, of the instrumental cause of sanctification.

Thirdly, of the great importance of sanctification.

1. The *Author* or the originating cause of sanctification. " The very God of peace sanctify you wholly." The sanctification of the believer is attributed to all three persons of the adorable Trinity. In Jude we are said to be " sanctified by God the Father." In First Corinthians we are said to be " sanctified in Christ Jesus ;" and in First Peter our sanctification is said to be through the *Holy Spirit.* God, the Father, chooses us, calls us, separates us unto himself. He is the originating cause of sanctification. God, the Son, by his precious blood, cleanseth us from sin, and God, the Holy Ghost, applies the wonderful efficacy of the blood to our moral purification. " O the depths of the riches of the wisdom and of knowledge of God !"

"Suppose," says Spurgeon, " to put it as plainly as we can, there is a garment which needs to be washed. Here is a person to wash it, and there is a bath in which it is to be washed—the person is the Holy Ghost, but the bath is the precious blood of Christ. It is strictly correct to speak of the person cleansing, as being the sanctifier ; it is quite as accurate to speak of that which constitutes the bath, and which makes it clean, as being the sanctifier too. Now, the Spirit of God sanctifies us, he works effectively ; but he sanctifies us through the blood of Christ, through the water which flows with the blood from Christ's smitten side. To repeat my illustration, here is a garment which is black ; a fuller, in order to make it white, uses nitre and soap, both the fuller and the soap are cleansers ; so both the Holy Spirit and the atonement of Christ are sanctifiers." "We delight to magnify," says the same great preacher, "the work of Christ for us, but we must not depreciate the work of the blessed Spirit in us. He finds us lepers, and to make us clean he dips the hyssop of faith in the precious blood of Christ, and sprinkles it upon us, and we are clean. There is a mysterious efficacy in the blood of Christ, not only to make satisfaction for sin, but to work the death of sin. The blood appears before God, and he is well pleased it falls on us—lusts wither, and old corruptions feel the death blow."

This is the way God sanctifies us. It is through the blood that he makes us "partakers of his holiness." It is by this blood that he has created over again his image that was effaced. There is no washing away of iniquity, except in this precious blood. To this fountain God calls the sin-stained soul, that he may wash it " whiter than snow." St. Peter speaks of us as "elect according to the foreknowledge of God the Father, unto sanctification of the Spirit, unto obedience and sprinkling of the blood of Jesus Christ." St. John says : " The blood of Jesus Christ his Son cleanseth us from all sin."

Hence we sing, perhaps more frequently than we do any other strain,—

"My dying Saviour, and my God,
Fountain for guilt and sin,
Sprinkle me ever with thy blood,
And cleanse and keep me clean.

"Wash me, and make me thus thine own,
Wash me, and mine thou art ;
Wash me, but not my feet alone,—
My hands, my head, my heart."

2. We notice the instrumental cause of our sanctification. As in justification, so in sanctification, *faith* is the instrumental cause. In the case of

justification, the Papist contends that faith alone is not sufficient,—that we grow into a state of justification by means of works. But the Protestant says, "Nay, by the deeds of the law can no man be justified." "Being justified by faith, we have peace with God through our Lord Jesus Christ." Good works can only be the fruit of faith. "With the heart man believeth unto righteousness,—*i.e.* unto justification. And here lies the great battle-field on which the true Church of Christ contends with the mighty Babylon. Luther, as we have already quoted, said that justification by faith only was the article of a standing or a falling Church.

Alphonsus Liquori, in his history of the Council of Trent, says that this doctrine was "the trunk whence almost all the errors of the modern heretics sprung." He was right; for if the blood of Christ, applied through faith, cleanses from all sin, then farewell to penances, pilgrimages, purgatory, indulgences, absolutions and masses. This is emphatically true. Just as this doctrine is held and prominently presented will you find real spirituality, real living power. In its absence you will have forms and ceremonies, ignorance, superstition and death.

The same truth applies to *sanctification.* The real difficulty we find in presenting the salvation of God to the inquirer, and which hinders his conversion, is this way of faith. We cannot make him see it is of faith, and of faith only. Hence his groans, his tears, his weary efforts to mend his life, and, in some measure, fit himself for God's acceptance. When at last the way of faith is revealed to him by the Holy Spirit, the work is done, the weary one is at rest, the wretched one has peace with God.

Exactly so is it with sanctification. Works have no more to do with the sanctifying of the soul, than they have with the justifying of the soul. Faith must be the instrumental cause in the one as well as in the other. If it be by faith, then it is no more of works. The provision for our sanctification has been made, and faith must receive it. Faith is the hand by which we grasp the Saviour, making him, with all his wealth and all his righteousness our own; so that in *having him,* we become both righteous and rich. Faith is the tendril by which the branch of the vine clings around their all-supporting stem ; it is the system of *nerves* by which all the parts of the body are consciously connected with the head. It is the great artery—the great *aorta* by which from the *heart* life is conveyed ; so that by its habitual action the very lowest extremities are continually invigorated and warmed. If it be of faith, then it must be instantaneous. Works require time for their execution. Faith, on the contrary, is an act of the soul. In a moment the soul, by the exercise of faith, can " wash and be clean."

3. We were to notice, thirdly, the *importance* of this doctrine of *santification.*

The importance of this work of divine grace will be seen if we consider—

First, that the sanctification of the believer is *the one grand design of our salvation.* I open the Bible and I read: " For whom he did foreknow, he also did predestinate to be *conformed to the image of his Son.*"

" For we are his workmanship, *created in Christ Jesus unto good works,* which God hath before ordained that we should walk in them."

I moreover discover that the purpose, the sovereign and eternal purpose of God, so connects our santification with the death of Christ, as to make the former one great end for which the latter was endured. In Ephesians we read: " Christ also loved the Church and gave himself for it, that he might sanctify and cleanse it with the washing of water by the word." In St. Paul's epistle to Titus we also read : " Who gave himself for us that he might redeem us from all iniquity, and purify unto himself a peculiar people, zealous of good works."

We are further taught that to this sanctification we have been called by divine grace. How beautifully does the apostle set this before us in the commencement of some of his epistles ! He writes to all that are in Rome, " Beloved of God, called to be saints "—or holy ones. And, " Unto the Church of God which is at Corinth, to them that are sanctified in Christ Jesus, called to be saints."

Thus brethren, the word of God teaches, in no unequivocal terms, that God's everlasting love has been fixed on us, and his Son sent to die for us, and his Spirit to call us from our apostate state, not only that we may be delivered from the punishment due to sin, but that sin may be destroyed. " Deliverance from sin," says Knapp in his " Christian Theology," " belongs as really to the redemption of Christ as deliverance from punishment. If Christ had not shown us by what means this deliverance may be secured, his work of redemption would have been incomplete, and his atonement in vain."

2. The importance of sanctification may be seen by a consideration of the *holiness of God.*

God is revealed to us as necessarily holy,—as the source of all holiness wherever it exists. His displeasure toward sin has been manifested in the most expressive and awful manner. We are assured that he is of purer eyes than to behold iniquity with either pleasure or indifference, and that nothing that is unholy shall ever stand before him. Revelation also informs us that when God proposed to save sinners, so directly was sin opposed to his holiness, that, before any hope of salvation could be cherished, or any offer of mercy made to man, his only begotten Son must become the sinner's surety, and, by dying in his stead, endure the penalty of the broken law, satisfy the claims of offended justice, and proclaim the purity of the divine character to every province and subject of the divine dominions.

3. The importance of sanctification is evident from the fact that the word of God sets before us the life of him who " was holy, harmless, undefiled and separate from sinners," as the great pattern of our lives.

Throughout the whole of his history he " did no sin, neither was guile found in his mouth." Whether he had to suffer the contradiction of sinners against himself, or endure the unfaithfulness of his disciples—whether living or dying, the same purity of character, and the same steady obedience to the divine will were always manifest. Dwell, brethren, on the life of your Master as recorded in the Gospels. Go with him to the scenes of mirth, and thence to the abodes of sorrow. Learn how he conducts himself as a son, a brother, a friend, and as a citizen. In every circumstance and station of life watch him, and then " purify yourselves, even as he is pure," for he has set us an example that we should follow in his steps. Upon nothing short of this does the word of God insist. No feature in the character of Jesus must be wanting in the Christian. " Let this mind be in you which was also in Jesus Christ." " If any man have not the spirit of Christ, he is none of his."

4. Sanctification is manifestly important, because *holiness and usefulness* are closely associated. It is not intellect, however brilliant ; it is not genius, how-

ever wonderful; it is not eloquence, however captivating, that will accomplish the most good in our world. Simple goodness, holiness of life, and entire consecration will yield a power for God with which genius and education cannot compete. The men who have cleansed the moral atmosphere of society, who have subdued the opposition of wicked men, who have reclaimed the wandering and saved the lost, were men of holiness. All experience teaches that holiness and success are linked together. There may be exceptions; but this is the rule. Thousands of witnesses may be summoned to show "whom God sanctifies for his work, him he also glorifies with success."

5. We may judge of the great importance of sanctification from the fact that *holiness and prevalency in prayer* are closely united.

Prayer is prevalent with God just in proportion as we are sanctified. It is the "effectual fervent prayer of the *righteous* man that availeth much." "If I regard iniquity in my heart, the Lord will not hear me," cries the heaven-taught Psalmist, and it is the almost universal conclusion that "God heareth not sinners, but if any man be a worshiper of God, and *doeth his will*, him God heareth." "The hearing of prayer is promised to the widest extent, but nevertheless it has its limitation, in the fact that only such prayer is spoken of as proceeds from inmost unison with Christ." (Tholuck.) Hence, our Lord says: "If ye abide in me, and my words abide in you, ye shall ask what ye will, and it shall be done unto you;" and bearing this condition in mind, the beloved disciple writes: "And whatsoever we ask, we receive of him, because we keep his commandments, and do these things that are pleasing in his sight"—(1 John 3: 22.) To have power with God in prayer, talent is not needed; eloquence is not required; forms and ceremonies, times and seasons, are not necessary; but a holy heart is absolutely essential. "Having, therefore, boldness to enter into the holiest by the blood of Jesus, by a new and living way, which he hath consecrated for us through the vail, (that is to say his flesh,) and having a high priest over the house of God, let us draw near with a true heart, in full assurance of faith, having our hearts sprinkled from an evil conscience, and our bodies washed with pure water."

6. The importance of sanctification may be seen from the *happiness* it imparts. God is called "the blessed God." He is happy because he is holy. The angels are everywhere represented as being filled with pleasure, with holy ecstacy and burning zeal. They are happy because they are holy. Holiness must always be a joy-giving principle; and yet thousands of Christians are not happy. Oh, how many are cold, spiritless and lukewarm without knowing anything of that spiritual, holy joy which comes of a close walk with God! How many are daily undergoing a slow process of corrosion, as it were, for the want of a full assurance of faith! They live on—a spiritless, uninfluential life, fretting themselves and fretting others, especially those whom they are most strongly bound to soothe, and cheer, and animate,. There are thousands of homes throughout our land that are clouded with sadness, filled with discontent, alienation, and strife, each one of which might be transformed into a paradise of peace, and love, and beauty, by the introduction of this grace of sanctification.

7. The importance of sanctification may be further argued from the consideration that it is the *only bond of Christian union.*"

A variety of plans have been suggested by great and good men, to bring together and unite the different denominations of evangelical believers: but they have all failed. The reason for these mortifying failures does not grow out of the undesirableness of Christian union, but from the impossibility of creating *uniformity* in the expression of belief in the constitution of the Church, and in the *administration of the ordinances.*

At last we have discovered a basis for Christian unity. The sanctification of believers of every name, create a unity in the great Christian brotherhood, such as no creed has ever been able to accomplish. Here, in this great National Camp-meeting, we have such an exhibition of Christian unity as thrills one's heart to behold. A unity not in ordinances; a unity not in Church government; a unity not in the forms of worship; a unity not in the mere letter of the creed—but in something sweeter, dearer, and more enduring than these: the washing of the blood of Christ and the baptism of the Holy Spirit. As it is the nature of sin to separate, disintegrate and repel, it is nature of holiness to unite, adjust and harmonize. We have found it to be so. Hallelujah!

> " We are one in Christ below,
> In hope and consolation;
> Though garb and colors show
> Shadows of variation."

8. The importance of sanctification is manifest from the fact that holiness is always set before us as an essential qualification to the enjoyment of heaven.

A title to this inheritance, a meetness of personal character, the word of God assures us, is absolutely required ere we can appreciate its excellency, engage in its duties, or enjoy its blessedness. It represents heaven as the " holy city."—the " inheritance undefiled," its inhabitants as clothed with white robes, and as praising God because he is holy; and it positively and in the most unqualified manner asserts that "without holiness no man˙ shall see the Lord." We may fiind admission into heaven as the poor and the despised, the neglected and the persecuted, but we cannot enter heaven without holiness. Our garments must be white and shining, or the gates will not open to receive us.

Thus, men and brethren, the sanctification of the believer is the one grand end of salvation. It entered into the counsels of the Holy Trinity from all eternity. It is intimately connected with the fore-ordination of God. It is the object for which the Christian is called, justified and pardoned. " For what would be our justification," says Mr. James, " what would be the robe of Christ's righteousness to us without the holy nature, but the vestment of scarlet and gold thrown over a body affected with leprosy?" " What is it," asks another, " but the dressing an Ethiopian in white garments and calling him white?" No, this is not God's method. The purpose of God in salvation extends far beyond this. God's creating purpose is gained; his restoring purpose is fulfilled; the redeeming love of Christ is glorified; the sanctifying work of the Holy Spirit is magnified, when his people are made holy. Cato is said to have commenced all his speeches in the Roman Senate with these words : " *Delenda est Carthago*," Carthage must be destroyed. Sin is the Christian's Carthage ; it is ever making war against him, ever impeding his progress, and imperiling his safety. God says "It must be destroyed." I hear it whispered by the sighing winds in Eden's blighted bowers,—" Sin must be destroyed ;" I hear it murmured by the side of Abel's altar,—" Sin must be destroyed ;" I hear it thundered out from the blazing Mount of Sinai,—" Sin must be destroyed ;" I hear it sobbed out from the quivering lips of Calvary's victim,—" Sin must be destroyed ;" I hear an apostle enunciating it,—" Likewise reckon ye also yourselves to be dead indeed unto sin, but alive unto God, through Jesus Christ our Lord." Amen! my soul responds, Amen! Here let sin be slain. Here, in this great congregation, let sin die within my heart. Here, O Lord, I present unto thee myself; my soul and my body, to be a reasonable, holy and living sacrifice unto thee forever.

Brother, "It is the will of God, even your sanctification." It is the aim of the Holy Spirit to do far more for you than merely to save you from hell. He aims to sanctify your soul to such a degree that you shall be lovely in life, gentle in disposition, humble in mind, pure in heart, and filled with all the fruits of holiness; loving holiness, living holiness, breathing holiness, thinking holiness, speaking holiness; and then—when time is no more—to raise your body from the sleep of the tomb, and make it like the glorious body of your Lord and Saviour. Brother do you believe this to be the will of God concerning you? Do you believe to-day that Christ is a Saviour "able to save to the uttermost all that come unto God by him?" Then why not come and trust him? Why be satisfied with any experience that does not secure holiness of heart? If you have not this, come, I beseech you, to the fountain to-day. It was opened for sin and uncleanness. It was opened for you.

THE PRAYER MEETING.

Rev. L. R. Dunn came forward, as the Dr. closed his tender and powerful appeal, saying: "In other days I was intimate with Dr. Levy. We used to labor together, as pastors, in the same city. and when I was seeking the blessing he has preached to us about, and urged on all here this morning, he was watching me.

" We can hardly realize how many are watching our movements. Three worlds are interested in everything we do, or say, or think.

" I believe one great reason why so many find it difficult to obtain sanctification is, because they are not clear in their justification. I am satisfied that a fully justified soul is one that always earnestly desires holiness. Many people experience religion; but they fail to go on to perfection, and consequently are turned aside into the wilderness—a waste, howling desert of " sins, and doubts, and fears." One of the most important things this world needs at present is, that the two-thirds of all our church members, living in an uncertain experience, should be clearly and soundly converted.

Voices—" That's so."

" I was converted at the age of fourteen, and in a very short time I was crying out for heart purity. Satan here interposed, saying ' Look at brother A, and at sister B. They are old members of the Church, and they say nothing about it. Is it not pretentious, and presumptuous in you to begin talking about holiness?' How many are now here before me who are members of the Church

10

and yet are not clear in their justification—have not to-day the witness of adoption ?"

He then proceeded to describe the sad condition of such, and said the first step they should take, ought to be to the altar of prayer, and to the blood, seeking a touch of refining fire. " Fire," shouted Mr. Inskip, ' yes that's it. That is what is wanted here—refining fire. I have been waiting to hear this point touched. There are people all around here, lukewarm, if not dead. Lord send down upon us this holy fire !"

The altar being hastily cleared, many came and knelt in deep contrition. The whole scene in front of the stand became transformed into a praying circle. Each for himself prayed. Bro. Inskip, who now had the meeting in hand, cried out—" Let us all pray together in these words—' Jesus save me now.' " " Come," he continued, " put faith into it, and say—' Jesus, saves me now.' "

The declaration, uttered simultaneously by hundreds, rose into a confident, triumphant shout.

" We have the word of God for it," continued the leader. " Let us repeat it —' The blood of Jesus Christ, his Son, cleanseth me from all sin.' " This was spoken in concert.

" How many of you will now rise up and say it loud enough for all present to hear you ?"

One after another stood up, repeating this passage, as applicable to themselves. Men and women, ministers and members, declared the fact, and God attested his own truth in bestowing great freedom, light and power, while confession was thus made unto salvation.

The noon hour had come and passed ; but all oblivious to dinner, or other duties, the congregation remained together. Some were still kneeling and praying to be made every whit whole, and it seemed to be the settled purpose of their hearts not to leave the spot until they too could " tell to all around," that this mighty work had been wrought within them.

Among those suddenly awakened was a lady who, when pointed to the Lamb of God, believed and was filled with sensations of new found joy. Her companion, a young man, looked on uneasily. He seemed not to comprehend the situation. He was urged to kneel and give his heart to God. Suddenly an apprehension of his condition as a sinner flashed on his mind, and he began to pray. His expressions were out of the prescribed formula ; but God heard him. Before leaving he learned to trust in Jesus, and we hope he is now happy in the life of love.

MONDAY AFTERNOON, 1½ O'CLOCK.

SERMON BY REV. WM. NAST, D.D., EDITOR OF THE *"CHRIS-
TIAN APOLOGIST,"* CINCINNATI, DELIVERED
IN THE GERMAN LANGUAGE.

*As Moses lifted up the serpent in the wilderness, even so must the Son of
man be lifted up : that whosoever believeth in Him should not perish, but
have everlasting life.* JOHN iii., 14, 15

These words form the conclusion of our Lord's memorable conversation with
Nicodemus. This sincere inquirer after truth came to Jesus with the confession, " Rabbi, we know that thou art a teacher come from God, for no man can
do these miracles that thou dost, except God be with him." By saying this
he acknowledged the miraculous works of Jesus and the divine authority of
his teaching, while his colleagues in the Sanhedrim, the rulers in Israel, utterly
rejected his divine mission. Surely, it was no little thing for a man like Nicodemus to confess this ; but much as this confession of the well-instructed and
upright Jewish scribe implied, he was yet very far from understanding what
was necessary to enter into the kingdom of the Messiah, concerning the nature
of which he came to Jesus for instruction. Before he was prepared to receive
more light in this direction, he must learn to understand that *he himself needed*
to enter into that kingdom ; he must know and feel himself to be a lost sinner,
whom Jesus came to save. Jesus, therefore, interrupts him in proposing his
queries, makes no account of the acknowledgment of his divine mission, and
tells him abruptly, " Verily, verily, I say unto thee, except a man be born again,
he cannot see the kingdom of God." To be born again was a phrase which
was not entirely unintelligible to Nicodemus. He knew, that of proselytes to
the Jewish faith it was said, " They were born again ;" a figurative expression
for the radical change that took place with them when they were converted
from their idols to the only true and living God, and were received into covenant relation with the God of Abraham, Isaac and Jacob. If Jesus had spoken
these words to a heathen, Nicodemus would not have been surprised. But that
such a radical change as this figure implied, in order to be able to enter the
kingdom of the Messiah, should be required of *him*, a son of Abraham, a ruler
in Israel, a believer in the Lord and the prophets,—this declaration of Jesus
was entirely unexpected by Nicodemus ; it was shocking to him ; he was irritated, as people get irritated to this day, when they are told they need a radical
change to be saved ; and by his reply : " How can a man be born when he is
old ? Can he enter the second time into his mother's womb and be born ?" he

told the Saviour, that he considered the demand he made of him as unreasona-
ble as to demand of an old man literally to be born again by his mother. We
cannot understand the reply of Nicodemus in any other way. Surely he could
not think that Jesus meant to require a new birth in the natural sense. His
reply was very disrespectful. and in utter contradiction to the confession he had
just made. The Saviour, however does not reprove him, but simply repeats the
demand, adding some explanation: " Verily, verily, I say unto thee, except a
man be born of water and of the Spirit, he cannot enter into the kingdom of
God." By saying to Nicodemus. " A man must be born *of water*," Jesus evidently reminded him of the baptism unto repentance which John the Baptist
required *of all Israel*, in order to be prepared for the kingdom of God, which
was at hand. John the Baptist was sent to awaken the people to a sense of
their guilt and uncleanness, which they were to confess by submitting to his
baptism unto repentance. But Luke tells us that "The Pharisees and lawyers
rejected the counsel of God against themselves, being not baptised of him."
They considered themselves possessed of all needful preparation for the kingdom
of the Messiah. And to those of the Pharisees and Sadducees who came to
John's baptism. perhaps only as spectators, the Baptist said : " Think not to say
within yourselves, we have Abraham for our Father, for I say unto you, that
God is able of these stones to raise up children unto Abraham." Of all this
Jesus reminds Nicodemus by saying, "a man must be born of *water*," and when
he adds " *of the Spirit*," Nicodemus was reminded of the Baptist's testimony :
" I indeed baptize you with water unto repentance, but he that cometh after
me shall baptize you with the Holy Ghost and with fire." He was reminded
of the Old Testament promises which were to be fulfilled in the time of the
Messiah : "I will put my Spirit within you and cause you to walk in my statutes,
and ye shall keep my judgments and do them." The *mysteriousness* and *free-
ness* of this spiritual change Jesus compares to the blowing of the wind, and
its necessity he demonstrates by saying, "That which is born of the flesh, is
flesh, and that which is born of the Spirit, is spirit. Marvel not that I said
unto thee (even unto thee, Nicodemus,) ye must be born again."

And what does Nicodemus answer *now ?* He says, " How can these things
be ?" Does he mean to reiterate his doubts of the necessity or possibility of being born again? We cannot understand him so. Jesus had not spoken in vain
to Nicodemus The knowing Jewish Rabbi has become an humble disciple,
inquiring after the way by which this new birth is to come to pass. After having convinced him of the necessity of the new birth. and awakened in his heart
a desire for its experience, the Lord first reproves him justly, that he, a master
in Israel, should not know that the new birth, spiritual religion, the righteousness before God, can be attained in no other way than by faith in the promised
Messiah ; expressing also surprise, why in coming to him as a teacher come
from God, Nicodemus did not recognize him, of whom Moses and the Prophets
had testified, and to whom John the Baptist pointed so unequivocally as the
Son of God, the promised Messiah, the Lamb of God that taketh away the sin
of the world; and then he closed his instructions by telling him that the Messiah came not to sit on David's throne as a temporal king, but that the Son of
man must be lifted up, even as Moses lifted up the serpent in the wilderness,
that whosoever believeth in him should not perish, but have eternal life; even
as every Israelite that was bitten by the fiery serpent, when he looked upon the
serpent of brass lifted upon a pole, did not die.

May the Holy Spirit show us what the Saviour wants to teach us, by comparing his being lifted up on the cross, and our believing in him, with the lifting up of the serpent of brass, and the Israelites being commanded to look upon it and be saved! Let us look at the principal points of analogy in this typical representation.

1. There is a striking analogy between the degenerate condition of the bitten Israelites and our condition as sinners.

Deadly and inexpressibly painful was the bite of those fiery-serpents, so called either from their appearance or from the effects of their bite. What a picture of that wider and more terrible desolation caused by the bite of that great serpent, the devil, who has infused his poison through the whole nature of every man, producing sin, sorrow, pain and death! How much more intolerable is the agony of the soul under a consciousness of the displeasure of God than the most excruciating pain of the body! And what is the death of the body compared to the eternal death of the soul to God,—the eternal woe of the soul succeeding the death of the body! Moreover, the plague of the Israelites, general as it was, yet does not seem to have been a universal one; it is not stated that all the Israelites, without exception, were bitten. But that which afflicts us as sinners, is universal. Death has passed upon all men, for that all have sinned. They are all gone out of the way; they are together become unprofitable; there is none that doeth good,—no, not one. In every man "the whole head is sick, and the whole heart is faint," and all men in every age and nation are by nature the children of the wicked one, exposed to eternal perdition.

2. The bitten Israelites could not be saved in any other way but by the remedy which it pleased God in his wisdom to devise.

If the Israelites had refused to make use of the remedy provided, they had to perish; there was no help for them. In like manner sinners cannot be saved in any other way than by Him whom God hath set forth to be a propitiation through faith in his blood. There is no other name under heaven given among men by which we must be saved. As God would not save the Israelites in any other way than by the remedy provided by him, so there is no salvation possible to sinful man in any other way but by believing that Jesus died for sinners. As Moses lifted up the serpent in the wilderness, even so must the Son of man be lifted up. Whenever Jesus speaks of his suffering and death, he uses the word "must," representing his death on the cross as the inexorable condition of the sinner's salvation. To redeem us from the curse of the law, he must be made a curse for us. Though Christ saves us as Prophet, Priest and King: though he is made unto us of God, wisdom, righteousness, sanctification and redemption; yet all these saving acts and offices of Christ are based upon his having been lifted up; and that his being lifted up means nothing else than his vicarious death on the cross, the beloved disciple assures us expressly by saying that when Jesus said: " I, if I be lifted up from the earth, will draw all men unto me," he signified what death he should die.

3. There is an analogy with regard to the use of the remedy which God chose for the bitten Israelites and the poor sinner.

What did God mean by this strange, mysterious object-teaching in the wilderness? When Moses prayed for the people, the Lord commanded him " to make a fiery serpent and set it upon a pole; and it shall come to pass that every one that is bitten, when he looketh upon it, shall live." It was evidently a test of faith for the Israelites. When they looked upon this lifted-up serpent of brass, the harmless image of the fiery serpents from whose bites they were suffering, they should look upon it as a pledge that Jehovah had secured their full recovery from the deadly bite; that his anger was turned away, and that he would heal every one who, looking upon the sign he gave, trusted in the promised salvation.

But this was a very strange way of saving the Israelites. It required strong faith to expect recovery from the use of such a remedy. No doubt many objections against it were suggested to the Israelites, though we read of none foolish enough to yield to them. "Of what use can it be to look upon this image? Is it not contrary to God's bidding, to make any image, and to expect help from the use of images? And why should we look upon the image of the serpent, the emblem of sin and Satan?" Moses himself might have hesitated. It was almost as severe as a test of faith, as the demand made of Abraham to sacrifice his own son. But as Abraham, so was Moses and his people assured that God had spoken. There was no other help offered by Jehovah. And does this way of saving the bitten Israelites not bear a strong resemblance to the way God proposes to save the perishing sinner? He who knew no sin, but came in the likeness of sinful flesh, who was made sin for us, that we might be made the righteousness of God in him; who was made a curse for us that we might be redeemed from the curse of the law; he is lifted up on the cross as a pledge that the debt is paid, that Satan is trodden under foot by the seed of the woman, that the blood of Jesus cleanses from all sin, extracts all the poison; that salvation from sin, from its guilt, its power, its pollution, salvation to the uttermost, is secured for all that will trust in the divine promise.

Though there is a difference in the type and antitype with regard *to that which constitutes the remedy*—the remedy in the type appearing in the likeness of that which produced the malady, while in the antitype, in Christ, the remedy appears in the likeness of him that is to be healed—which difference arises from this, that the poison of the serpent could in no other way be extracted from human nature but *by Christ assuming that nature*; yet a striking analogy between the type and the antitype, even with regard to the form in which the remedy is represented, lies in this, that as it pleased God to save the Israelites by looking upon an object which appeared to them utterly inadequate and offensive, so it has pleased God to save sinners by a method which is to the Jews a stumbling-block and to the Greeks foolishness!

4 In conclusion let us look at the striking analogy of the type and antitype with regard to the suddenness and perfection of cure which they obtained who made use of the remedy offered to them.

"It came to pass," we read in the account of the wonderful transaction in the wilderness, "that if a serpent had bitten any man, when he beheld the serpent of brass, he lived." They were healed and lived in all stages of the fiery disease, some just bitten, some writhing in torture, some fast sinking into death, little children, strong men, delicate women. They are all in consternation and torment, but they look; perhaps they can but lift the half-closed eye; but they catch the sight of the brazen serpent, and one glance avails—they live! In an instant they are saved at the very portal of death.

Just so it is with the great salvation which Jesus has wrought out and offers to every sinner. What the looking on the brazen serpent was to the bitten Israelites, faith in Christ is to the sinner. The salvation which Christ offers to us, whether it be from the guilt of sin or from its power and pollution, whether partial or full and entire, is to be obtained in no other way but by believing that as God was in Christ, reconciling the world unto himself, there is nothing that hinders him to save us now either from the guilt or the power of our sins, provided we are willing to depart from all sin to the extent of the light that God has given us, and to consecrate all we are and have to his service.

An appropriating, saving faith in Christ is sometimes called coming to him, at other times receiving him, or accepting the invitation to the great supper, or eating his flesh and drinking his blood. Here it is represented under the figure of simply looking on him, perfectly helpless, casting away all confidence in help from any other source, sinking into both his arms as our only, our last refuge.

It was just at that moment, when we utterly despaired of all we could do, when nothing more was left to us but simply to look upon him who died for us, looking upon him like the penitent thief on the cross; it was in that moment, that we heard his pardoning voice, that we passed from death unto life; that we were justified freely by his grace. And just in the same way as Jesus saved you from the guilt of sin, when you looked upon him as your righteousness, so he is ready to save you from the indwelling of sin, from the last and least remains of the carnal mind, when you look upon him as your sanctification, when you believe his promise to cleanse you from all unrighteousness and impurity.

From the beginning to the end we are saved simply and only by looking unto Jesus, the author and finisher of our faith. "Look unto me and be ye saved, all ye ends of the earth!" Are you yet an unpardoned sinner? Look unto Jesus, who is exalted a Prince and Saviour, to give repentance and remission of sins! Penitent sinner, stop looking upon your sins! Look upon him that died for you, the just for the unjust. What would it have helped the bitten Israelites to look upon the terrible wounds received from the fiery serpents? Justified believer, look upon him who shed his precious blood to redeem you from all iniquity, to wash you from all impurity. Do not rest short of full salvation. You must have it in order to see him in heaven ; for without holiness no man can see the Lord. None but the pure in heart shall see God. You need this heart-purity now. You can have it now, if you seek it by faith. Look away from self; look simply and only unto Jesus ; expect this, as you did justification, by faith. Sanctified believer, look unto Jesus from moment to moment, to be kept clean, and to be changed from glory to glory into his full image. As soon as you look away from Jesus, you sink, like Peter on the water.

Glory be to Jesus! As he has come to save all men, so he is able to save to the uttermost, fully, through and through, and forever; or, as Luther translates it, always, under all circumstances, and at all times, all that come unto God by him. Yea, "Unto him who is able to do exceeding, abundantly above all that we ask or think, according to the power that worketh in us, unto him be glory in the church, by Christ Jesus, throughout all ages, world without end. Amen."

THE WORK ADVANCING.

While Dr. Nast was addressing the Germans in their own rich and unctuous vernacular, and Mrs. Inskip was busy with her children's meeting, and the members of the National Association were secluded in prayer and counsel, a mighty influence prevailed at the Landisville meeting tent. The exercises had been opened with prayer by Rev. S. W. Brown, and immediate answers were realized.

Brother Thompson observed—"We get our richest blessings in the humblest frame of mind. Let us take the lowest place to-day."

Sister Amanda Smith then led in one of those simple prayers that carries the soul right to the mercy-seat.

Brother Brown, in reference to his experience, said: "I used to live such a wavering life—sometimes with Mary at the Saviour's feet, sometimes with Peter afar off; but, thank God, I found a better way. The thought occurred to me: Why should I carry a burden when Jesus is able to carry it for me, and wants to do it? Two tipsy men were rowing a boat, but it would not move; so they fell asleep, and in the morning they found out that they had never pulled up the anchor. So it is with many. They want the blessing of holiness, but they have not pulled up the anchor. God had to put me to a great many *tests*, to see if I would do so. Thank God, I did!"

Sister Smith said: "We often come up against something when we are consecrating, and we can't get any farther until we give it up. People ask me to pray for their children, when they are not saved themselves. I was praying for a family in New York, and I could not pray in faith. I seemed to pray up against something; my faith could not take hold. I was invited to call one morning, and was shown into the parlor. Then I found that they had a party the night before; and there were the billiard tables. I said at once, 'Now I know what I was praying against.' We must lay aside these things, and become very peculiar for God.

"I was praying for a young lady, and I asked, 'Do you believe God hears your prayers?'

"'Yes.'

"'Does he answer?'

"'Well, I don't expect he will just now.'

"How many there are of this kind! We must wait in hope, as they did before the Pentecost.

"I feel quite a burden for some one that is unconverted. Are there any here who desire us to pray for them?" A number rose up. A brother said, "I am going to leave, and I want you to pray for me. I came here for a blessing. I am tired of this kind of life. I want to be fully the Lord's."

Then followed a precious season of silent prayer, and in the midst of it a sister sang, sweetly and softly,

> "My all is on the altar;
> I'm waiting for the fire;
> Waiting, waiting, waiting,
> Waiting for the fire."

The fire came. Many hearts were melted. The tears flowed; shouts arose, and the "Spirit of burning" was sensibly felt on every soul.

SERMON BY REV. J. E. SEARLES.

MONDAY, 3 P. M.

" I am crucified with Christ," &c.—Gal. 2: 20.

After some preliminary remarks respecting the origin of the passage read, the speaker proceeded to say: This text is of peculiar interest, because it sets forth St. Paul's experience of the higher Christian life, embracing what we denominate entire sanctification—comprehended in the idea and fact of the death of self, and a new divine life through faith in Christ.

To make this subject plain, I propose to show first, what this experience is not.

1. It is nothing that can be originated or produced by the observance of religious ordinances, or any Church services whatever. All who may be depending on these things for religious experience will be sadly disappointed. These ordinances and services are only guide boards leading on to the realization of the experimental in religion, but can never produce it.

In this connection I would also say, that there is nothing in religious duties to nourish or perpetuate this higher-life experience. Duty may be, and is in many cases, a mere performance. At best, Christian duties are only channels through which God conveys grace and blessings to the soul. Christian duty has no real significance apart from the fact that religion is a reality. Many blunder here. Instead of looking to the Holy Spirit for his blessing, they depend on doing duty, and backslide in heart.

2. The great act of consecration is not this experience.

Entire consecration of all to God is indeed a great work. It is easy to say the word; but to really make it, embracing not only all we have, but our entire being for all time, whatever may transpire, is an act requiring the whole strength and effort of the soul, and the intensest sincerity. But such consecration in its best sense, is only our own act, and falls infinitely short of the experience contemplated in the text.

3 This higher experience is not merely being cleansed from sin. It includes this. Being cleansed from all sin is indeed a great experience. My soul shall never forget the day when this blessed experience became my own. But being cleansed from sin is only the negative part; it is only the removal of the rubbish, the defilement of the soul—something we have no business with, it is our shame and ruin.

St. Paul's standard of experience is infinitely higher—hear him: "I am crucified with Christ, nevertheless I live; yet not I, but Christ liveth in me."

This higher-life experience of the apostle produces a complete revolution in our whole being. Pardon, consecration, and cleansing, therefore, only prepare the human temple for the incoming Christ-life.

This higher life experience is not the doing of religious duties. It is not the consecration of all to God. It is not merely freedom from sin ; but it is the death of self, the carnal mind, and the reception of Christ into the soul, who is the true God and eternal life. Thus the life we lost in Adam, comes back to us *in* and *with* Christ.

Some persons, not a few, hold that salvation is a completed work in regen-. eration, and that sanctification is the subsequent growth or development of that work into pure Christ-like spirit and practice. Here I blundered, and tried to struggle up to the higher attainments for long years never to be forgotten, with the sad experience of finding myself less advanced than when I commenced ; but often reproaching myself for many sad failures. But I was honest in my views, for it seemed to me to be a reproach to Christ to say there remained any sin in the heart of a person whom he had saved. And yet I was not satisfied with myself, finding a tendency, a leaning in my nature to sin. But I embraced the theory that this evil was in my animal, or human nature, and I must make the best of it ; for that nature was not a subject of grace, but must be kept under ; and at last death would bring deliverance. And, with a good deal of triumph, I would ask professors of sanctification : How can Christ and sin dwell in the same heart ? If a justified soul is not saved from all sin, how can that soul go to heaven ? But God has enabled me to see these things in a clear light since. For the help of any who may have these troubles of mind, let me explain : Christ does not dwell in a heart where sin is allowed ; but he does dwell in every believing heart where sin is resisted.

But how can an unsanctified believer go to heaven? There never was such a one who went to heaven.

Observe : All justified persons are in the same moral relation to God as a little child. But we have the fullest evidence of depravity in the little child. Jesus, however, says, " Of such is the kingdom of heaven." Now if the little child die, not having actually sinned, the Redeemer takes the responsibility of purifying and bringing him to heaven. So with the convert dying before he has the opportunity to seek sanctification ; Christ will also sanctify him unconditionally and take him to heaven.

So also if a believer really maintain his justification, that relation to God secures to him the promise of the full salvation of his soul. " He which hath begun a good work in you will perform it until the day of Jesus Christ." It is God's plan that the justified should go on immediately to the higher-life experience. It is doubtless exceedingly difficult for any to long keep their justification unless they are seeking to advance in the divine life ; and to keep in the sanctified state there must also be a growth in that grace.

These facts account for the low state of piety and the frequent backslidings in the Church. Converts are left to get on as best they can in their merely justified state. They are not taught their privilege and duty to be fully saved. It is not at all marvelous that with the remains of the carnal mind in their hearts, and the sad example of the mass of old professors before them, that they should fall away and lose their religion.

Here then we see the need of a second work, and deeper experience of salvation. There is in human nature an inborn will, a tendency to sin This is the occasion of most of our trouble and hindrance in the divine life. It stirs in the heart sometimes in the rising of anger, or pride, or envy, or self-will or love of the world, or unbelief. We may not allow these things; we fight them down; we are often ashamed of them. But the existence of this evil nature not being the result of our transgression, but being born in us, consequently it does not affect our justified state. But being an inborn evil, it cannot be pardoned like actual sin; and being also inbred sin, attaching to our moral nature, it cannot be lived out, or extirpated by any act of our own; but puts us in peril while it remains in us, ready to spring up at any moment when we cease to watch it. This inward evil can be removed only by crucifixion—separating it from us by the power of the Holy Spirit applying the blood of Christ.

Two deaths are necessary to entire sanctification—the death of Christ *for* sin and our death *to* sin. Our death to sin is after the manner of Christ's death *for* sin; it is imperative and voluntary—*i.e.* the law demands it; and we also choose it, and say, " Not as I will, but as thou wilt." This death of self is absolutely necessary to the incoming of the Christ-life. While there remains evil in our heart, the fullness of the Christ-life cannot come in; but when the heart is cleansed, emptied, self and inbred sin removed, then there is room for Christ to reign entire. Then it is, and not till then, the other— the positive part of this great experience is effected, and we are enabled to say, I am not only " crucified with Christ," my old self is no more—is dead; " nevertheless I live, yet not I, but Christ liveth in me." What is the result? Then we have the meekness of Christ; no more flashing out of anger. We have the patience of Christ; no more fretfulness or sourness. We have the submission of Christ; no more self-will. We have the humility of Christ; no more pride and vanity. We have the love of Christ; no more envy or hatred. There is no more desire for the world's vain pleasures. How can there be if Jesus fills the heart?

When Christ lives in us, then there is no more trying to love God; but love springs—wells up spontaneously. This is a style of religion that goes without trying. This Christ-life is a sovereign power in the soul, impelling it onward in the King's highway, shining more and more. You may be tempted from without to be angry, to be proud, to indulge your appetites; but there will be no inward struggle. The inward presence of Christ is the victory.

But the great question is, How may this great experience be obtained? This is the plainest part of the subject.

St. Paul says: " The life I now live (*i.e.* this higher life), I live by the faith of the Son of God, who loved me, and gave himself for me." It is by simple faith founded on the atonement, and personal love of Jesus, "who loved me and gave himself for me." Mark: Faith that seems so difficult is easy when all the hindrances are removed.

But the crucifixion of self must precede faith. No heart can believe into which Christ cannot come. This is the struggle—*not* faith. But this great *I* must go down! Self must be killed. Can't get rid of it in any other way. " I am crucified" (Paul says)—not bound, not wounded, *but killed*— crucified to the world and sin. Unbelief is the last relic of an evil heart that is given up. But when all is given up, then comes the resurrection— then the fullness of the Christ-life comes in and fills the soul. This resurrection is in the likeness of Christ. Then perfect love rises to the throne of the soul, and rules with the sceptre of God. Now the soul moves from a power within—not from outward motives.

Christ, therefore, dwelling in our hearts here, is the true higher-life. This is the great salvation—this is the highest experience of a human soul, until we behold the Lamb in his glory, and sit down with him at the marriage feast.

This great experience is the privilege and duty of all the followers of Jesus, fitting them for usefulness and heaven.

The question, "Who is now willing to die—die utterly to self and sin, that he may realize this new life in Christ?"—was pressed home at the close of the sermon. To many, this "one thing needful" became the great object of desire; others, alas! feared the grave of earthly hope, and shrank from the duty and privilege so plainly presented. With them the moment passed, and the opportunity was lost forever.

The Preachers' Meeting, at 6 P. M., was attended with special tokens of the presence of Jesus.

MONDAY EVENING, 7½ o'clock.

SERMON BY REV. I. SIMMONS, OF BROOKLYN, N. Y.

" *But if we walk in the light, as he is in the light, we have fellowship one with another, and the blood of Jesus Christ, His Son, cleanseth us from all sin.*"—I John i., 7.

Before entering upon the discussion before us, I call you to notice a few facts concerning it. You observe that herein is stated a positive declaration of a moral condition. It is not a promise, though the Scriptures abound in promises relating to the state here expressed. But in this text God makes a distinct statement of a fact, and it comes to us with all the force of the Omnipotent word. It is also a declaration in which the three persons of the adorable Trinity are involved. We are to walk in the light, to have fellowship with God, and be cleansed by the blood of his Son. Oh, what a salvation is ours that results from the active co-operation of the entire Godhead!

And then, again, this is a declaration made concerning men. Whatever great and glorious communication God makes to the beings of other spheres, or to the saints and seraphs in heaven, we do not know ; but this we know, that if we walk in the light with him, the blood of his Son does now, while we thus walk, cleanse us from all sin. But you will observe the declaration is not simply to man as such, but to man in the possession of grace, and in the experience of some measure of fellowship and acquaintance with God. Glance at the context, and this point will appear plain. "This, then, is the message which we have heard of him, and declare unto you, that God is light, and in him there is no darkness at all. If we say we have fellowship with him, and walk in darkness, we lie, and do not the truth. But if we walk in the light as he is in the light, we have fellowship one with another, and the blood of Jesus Christ, his Son, cleanseth us from all sin." Now this must be addressed to all believers, for only they claim to have fellowship with God. Sinners make no such claim. The carnal mind is at enmity with God, and has no companionship with him in the sense of this passage.

Again, this is a declaration of a progressively present moral condition. I insist with all emphasis that the power of this text is not that it is historical or prophetic, but that it is a constantly present work. The blood *cleanses;* not *has*, or *will*, but *does!* It does so each moment, so that the trusting soul has but to fix its gaze upon a present cross, a present sacrifice, and be each moment cleansed. This is God's way. He takes it to us as a determined law—a law as positive as any law of cause and effect. If we walk in the light, follow the Spirit, through the word, the cleansing *must* follow. But some effects follow their causes at long intervals. The effect of seed-sowing, under proper conditions, is harvesting : but four months must elapse. Not so with this law. The effect and the cause interblend. There are operations in nature that illustrate this. The barometer immediately acts with the changes of the atmosphere. So, while we walk in the light, immediately and in closest conjunction with the fulfilled conditions of the law of holiness, the blood cleanses.

And now I call you to notice a few specific features of this moral condition : " The blood of Jesus Christ, his Son, cleanseth us from all sin." And the first point that attracts us is its comprehensiveness. " All sin!" There is one passage in the Scripture more frequently misquoted than otherwise. It is John's announcement of the Lamb's mission among men. He said, as he pointed to the Saviour, just baptized into his earthly ministry, " Behold the Lamb of God, which taketh away the sin of the world." We misquote, and say " sins." The fact is true, but we weaken the idea in this rendering. He does take away " sins ;" he covers them with his blood, and they are never remembered against us ; but " sins " are the fruit of sin, and the removal of sin as a principle, a radical and dreadful soul-disease, is the fundamental will of the atonement. The blood cleanses not merely from sins committed, but it goes down also to the foundations of corrupt, sinful nature, and takes away the sin of the heart, and thus the sin of the world. *All* sin ? Yes, *all* sin. Glory to the Lamb forever !

There are some mighty words in Scripture. In nature, we find the great Creator stooping, with infinite tenderness, to construct and protect the delicate lily, and we behold his tremendous energies illustrated in the vast forms of river, and cataract, and storm. So there are sweet and delicate sentiments here in this Bible, that breathe the heavenly tenderness of the heart that spoke them ; and there are also mighty words that come sweeping along with all the fullness and grandeur of the Divine Omnipotence. They are the Amazons and Mississippis of grace. Such words are these: " Whosoever," " Whatsoever" and this mighty word " *All*" in the connection here found. It proclaims God's intent. *All sin* is to be cleansed away. It may have had forty years the start of Jesus in your soul. It may have intrenched itself behind strong fortifications, and wrought itself into the most degrading and controlling appetites, until your eye is full of lust, and your thoughts full of

evil; until your imagination is utterly covered with corrupt pictures, and
your affections are trailing along the track of the lowest objects; until your
whole spirit, soul and body are subjected to the foulest depravity—the blood
can cleanse it all away. It can enter the imagination and paint there the
pictures of heaven. It can enter the mind and subject every thought to
God. It can purify the body and purge the affections. It can seize the
fiery steeds of appetite and passion, and curb them into the sweetness of
heaven. *All* sin is under the control of the blood. To remove it, all and
forever, the mighty victim died!

This is the pivotal idea of the gospel. To this every experience of grace
points. This was the sum of the war-challenge made by God to Satan amid
the devastations of Eden To this end the battle wages. Every victory is a
prophecy—and only a prophecy—of this the crowning victory, that *all* sin is
cleansed away. A conquering army may pursue the foe from one point to
another, raising its triumphant banners at each stage of its progress, but if
at last the war settles into a siege, the shout of final conquest delays. A
besieging army is defeated as long as it remains necessitated to that condition.
It is not until it has planted its banners over the last citadel to be surrendered that it can raise the full shout of complete victory. Oh, beloved, as
long as Christ is held as a besieging army in relation to any unsaved part or
faculty of our being, we cannot raise the shout of complete triumph! We
have had victories, many and glorious, but at the unsurrendered point there
is the silence of defeat. Let the blood come to that point. Let Christ in;
let him in now, and you will have the gospel shout ringing through every
fibre of your being; a present shout, echoing every moment, increased by
every new faculty and possession as it comes into consciousness and is put
under the fountain. "The blood of Jesus Christ, his Son, cleanseth us
(me) from all sin." Oh, hallelujah to God for the power that bestows on us
the privilege of proclaiming such a victory!

2. I ask you to notice now the peculiar physical term employed to denote
this moral condition. The blood *cleanseth!* It makes clean by washing.
Washing always means purification. It would be absurd to think of washing
if cleanliness was not the intent. And, in washing, the removal of *all*
impurities is the purpose, according to the capacity of the agencies used in
the process. If there is failure, it must be in these, for all the declarations,
the commands, the promises, the symbols and the experiences of the gospel
announce purity of heart as our privilege and duty now, while in the flesh.
And, all glory be to Jesus forever, multitudes of witnesses *do* testify to the
possibility of this state by a clear and conscious enjoyment of the experience.

But perhaps you point me to some who claim this cleansing, and have
certain weaknesses and infirmities. Well, what this blood proposes to do is
to cleanse, to purify; and there may be infirmities growing from ignorance, a
lack of judgment, or other similar sources perfectly compatible with such
purity. When a garment is washed it is thoroughly clean, but the holes in
it are to be repaired by other appliances than water. So it may be true that
some defects exist where the Divine cleansing has been wrought. But I
affirm it here as my positive conviction that a pure heart will wonderfully
correct other powers that need other repairs beside cleansing. This salvation
is for the character. God does not propose to make a man an astronomer or

a scholar of secular knowledge by washing him from sin, neither does he promise in this cleansing to substitute it for all other modes of culture and effort in attaining proper results. It is *cleansing*—a purifying of the entire being—a washing of spirit, soul and body.

But this cleansing implies strength as well as purity. To no small degree is every faculty of the nature empowered by the removal of all sin. A pure imagination is a vigorous one. Images of the beautiful, and pictures by the divine limner are all over its walls. The intellect may not have been trained in the scholastic halls, but its thoughts, springing from the pure inspirations of God, are strong and healthy. The affections, no longer weakened by twining around forbidden or doubtful objects, are raised to an intensity of strength hitherto undreamed of. In fact, every power is renewed with a vigorous vitality. The proper passions and appetites are gloriously intensi- fied in their several directions of exercise. Every love is deepened and strengthened. You loved deeply and truly as you plighted your vows at the marriage altar, but I assure you the cleansing blood of Christ will make that love deeper and richer than ever it was before. If it does not, your experi- ence will not be like mine. Oh, how we love, when we love with a cleansed heart!

3. I want you to observe, in the next place, the remarkable instrument- ality by which this moral cleansing is effected. The *blood* of Jesus Christ! Wonderful arrangement, this! Sinners saved, sinners purified by blood, and that the blood of the Son of God! This is a mystery too deep for solution. I cannot measure the mighty meaning of this symbol. I can see how water can be the symbol of purity. I can understand how the clear, sparkling water can wash and cleanse, and thus be used as a symbol of spiritual clean- liness. And so I come to catch the spirit of the promise made through the prophet of old: "I will sprinkle clean water upon you, and you shall be clean. From all your filthiness and from all your idols I will cleanse you."

And I can see the symbolic use of the element of fire, through the Old and the New Testament. Fire is a purifier. It will hold the native metal in its fiery grasp, until the sordid and base therein is burned out, and the refiner can see his face reflected in the purified material. I can somehow appreciate that when the pure God would descend to this sin-defiled earth, the symbol of his presence should be fire. When he would guide, it should be with a pillar of fire; when he would vindicate his pure authority, and leave himself a testimony in the midst of idolatry, he came in showers of fire; when he would purify his chosen ones, he permitted them to be thrown into the burning furnace, and then walked sweetly therein with them, that they should not be harmed. Flames of fire, pillars of fire, tongues of fire! Great symbol of purity, we see it in every dispensation; but here is a symbol with a deeper significance. It appears early in human history. It is by blood we come to God and are made pure. Abel was accepted because his sacrifice could bleed. The angel saw the sprinkled blood as he went on his errand of death among the dwellings of Egypt. He wondered as he oked, and he wondered again when he saw the mighty Victim on the cross, sprinkling the throne of grace with precious blood for sinners shed. Oh, what heaps of sacrifices along the ages! Blood, blood, everywhere! The new Tes- tament opens, the new dispensation comes, and still the blood appears. But now the symbolic idea has gone. And the atonement uncovers its mighty mysteries: "If the blood of bulls, and of goats, and the ashes of an heifer sprinkling the unclean, sanctifieth to the purifying of the flesh, *how much more* shall the blood of the Son of God, who, through the Eternal Spirit, offered himself without spot to God, purge your consciences from dead works to serve the living God!" Oh yes, it is by blood you are to be purified! Oh, my soul, what does it mean! I go to the Mount of Calvary, and I kneel amid the bones of crucified criminals, by the death-bed of God's only Son, and I ask, what is all this for? and he answers, "All for thee; for thy pardon, for thy purity!" Yes but my sins are as scarlet! "Yet I will make them white as snow." But they are red like crimson! "Yet I will make them as wool." Oh, let all my powers give him glory! His blood does fully save. It cleanses even from all sin. It is by blood then. The cross at the beginning, the cross in the progress, and the cross at the end. We shall never get beyond the blood. A voice from the other side of the grave attests this. I look beyond the river: I see those golden gates, not left ajar, as the poet sings, but lifted high, and as I am looking far up the shining sea, I see the countless host of pure ones bowing before the exalted Lamb. I hear the burden of their song: "Unto him that loveth us and washeth us from our sins in his own blood .. unto him be glory and dominion forever!" And to this our hearts respond. We are washed, we are cleansed by blood. All glory to the Lamb; the saints in heaven, and the saints on earth have this one song: "The blood of Jesus Christ cleanseth us from all sin."

II. With this cleansing is an associated moral state, most precious and blessed. It is soul-fellowship with God. In this practical and material age the tendency is to hurried devotion. No objection is taken to family prayer, and a daily chapter in the Bible and a weekly religious meeting, with a few other ordinary observances, but we are advised to be careful of protracted communion before God less we become mystical and unpractical. Now I have a strong confidence that great religious power comes through a proper observance of any spiritual means, there is power in brief ejaculatory petitions and praises lifted up on the street, in the office, and in the home; but if you want close and intimate fellowship with God, you must tarry with him. And as the blood cleanses you, you will do it. You will long to do it. Oh, the giant saints of the earth have waited in the heavenly presence until they have caught the heavenly glory and power. And we must do it if we would know the fullest joys of soul companionship with God.

Such fellowship as this is the ground of spiritual conformity with God. We take on his glorious nature as the weaker is lifted into and becomes absorbed into the stronger. We become partakers of his choice bestowments; yea, it is in this close fellowship of a cleansed heart with God that we come really to see him. The pure in heart see God. They think like him, they act like him, they feel like him, in the measure that his Holy Spirit can occupy and work out through their human faculties.

Again, this fellowship is the foundation of spiritual beauty. Oh, the beauty of holiness! Oh, the beauty of a soul that is cleansed, and whose intercourse with the Father through the Eternal Spirit is expressed by the words, "Fellowship with God." And the soul's precious fellowship with God makes a beautiful transformation of every part of us. I have seen the most homely faces radiant with beauty as the blood-washed soul within has leaned in trustful communion upon the bosom of its God.

And herein is spiritual strength also. The power that accompanies us and measures our need in every place, comes from keeping our cleansed soul in constant communion with God through the Spirit. Oh, how small our earthly and satanic antagonists seem when we have come from a waiting upon God! Oh, let us *wait* upon him that he may renew our strength!

III. But, beloved, notice the conditions of this cleansing and communion. "If we walk in the light," we must follow the Spirit. The Spirit is light. *Walk* in it, and it will lead to and apply the blood. But observe the light is always through the word. "Ye are clean through the word," says Christ. And again, "Sanctify them through Thy truth; Thy word is truth." If you follow the Spirit as it illuminates the word, and follow it with all self-dependences removed, you will come right to the cleansing fountain.

As you are frequently told by those who have experience of this precious grace of a cleansed heart, the Holy Spirit will lead you to receive heart-purity through simple faith in the promise of God. And, oh, it is the joy of my heart to-night to add my testimony to others, confirming thus their experience and the word of God! I had lived a life of justification for several years, having many previous experiences of the love and favor of God. But my soul often longed and hungered for heart-purity. A few years ago I attended a camp-meeting in Connecticut, and resolved by God's help, I would enter into the desired rest. I retired to the woods, knelt upon a flat rock, and, writing out a covenant on the fly-leaf of my Testament, I commenced to pray; and I prayed until it seemed as if my soul became as dry and barren as a desert. I felt worse than I did before I began, but I resolved to pray on; for to live longer without the blessing I could not. At last the word came, "you have asked, now believe." I said, "I will, I do believe. The vow is made and God accepts the offering, and the blood does now cleanse me from all sin." I arose and returned to the encampment. A strange barrenness possessed me, but a quiet, subdued softness of soul was beneath it. Five hours passed, and still I said, "'Tis done; the blood does save;" when as I was singing the couplet:

> "And there *do* I, though vile as he,
> Wash all my sins away,"

the baptism came—the witness was given. Hallelujah to Jesus! He saves me to night. Now I tell it everywhere, in my pulpit, in my pastorate, in my family, I love to tell it, and that it comes by simple faith. Oh, let us come this moment, and standing upon the promise, lighted up by the blessed Holy Spirit, let us now give ourselves away, and believe that the "blood of Jesus Christ cleanseth us from all sin!"

———

The foregoing discourse was listened to with delightful surprise. The preacher was a stranger, but immediately won the entire sympathy of the large body of ministers around him, and elicited, by the force, fluency, and convincing earnestness of his words, the undivided attention of a very large audience. Brother Inskip said, at the close of the sermon, "I do not see why we cannot all be saved to the uttermost this very night. I wish I could

tell you what I said when I was seeking religion.   A class-leader came along
where I was kneeling, and asked me :

"'Boy, dost thou believe that God is able to save thee ?'

" I answered, ' Yes.'

"'Dost thou believe that he is willing to save thee ?'

" Yes."

"'Well, my lad,' he said tenderly, 'do you believe that he *does save you
now ?*'

"'Yes'—and I was saved in a moment.   Now, just what happened when
I said ' yes ' I never could tell ; but it brought salvation.

" God put me in a corner once.   I was telling the people how they must
lay aside every weight, and let go all for Christ; and the Spirit said distinctly
to me, 'Do it yourself.'   I could not refuse; so I replied, ' I do, here and
now, consecrate my whole being to God.'

" Then a thick darkness gathered around me.   Not a ray of light.   Still,
I felt I must go forward, although I could see nothing to step out upon.   So
I went forward and said, ' I declare that I am now and forever all the Lord's.'
In a moment God let a little heaven burst in upon my soul.

" There are people on this ground who are high in position in the Methodist
Church, who are opposed to this experience, and to these meetings.   They
know they are not fully saved, and their children are not saved.   They know
they are in their children's way, and it is fearfully possible they may see them
lost, and the blood of their own children will be upon their heads.

" O Lord, take hold of these people !   Who is on the Lord's side ?   How
many of you do feel that you are fully cleansed by the blood of Christ ?
Raise your hands."

Many hands went up.

" Do you know this, without a doubt?"

Affirmative answers were given.

" Now I want to know how many of you desire to have this experience to-
night.   Raise your hands."

The hands were lifted.

" But your neighbors and your children may not know that it is your hand
that is raised.   Will you stand up?"

A large number stood up.

" Do you mean to say that you want it *now ?*"

" Yes."

" If any of you are ashamed of your position, and prefer to sit down, you
can do so."

We noticed but one person who sat down.

" Now come forward and let us have a season of prayer.   Each one must
pray and believe for himself."

After a short interval, Mr. Inskip announced—"I have a telegram from our Heavenly Father. It is this : ' Every one that asketh receiveth ' Here is another : It reads, 'Ask what ye will in my name, and I will do it.' Telegrams come fast. Here is another."

He thus proceeded to announce promises, which were appropriated by the kneeling multitude around him, until it appeared as if the mighty power of God rested on all present. People were so wrapped up in contemplation, or excited by new sensations, that they were weeping, shouting, or silent and prostrate on the ground, with a consciousness that God was nigh to save.

" This is but the beginning of victory," said Brother Inskip. " I expect to see this ground inundated with salvation, and every one of you so filled with heavenly unction, that you will go around these tents and cottages, and bring every sinner to Jesus.

"Now sing the doxology. Sing it again ; you did not all sing. Every voice and every heart ring it out—

<blockquote>" ' Praise God from whom all blessings flow.' "</blockquote>

SEVENTH DAY.

TUESDAY MORNING.

After a refreshing season of prayer, it was proposed that those who had just been blessed, speak first.

A preacher : " I feel that I have been invited specially to speak. I have just been blessed. I have been a mourner here. I wanted a new touch of power. There has been too much sourness about me. In our work we meet with peculiar obstacles—men still clinging to the Zinzendorf theory, who ought to know that it has been exploded a thousand times, as mischievous and false. I want more sweetness of temper. I sent in a request yesterday for prayer. You heard it read, and probably joined in prayer for that Central Pennsylvania Conference preacher. I am the man. I became sick. This is how God answered it. I got very sick. I died unto sin last night. In looking for a promise, the Lord gave me this—' I will circumcise thy heart,' &c. I said amen, Lord! Then the bottom of glory fell out, and down came the power, streaming all over me.

I want to be so filled that I shall fear neither men or devils, and see this cause go on. O God—my Father, my Redeemer, my Comforter, glorify thyself in me !"

"I have been pointed out as the 'rowdy Methodist,' because I have to make a joyful noise unto God. Brethren, he has given me a perfect hatred of the things I once loved, and put in me a conscience quick as the apple of an eye, the least approach of sin to feel."

"I almost envy this brother who has just spoken. I feel that after leading a class twenty years without seeking for myself, or telling others of the sweet joys of purity, I am one of the meanest men in the world. I am in a condition now, blessed be God! to do a little better."

"Two years ago the blood cleansed me, and I have been endowed here with power to hold up the banner of holiness when I return home."

Others referred to similar experience—the need of more power.

"You see here," said a Presbyterian layman, "a brother who has been driven out of his Church for professing the grace that fully saves. Glory to God, I feel I can go back in the face of it all, and tell them I am sanctified—as Paul prayed—sanctified wholly."

"I rejoice that I can return and tell my class that I am saved—cleansed from all sin. Yes, from all sin."

"Three of us, leaders, came up to this feast of Pentecost, to obtain full salvation. Glory to Jesus, he has saved us all, and filled us with perfect love. I feel now like a man who has plenty in bank that he can draw upon whenever he needs it."

Bro. White—"I gave a word of testimony this morning, and wish now to make a correction. I gave all up—goods, time, family, self, all consecrated. Yesterday, as sister Smith prayed, the power I so much lacked came on me—courage to be crucified for Christ, if necessary. I raised my hand, determined to die rather than go back. Last night there came a tide of faith. 'What are you going to ask?' was suggested. 'Courage, power, the sanctification of my whole Church.' I'll believe God if it costs me my life. Whenever I am tempted to falter, wherever I am, I'll hold up this hand, and keep it up." Shouts of ("Amen!")

"I, too, had to die. Death must come before resurrection. Now I live; yet not I; Christ lives in me." Singing—

> "The cross for Christ I'll cherish,
> Its crucifixion bear:
> All hail reproach and sorrow,
> If Jesus lead me there."

Spontaneously every hand went up as these lines were sung, and as the chorus was repeated the whole congregation, weeping, shouting and vowing fidelity to Jesus, started to their feet.

ANOTHER LOVE-FEAST.

Bro. Inskip conducted the services at 8 A. M., which assumed the character of a genuine love-feast.

After a hearty hymn and prayer, passages of Scripture were called for and given by the people, some rising in the most remote part of the audience to quote a text, which might be profitable for doctrine, reproof, encouragement, and instruction in righteousness.

"Now," said the leader, "of necessity the testimony must be short. Twenty five-minute speeches here would occupy an hour; may we not have fifty or sixty in that space of time? Let us try. I am gloriously saved this morning!"

"Fourteen years ago I started on this line. Instead of seeking Jesus, he sought me, and he saves me now."

"I did not come here to enjoy the society of friends, or the recreations of the tented grove; but to find this great salvation. I can testify, he saves me wonderfully."

"I love God with all my heart, and my will is sweetly lost in his."

"I take no credit (said Bro. Barker) for loving Jesus; but it is an infinite mercy and condescension that Jesus loves me, for I was such a miserable and unlovable creature."

"In the midst of all my cares (Bro. C. I. Thompson) providing for the temporal wants of the people here, I have been sustained and sweetly saved, as if I had no care or trouble. Praise the Lord."

"I bless God that I know for myself, the blood of Jesus cleases me."

"I feel a constant shrinking to go forward. It seems I need more grace than anybody else, but I have learned here to trust Jesus fully, and I know he will not let me fall."

"When I draw nigh to God, he draws nigh to me, and I love to trust him."

"Years ago I read Timothy Merritt's book on holiness. I had no one to inquire of as to how I might obtain this great blessing; but I wrestled in prayer before God at my home, until he filled my soul with perfect love. I went to my pastor and told him what I felt. He asked me: 'Do you feel any more rising of anger or pride?' I said, 'No.' Then said he, 'You have the blessing, and the witness of it will come.' It did come, sure enough. Sometimes the flame burnt low, but I nursed it up. I had to testify all alone, and doing so I never lost this pledge of love. I can now rejoice in the salvation of all my children, and the raising up of a great cloud of witnesses to the grace that saves from all sin."

"I have enjoyed full salvation for five years, but never quite so full as now. It is pressed down, shaken together, and running over. All is well. Bless the Lord."

" The highest aspiration of my heart is to say in downright sincerity and re-signation, ' Thy will be done.' "

" Jesus saves me all the time."

" I used to have daily concern to keep my religion; but now all anxiety is re-moved; I trust Jesus and my religion keeps me."

> "The peace of Christ makes fresh my heart,
> A fountain ever springing ;
> All things are mine since I am His,
> How can I keep from singing."

" Praise God ! I cannot keep from telling my friends and neighbors how precious Jesus is, and they rejoice with me."

" I used to drink wine, and all I gained was headache ; but this wine of the kingdom makes my heart glad. And it is without money and without price."

" No, brother; it cost the great price of Jesus' blood—

> "Jesus' blood hath healed my wound,
> O the wondrous story ;
> I once was lost but now am found,
> Glory, glory, glory !"

" I can say I am saved. Jesus died to save, and I believe it; but I cannot say I am cleansed.

Bro. Inskip—"Believe that, too, sister, and declare it—the blood cleanses."

" I was two whole years dying. I now feel that I am dead to sin. I am nothing at all. Jesus Christ is my all in all. He lives in the temple of my heart."

" Forty years," said Dr. Nast, " have I been learning the depths of this re-deeming love; how it reached down even to me. Two years ago I began to learn the *heights* of this love. I am also trying to comprehend its length and breadth. O what a theme for eternity !"

" When I heard the request read for the entire sanctification of a class leader, I thought it was surely me was meant; and whether or not, I felt I must have this blessing. Help me by your prayers."

" Jesus is mine. His love fills my heart."

" I only want to say, I am a poor sinner, saved by grace; but, O how rich and free this grace has been manifested to me. I am all the Lord's."

Dr. Levy —"I am glad to hear one of the members of my church testifying for Jesus and full salvation here. At this meeting I have received a rich bap-tism of love. Go out in the early morning, and you will see a dewdrop on every blade of grass; look again in an hour or two, and you will find the sun has absorbed them all. Just so the Son of Righteousness has taken us all up into himself."

Bro. Foote—"There are some doctors of divinity for whom I have a pro-found respect, but as to you, Dr. Levy, my heart's strongest tendrils entwine around you with the sweetest tenderness, and the purest affection." Here these two brethren clasped hands, then placed their arms around each other's neck, while the faces of the people were bathed in tears, and shouts arose all over the congregation. The impulse of the two manly Christian hearts, leading to such a loving embrace, affected all, and was but a representative act; for all were melted and drawn by the same spirit to love one another.

Bro. Searles—"I have been wonderfully blessed at this meeting. In my early experience I used to shout a good deal; but I was fully sanctified in such a quiet meeting, that if anybody had spoken aloud to me it seemed as though it would have killed me. I enjoy a quiet or a noisy meeting, just as it comes; for I am in harmony with whatever course the Spirit leads."

Bro. Davies—"There is a deep, surging river of salvation flowing through my soul. It runs so deep it makes but little noise, but it still flows on."

Bro. Inskip—"God bless you, Bro. Davies."

A minister—"I heard Father Merrill, of New England, once exclaim, ' O the luxury of a tender heart!' I am enjoying that luxury to-day. The timidity of my nature is being overcome by a sense of obligation to honor the Lord who bought me. I am following on to apprehend that for which I am apprehended; and if in anything I be otherwise minded, God will reveal even this unto me. This passage suits me so well it seems as if it was put in the Bible for me exclusively. It is encouraging to know that if there is anything I have not given up, God will make it plain."

Dr. H., of Baltimore, said he was living these times on "Hallelujah hill." "I was converted in 1836, was baptized into the spirit of labor in 1842, but not fully saved until ten years after. Then I was emptied of sin and filled with the Holy Ghost. For about a year I had been praying a hundred times, a day, perhaps, for this fullness. While in my office one day I received a wonderful blessing, and became so happy that I began to shout. One of my neighbors came in and inquired what was the matter. I told him I did not know, only that God had saved my soul. Ever since I have an illuminated Bible. I went to my pastor and told him my experience. He remarked, ' You have, no doubt, received a great blessing.' I said 'Yes, I have had many big blessings, but they were not like this.' That dear minister now understands it himself by a blessed experience."

Bro. McDonald—"I heard my pastor say, for I have a pastor—Dr. Steele of Boston—that it seemed to him God was trying an experiment with him, to see how much grace he could pour into his soul. It seemed at times he was sending through his nature a very Amazon of grace. This is not my experience, but God is pouring himself into my soul. I had a great conflict at the beginning of this meeting. Now I can help shout the victory. Glory be to the Father, Son and Holy Ghost!"

A German brother—"When Satan appears to intimidate me, I look to Jesus, and Jesus is the strongest. He is Satan's conqueror, and he is able to keep that which I have committed to him. I expect to gain the victory through his power."

"I can safely say, this morning—

> "My all to Christ I've given,
> My talents, time and voice,
> Myself, my reputation,
> The lone way is my choice."

A Presbyterian brother—" On last Sabbath I determined I would have this fullness if I had to be crucified. Then Jesus appeared a glorious Redeemer, and saved me to the uttermost. I know not what may happen in my surroundings; but now all is well. This is most like what I think Pentecost was, of any meeting I ever experienced before."

Bro. Inskip here arose and directed attention to another subject. " I am going," he said, " to put a strain on this meeting—a financial strain. You have been getting happy. Now let us see if you can stand your ground while a collection is taken up. We need some money to repair damages. About $200 have been expended on this Tabernacle, and more will be required to put it in order after the present meeting. We need $300. Are you willing to give this amount as a means of grace ?"

Yes, they eagerly entertained the proposition, and in a very few minutes the cry was—" Hold up; we have enough !"

While the rock had been struck and the stream was flowing, Bro. Perkins suggested that there was another claim on the kindness of the people. "Two of our brethren laboring here, are committed to the work of Evangelists without pastoral charge, or any regular means of support. Should we not make a contribution toward their expenses ?"

Responses were heard all over the congregation. Collectors passed round and received the free-will offerings for the object named, and in eight or ten minutes more *five hundred dollars* were reported as a contribution towards expenses of Messrs. Inskip and McDonald, the President and Vice President of the National Camp-meeting Association.

MEMORIAL SERVICES.

On the assembling of the congregation in front of the main stand, Mr. Inskip proceeded to speak, in a feeling and solemn manner of the deceased members of the National Association.

He said: "The National Association for the promotion of Holiness, was organized at Vineland. A committee at the Vineland Camp-meeting for the promotion of holiness, had been appointed, to make arrangements for a National meeting. That committee being called together, at the close of the Vineland meeting, resolved to hold another Camp-meeting the next year and a sub-committee was appointed to make the necessary arrangements. We knelt down there together, a few of us, and invoked the divine blessing upon us, consecrating ourselves before God, on our knees, for the work. The organization was formed in the act and attitude of prayer.

"It was suggested, while still on our knees, that we gather more closely together, (there were twelve or fourteen of us); we did so, at the same time joining hands, and entered into a compact, that by God's help we would sustain each other, by every possible means in the great work of spreading this blessed doctrine of entire sanctification. I suggested that we would meet with severe criticism, and be misrepresented; and we then and there covenanted never to answer any criticism that might be made.

"In that company were two who are now before the throne. One was Alfred Cookman, who led that little band in the prayer of consecration. It was the most sublime, comprehensive, faith-grasping prayer that I ever heard that man of God, so gifted, so earnest, so eloquent as he often was, utter. There knelt with us also the Rev. George C. Wells, a man of exceedingly great mental calibre, and of extraordinary pulpit ability. He was remarkable for directness of utterance, for clearness, for force. Cookman's last utterances combined, form the grand sentiment that has been reverberating over the country, 'I'm sweeping through the gates, washed in the blood of the Lamb.' Brother Wells, after a long, fearful and painful sickness, passed upwards to meet the blood-washed around the throne. His cherished companion said to him, 'What shall I write as your parting word to the National Association?' 'Tell them" said he, 'I am clinging to the cross, and as I am passing through the valley all is clear and light.' He lived well, and died better. We have a few resolutions of respect to offer, which we wish you to share with us as a declaration of our respect for and a testimonial to his valuable and noble memory. Our Secretary will read them."

Rev. George Hughes then read the following resolutions of respect, passed at the Landisville National Camp-meeting, in memory of Rev. George C. Wells.

Whereas a wise and yet inscrutable Providence has removed from our midst our beloved brother and fellow laborer, Rev. Geo. C. Wells, thereby subjecting his family to a heavy bereavement, and depriving the Church of a devoted minister; therefore

Resolved 1st, That while we bow submissively to the ordination of the Lord Jehovah in this matter, we are painfully affected by his removal from our fellowship, and admonished of the uncertainty of life, and the importance of constant readiness for our departure to the eternal world.

Resolved 2d, That inasmuch as our dear brother has been associated with us since the commencement of our organization, we recall with pleasure the many seasons of fraternal intercourse that we have enjoyed together, and we magnify the grace of Christ our Saviour, which enabled him in life to exemplify so clearly the excellence of entire holiness, and to labor so zealously for its promotion.

Resolved 3d. That we especially rejoice on account of his final triumph, and abundant entrance into the everlasting kingdom of our Lord Jesus Christ; and we shall ever cherish and hold in remembrance, as a precious legacy, his last message to us, declaring that he was "Clinging to the Cross," in death as in life.

Resolved 4th. That we tender to his surviving companion and the other members of his family, our sincere condolence in this deep affliction, praying that the God of all comfort may abundantly sustain them, and sanctify the dispensation to their present and eternal well-being.

Resolved 5th. That a copy of these resolution be furnished to the family of our deceased brother, and published in the *Advocate of Holiness* and our Church papers.

TUESDAY MORNING.

SERMON BY REV. LEWIS R. DUNN, OF ELIZABETH, N. J.

ENTIRE CONSECRATION.

" Who, then, is willing to consecrate his service this day unto the Lord ?"—
1 Chron. 29 : 5.

The occasion on which the language of the text was uttered was one of the grandest and sublimest in the history of the Jewish nation. At the close of a long, troubled, yet prosperous reign, in which the borders of Israel had been greatly enlarged, and the wealth of his kingdom vastly increased, David, the royal psalmist, had convoked a grand assembly at Jerusalem. It is described in chapter 28, verse 1. This council was not assembled for warlike purposes, nor for territorial enlargement or aggrandizement, but it was to provide for the erection of the most costly and magnificent temple ever erected in this world, the plan of which the Spirit of God had given to David, the consummation of which was to be effected by his son Solomon. When all were assembled, the king rose to his feet and addressed them in earnest words. He told them how he had longed to build this house for God, how the Lord had refused him permission to do this because he was a man of war and of blood ; how this work, by Divine appointment, had been entrusted to Solomon, and of the immense preparation which he had made toward it. He then gave a solemn charge to his son, and also a pattern of the whole building. Then follows an enumeration of the gold and the silver, and precious stones, and iron, and wood, which he had prepared. After all this he calls upon the people for their contributions. The amount contributed on this day, according to the calculation of some authors, was the enormous sum of $600,000,000, lowest, or $5,146,887,480, the highest. The offerings of the people were made with the greatest cheerfulness, insomuch that the heart of the aged king was overwhelmed with delight and joy, and he offered publicly both prayers and thanksgivings. And at his bidding the whole congregation arose and blessed the Lord God of Israel, and worshiped.

Our Lord Jesus Christ is building the most magnificent temple which this universe ever beheld. The richness of the materials of which it is being constructed, the immense, the infinite cost of this building of God, the grandeur and magnificence of the design, will occasion, at its completion, an outburst of praise from angel and archangel, seraphim and cherubim, and all the intelligences which God has made. Of this temple, that which Solomon built is only a faint and feeble type, while the gold and silver and precious stones sink into insignificance before its richer value and its greater glory. The foundations of this building are "the apostles and prophets, Jesus Christ himself being the chief corner-stone;" and the materials are "living stones,"—immortal spirits, each one of which is of more value than all the gold and silver in the universe,—purchased and prepared for this habitation of God by the infinite preciousness of the blood of Christ, and by the infinite wisdom and power of the Eternal Spirit. Here, then, assembled before God in this grand convocation, I come to ask you, "Who, then, is willing to consecrate his service this day unto the Lord?"

1. The burden of my message this day is *consecration*, what it *implies* and embraces, and *why* and *when* it *should be made*. The original meaning of the word is "to fill;" and the literal rendering of the text, as the margin shows, is—"Who is willing *to fill his hand* this day?" etc.,—*i. e.* to fill his hand with offerings to Jehovah.

When the priests under the former dispensation were consecrated, their hands were said to be filled with their office, their work and their offerings. The word is also used for the devotement of anything to God's worship and service. In this sense all the first-born in Israel, whether of man or beast, were to be devoted to the Lord. The tribe of Levi was taken in lieu of the first-born of Israel, and, in a special manner, devoted to the Lord. So the Nazarites of old devoted themselves to the Lord for a limited period, and fields, possessions and persons, in like manner, were set apart as belonging wholly unto the Lord. Under the present dispensation, every believer is set apart for God; is, or should be, devoted wholly to his service. This implies that God has a *right* to *demand* this consecration, and that we have the *power to make it*. These two things must ever be borne in mind. If there is any doubt about either of them, then the work will either be greatly delayed, or never accomplished. That God has the right to demand it, no one can reasonably doubt. But many doubt that we can comply with the demand. Of course, I mean that we have the power, through the redemptional work of Christ, which has procured the gracious agency of the Divine Spirit. No one is required to act, or expected to act, in this transaction without grace. Thus aided, I say, we can all comply with this command. To argue otherwise, would be to argue injustice on the part of God, for making a demand of us which we are by no means able to perform. There is not one now before me, there is not one in all this wide world, but who *can, if he will*, "consecrate his service this day unto the Lord."

2. This command *covers the whole being of man*, with all its *actualities, conditions, relations* and *possibilities*. But, primarily, it requires the *surrender of the heart*, or *the moral powers*. It is these which regulate and control the whole being. Hence, God's first requirement is, "Thou shalt love the Lord thy God with all *thy heart*." "My son, give me *thy heart*." Where the heart goes, there goes man's whole being. The moral powers include the *will*, the *affections* and the *conscience*. There is no obstacle in the way of man's salvation so great as that of an unsubdued and unsurrendered will. The whole stress of God's requirement is made to bear against this power. "Whoever *will*, let him take the water of life freely." And, "Ye *will* not come to me that ye might have life." In the one instance it is the great power which leads man into salvation, holiness and heaven; it bathes his parched lips, and slakes his feverish thirst with the waters of life; it plunges him into the purple flood, it encircles his brow with a diadem of glory; in the other, it raises a barrier, heaven high and hell deep, between him and the fountain of life, the cross of redemption and the gates of pearl, and determines his eternal banishment from God and from heaven. Wonderful is the power of the human will! In all his dealings with us, God recognizes this wonderful power which he has given us. Now, God requires the surrender, the consecration, first of all, *of our will*. He nowhere asks that this power shall be absorbed, destroyed or lost, any more than he asks that our memory, reason or imagination shall undergo such a change. In fact, *our wills can never be lost*. If we are saved in heaven, we shall have a will; if we are lost in hell, we shall have a will. What the Lord asks is that our wills should be surrendered, or subjected to his will; that they should act in harmony with his will; that there should be no controversy, no antagonism, no *war*, between his will and ours; that, like parallel lines, which run on forever without contact or conflict, so our will should run on to eternity in the same direction with God's. Is not this the import of the petition? "Thy will be done on earth, as it is in heaven!" Now there is not an angel nor an archangel in heaven without a will; and yet, that will is forever in harmony with God's. If it were not, there would be again "war in heaven," instead of the eternal calm which pervades the city of God.

The will is the keystone to the arch of man's being. It is the foundation stone of his whole mental and moral superstructure. If this is given up, or consecrated, all else will be laid upon the altar with it. The consecration covers, also, our *affectional powers*. Every human heart possesses these powers. But, alas! they are perverted, abused, degraded. Like the vine, designed to cling to the trellis-work or climb the oak, and thus mount heavenward; but which, torn from its supports, twines its tendrils around clumps of grass, or weeds, or earth—so the affections, having swung loose from God, cling to the low, vile, groveling objects of time and sense. Now the Lord asks and demands that these powers should be centred in and should cling to him. And, certainly, he is worthy of all our love.

The requirement also embraces *our conscience*. This wonderful power, this voice of God in the human soul, often abused, benumbed, blinded and seared, but which, ever and anon, asserts its supremacy and thunders down through every avenue of the soul—this power which is perverted by sin, prostituted to the service of Satan, God asks should be placed in his hands. He asks it, that he may remove from it the deep incrustations of guilt which cover it; that he may heal the deep scars which sin has burned into it, and that he may make it enlightened, quick as the apple of the eye, and soft and tender as the flesh of a smiling infant.

Now, then, we say that the surrender of these moral powers involves the surrender of the whole being; just as the surrender of Lee at Appomattox involved a surrender of the whole of the forces of the rebellion in the field and on the flood.

Here is a point where many persons are honestly mistaken. The question is pressed upon them of their duty to be wholly the Lord's. One begins to think of his tobacco, another of his cup, another of her dress, another still of her worldly amusements. And each asks, "How can I give this up?" And thus the mind is perplexed with what is, after all, nothing; comparatively but a trifle. To all such persons, we would say, first of all, give your *hearts* to the Lord; surrender your will, affections, and conscience to him, and all these things will come along in the train. Your great difficulty is not with these minor things, *it is with your will.* If you say, I *will* be wholly the Lord's, " I will consecrate myself to him wholly this day," all other difficulties will vanish as clouds when the sun has risen in his strength. I know there are many who think and teach differently. And their great stress is laid against this and that habit, against this or that article of dress. This is like beginning to cut down the tree at the outmost twigs. God does not cut down the tree of man's heart in that way. He strikes right at the very root, and severs even the tap-root with the power of his arm. There are others who are always laboring with the understanding and the powers of ratiocination, as if they were the grand barriers in the way of man's salvation.

But, as a rule, man's understanding is sufficiently enlightened, his judgment convinced. If the fool says, "There is no God," he says it "in his heart." If men decry the Divine Christ and his atoning sacrifice, and the transforming and sanctifying Spirit, it is because their "foolish hearts are darkened." So if men oppose holiness, it is because of the antagonizing elements of sin in the soul. The apostle declared that "by manifestation of the truth, he and his co-laborers commended themselves to every man's conscience in the sight of God." O, then, if my will is surrendered, consecrated to God, I see the affections of my heart lifting up themselves Godward and heavenward. I see conscience purified and enlightened, uttering God's voice and fleeing from the least approach of sin. I see memory bringing its stores and laying them on God's altar. I see reason, and judgment, and understanding, and imagination, all meekly bowing down, receiving the divine impression. I see the body, with its arms and limbs, with its tongue and voice, with its eyes and countenance, with all its parts and powers obedient to the dictates of God's king and priest, who, robed in vestments of righteousness divine, holds sway over all his passions and his powers. I see the family, the loving, gentle wife, the children,—even the darling babe, so much of an idol,—all, all are here upon the altar. And I see, too, business, wealth, honors, reputation, social position laid at the feet of Jesus, each ready to say, "Here are we, Lord, to help on thy cause, and advance the interests of the Redeemer's kingdom."

3. The command of God, requiring this consecration, is absolute; the performance of it by man is voluntary.

The command admits of no compromise. God never compromises with his creatures. In fact, Jesus Christ is the most uncompromising sovereign in the world. And yet, strange to say, some persons labor all their lifetime to compromise with God. They will do this if they can only be released from doing that. They will perform this duty, if they can only be excused from the performance of that. Some will give their money, if they can be released from giving their time; and some will give their time if they can only retain their money. Some will observe the outward form of religion, with tithe, mint, and anise, and cummin, if they can neglect the weightier matters of the law. But in the midst of all, and above all the clamor for compromise, Sinai's blazing mount still thunders out, and its voice is answered back from the blood-crimsoned brow of Calvary, "Thou shalt love the Lord thy God."

But man has the fearful power of obedience or of disobedience. He can, aided by divine grace, obey God's voice, or he can turn a deaf ear unto it, and refuse obedience to his requirements. And if this work is done at all, it must be done willingly. I know there are some who misquote God's word, and say, "Thy people shall be *made* willing in the day of thy power." But there is no such Scripture as this. In fact the utterance is as contrary to philosophy as it is to revelation. The very same verb is employed by the Psalmist in that Psalm as is used here in saying, "The people offered willingly." And the literal meaning of that passage is, "Thy people shall be *free-will offerings* in the day of thy power." It is in view of this that they shall shine forth resplendently and in countless numbers, as the dew-drops of the morning, in the beauty of holiness.

It was the beauty of the offerings brought upon this occasion, and what so affected the heart of king David, that the people presented them so cheerfully and so freely. God will never force the citadel of our hearts. He will never break open the door which leads into them. If we are ever consecrated to God, we must do it voluntarily and cheerfully. It is true that the results will be widely, infinitely different, according to the choice which we make. If we are "willing and obedient we shall eat the fruit of the land." But if we disobey, "tribulation and wrath, indignation and anguish, shall be upon every soul." While this is a matter of voluntariness, it is not a matter of indifference. I know there are many different degrees of this consecration, according to the light, the conviction, the faith of the true Christian. All who are in a sense true Christians, do not so clearly as some comprehend their privilege or their duty; their conscience is not so enlightened as others, and they consequently are held back from doing what they would otherwise cheerfully do, if the way of duty were made known to them. But, I will say this, that no person can be a true Christian who is not longing to be wholly the Lord's, and is not willing to give up all to him. And yet, what multitudes profess to be Christians who know nothing of justifying or saving grace!

4. Our *service* is to be *consecrated to God.*

This is the very idea here. What did David mean when he asked this question? Why, certainly, that his nobles, and princes, and captains should come forward and lay their offerings for God's temple at his feet. And this God requires of every one of us. We are to offer, or fill our hand willingly, freely, cheerfully, and without constraint, with offerings to the Lord; recognizing that all we have of right belongs to him (verses 11-14), and that all should be freely employed for his honor and glory. Time, talents, money, property, position—

everything, are thus to be cheerfully surrendered and constantly employed. Self is to go down, no matter in what form it has exhibited itself—self-pride, self-seeking, self-ease, self-indulgence, false ambition, envy, jealousy—and God alone is to be honored, worshiped and adored. Everything we can *give* for him, we are to give; everything we can *do* for him, we are to do ; everything we can *say* for him, we are to say. We are to own his right to every service we can pay. And this to a consecrated soul will be no hardship, but a delight—a " supreme delight." It will be done without murmuring, without grudging, or fault-finding—with full consent, with heartiness, and with songs of joy.

5. When this *act of consecration* is *performed,* it should be *for all time* and *for all eternity.* The act which it takes us so few moments to perform should bind us to the throne of God forever. Just as in the marriage bond the wife gives up herself to her husband, and the husband endows her with all his wealth of affection, as well as his worldly goods, so in " this great transaction" man gives himself up wholly to the Lord, and the Lord gives himself to man ; and just as ever after the mutual vows of the husband and wife are taken to love, to honor and to cherish—to forsake all others and cling to each other so long as life shall last, or until death them do part. Wherever they go they are to remember their vows, and to act accordingly. So the Christian is to remember his vows, and always and everywhere to feel, "I am my Lord's, and He is mine." Further still: if one or the other is guilty of a breach of the marital vows, the crime of adultery lies at their door. So God will charge his people now, as he did of old, with fornication and abandonment, if they break their vows to him and go after the vain things of this world. This covenant with the Lord is to be an everlasting covenant. To withdraw, or take back any part of what we have voluntarily surrendered to God, is robbery—is sacrilege. What we give to God is no longer our own. Indeed, it never was really our own (verses 12–14.) But God has required our acknowledgment of his right to us, and the relinquishment of our usurped right wholly to himself, as our absolute proprietor and Lord. When this is done, and the seal of God is placed upon us by the cleansing blood and the fire of the Holy Ghost, we are never, *never*, NEVER to take back what we have given up. Such is the consecration which God requires. Let us see:

II. *Why we should make it.* We are moved to this—

1. By the *highest considerations* of *duty,* of *interest* and of *gratitude.* The argument here is so plain, so clear, so frequently presented, that I need scarcely dwell upon it for any time. Our *creation* by the power of God gives to him of right the *absolute proprietorship of all our powers.* It is universally acknowledged that whatever is created, so to speak, by man's skill, or genius, or power, belongs to him of right. The name of the sculptor, painter, inventor, or the architect, or of the musical composer, is enstamped, or engraved, or printed upon all such productions. For instance, every one knows the " Greek Slave" is the work of Powers ; the " Heart of the Andes," of Church ; " St. Peters," of Michael Angelo ; "The Messiah," of Handel. No one else can lay claim to these works. So the name of God should be upon our forehead, upon the tablet of our hearts, and upon all the powers of our mind. (" His name in their foreheads," etc.) Any attempt to erase or obscure that name is a violation of the most sacred obligation, and is sure to be visited with the Divine displeasure. Oh, how sin, and Satan, and the world, and self, have labored to blot out the name of God from man's being and substitute their own names !

But let us see well to it that the name of *God* is restored to his own property, and that it be forever outshining from all the powers of our being.

But more than all this—more than the fact that " in His hands is our breath and all our ways ;" that " in Him we live and move and have our being ;" that every crumb of food which we eat, and every drop of water we drink, and every shred of clothing we wear, and our comfortable homes, are all from Him—is the higher, the more wonderful fact, *that we are redeemed !*

The two grand arguments presented by the apostle for our consecration are, first, " The mercies of God ;" and, second, " Ye are not your own—ye are bought with a price." Sin had doomed us to eternal slavery—to eternal damnation. But our Lord Jesus Christ has redeemed us ; not, indeed, " with corruptible things," etc., but with his own " precious blood." It required a sacrifice of infinite value to redeem immortal spirits, and that sacrifice the Son of God freely made. Here, then, is a *double* claim which God had to us ; an infinite claim, infinitely surpassing all other claims and considerations. Oh, then, not only our *duty*, but *gratitude*, calls upon us to make this consecration.

2. By making this, and having God accept it, we can only attain to the *highest condition and privilege of our being.* As the claims of God, founded upon our creation and redemption by his power, his wisdom, and his love, cover our whole being, so by complying with those claims we can only secure our highest well-being. This is true of our *physical nature.* We all know that sin has blurred, defiled, defaced, brutalized and destroyed the body ; how, that by impurity, intoxication, gormandizing, and abuse in multitudes of instances, this beautiful framework has been marred. Anger, malice, hate, revenge, remorse, envy, covetousness have left their stamp upon the countenance. The eye has become blood-shot, the limbs prematurely trembling, the blood poisoned, the nerves shattered, and the delicate tissues of the brain inflamed and deranged. How that it has been prostituted for the vilest and most unworthy purposes, deformed by the hand of fashion, or dressed like a doll, or disguised by a horrid mask. But the consecrated body is separated from all vile uses and purposes. It " is the temple of the Holy Ghost." And, although often frail, and feeble, and homely in its features, yet, the indwelling Spirit makes the eye to glint with his light, and the countenance to glow with his radiance, and the whole features to be overspread with his own loveliness and beauty. I do not mean to say, of course, that the body of the truly consecrated child of God will attain to the strength of the prize-fighter, or the swiftness of the pedestrian, or the so-called grace of the danseuse.

Nor do I mean to say that the body, which before its consecration to God has been wasted by disease, or poisoned by alcohol, or exhausted by debauchery, or brutalized by lusts, will be entirely delivered from the legitimate, and, in a sense, necessary results of its previous conditions. No. None of these things. But what I mean to say is this ; that that consecrated body will no more, forever, be brutalized by lusts, or swollen and disfigured by intoxication, or its throat be a chimney for the smoke, and its mouth a filthy mass of tobacco, or worn out by gormandizing, or shattered by dissipation, or frittered away by carking cares and overburdening anxieties. And, further, that if this consecration occur in early life, it will tend to produce those habits of cleanliness, temperance, chastity, and those habits of economy and thrift which will supply suitable clothing and food, and proper hours of sleep, so that long life will be generally the only legitimate result. This, indeed, is promised, "What man is he that loveth life, and desireth many days that he may see good?" "Keep thy tongue," etc. "With long life will I satisfy him, and show him my salvation." "Length of days is in her (wisdom's) right hand." "That thy days may be long," etc.

The body which belongs wholly to God will attain to its highest condition and best answer the end for which it was created. So, also with our *mental powers*. Grace will enlarge and expand them, and all will be employed for the honor and glory of God. The consecrated man may not have the most brilliant natural powers, or the most resplendent genius. It is not the mere accumulation of vast stores of learning, or the splendid corruscations of genius, which are the most highly prized by God. No; "With the talents of an angel, man may still be a fool." While many a saint with humbler powers, and scanty stores of human learning, may be truly wise in the sight of God.

He has the highest kind of knowledge—the basis, indeed, of all other knowledge. He knows God, and Jesus Christ whom he has sent. And, as far as possible, he will desire to know everything that will illustrate his character, his word, and his works. The truly consecrated Christian will endeavor to improve his mind to the utmost of its capability, and of his opportunity. Those capabilities may not be great, and those opportunities may be few, but he will employ them all in the acquirement of knowledge. His time will not be wasted in novel reading, or in poring over nonsensical and very often impure and obscene stories. He will only read and study what will be for the glory of God. He is the Lord's, not only for time, but also for eternity. He is preparing for a purer, higher, nobler sphere of being. And he sees before him a whole eternity for the development of his powers, and his growth in every department of knowledge. Then, in the consecrated mind and heart, the Holy Ghost abides, enlightening and clarifying the understanding, curbing, controlling, and chastening the imagination, counselling and directing the judgment, strengthening the memory and guiding the man of God into all truth. But if he never knows anything about theology, books of science and literature, he knows by experimental tests the truths of his Bible, and the preciousness and power of his Saviour.

This is neither an argument nor a plea for ignorance; but to show how these devoted powers may attain to their highest earthly condition. Cowper thus contrasts the conditition of a poor widow and Voltaire:—

"She knew, and knew no more, her Bible true;
A truth the brilliant Frenchman never knew;
And in that charter read, with sparkling eyes,
Her title to a treasure in the skies.
O happy peasant! unhappy bard!
His the mere tinsel, her's the rich reward;
He praised for ages yet to come,
She never heard of half a mile from home.
He lost in errors his vain heart prefers,
She saved in the simplicity of hers."

But, above all, our moral powers will reach their highest condition. The will in harmony with God's—the affections supremely and forever centred in him—the conscience ever answering to his voice, quick, and pure, and calm, and peaceful. So shall the will of God be done by him upon the earth, as it is in heaven.

12

3. Only by so doing can we reach the *highest state of blessedness of which our being is capable.* The sinful, worldly, ambitious and sensual man, each has his pleasure. It is not true to say that the world has no joy and sin has no pleasure. There are, to unrenewed, men pleasures of sense, of taste, and smell, and sound, and sight, and sensual gratification. There are also pleasures of mind, of the memory, imagination, understanding, and the powers of ratiocination, of analysis and synthesis. There are also pleasures of the heart, the hearth, and the home. Indeed, God often permits wicked men to have many pleasures and comforts of which his people are deprived. But, after all this is admitted, the voice of God is confirmed by the voice of universal history and experience, that "the world can never give the bliss for which we sigh." All the pleasures which man can derive from wealth, honor and sensual gratification, are as nothing in comparison with the bliss which the humble saint of God enjoys. One hour of communion with God, of the conscious sense of sonship and heirship, of the light of God's countenance and the glory of his smile, of the unspeakable peace and the unutterable joy of the Holy Ghost, full of exultant hope of the eternal life, infinitely outweighs all the transitory pleasure which earth can give. Such bliss is the bliss of the saints; aye more, it is the bliss of the angels. Aye more, it is the bliss, the joy of God! O, if I could call down an angel from the throne now! but I have no need to do this, for they are here; but, if I could make one to appear before you, and speak to you, I would ask him, "What makes you so happy? Why is eternal sunshine upon your face? Why is heaven ever beaming from your eye? Why is your overflowing heart ever bursting forth in songs of joy?" Would he not answer, substantially, "Because I am wholly the Lord's, and all my powers are ceaselessly employed in his service." So will it be with us if we are wholly given up to God.

4. Only by so doing can we attain to the *greatest degree of usefulness.* Our real usefulness will be proportioned to the degree of our devotion to Christ. I know that I shall be met here, right on the threshold of this statement, by the counter-assertion that many ministers of evidently little piety have been greatly successful as evangelists, and have been instrumental in the conversion of more persons than some who are known to possess greater piety. There have been instances of this kind, I know, which have staggered the faith of many a truly devoted minister. But, after all, has not this so-called usefulness been more apparent than real? Have not the results been ephemeral? Or, if permanent, have not the real agents been kept out of sight, while the visible agent has received the glory and the applause? But, on the other hand, is it not true—true as the word of God can make it—that his chosen ones, as they go forth, shall "bear *fruit*, and that their *fruit shall remain?*" Have not all the great, mighty, moral movements of the world been commenced and carried forward mostly by consecrated men—men deeply devoted to Christ? True Christians in every degree of their experience are useful, from the merest babe in Christ to the brightest and maturest saint. But oh, how much more good we might do as ministers and as laymen and women of the Church if we were wholly the Lord's! Here, for instance, is a machine, well-designed and really of great capacity to accomplish a given result. But some of its parts are out of place—some of the wheels are clogged—and there is friction between the parts. It is doing something; but if it were in complete order, how much more it would accomplish! Here is a fruit tree, well shaped, and planted in a good soil. It bears some fruit, but it is nothing to what it is capable to bear,

and the fruit is not of the quality which it might bear. It is untrimmed, and useless shoots are drawing away its life. Worms are at the root, or are concealed in the bark. Now, let the tree be put in condition, and its branches will bend under the burden of luscious fruits. Here is a battery; it may be small—it may be made, in a lady's thimble, of sufficient power, it is said, to send a single message across the Atlantic. Well done for the little battery! But let it be enlarged, and day and night it will be flashing messages over continents, islands and seas. So with the Christian. He is—he must be—useful with a little light, a little grace, a little power. Nor is his limited experience or attainment to be despised. But he knows, and we all know, that if that light were nearer the perfect day, if that grace were all-transforming and sanctifying, and if that power were greatly augmented, how greatly his usefulness would be increased!

III.—When, then, should this *consecration be made?* " *This day.*" 1. Because *every moment* of our *conscious being* that we have *delayed doing it,* or *refused* to *do* it, we have been *defrauding God.* We know that the demand which God makes of us is right and reasonable. "*He justly claims.*" If this be so, then the question admits of no delay. We ought not, in any instance, to hesitate where right and moral honesty are concerned. The simple question settled, " Is it right?" then everything else follows. The wonder is that we have delayed doing this so long. And yet, with most professing Christians, this has not been *wholly* neglected. Before conversion there was a giving up to God—a consecration to his service; and since that time your minds have doubtless been frequently drawn to consider the importance of a more complete and perfect surrender. You have thought about it, talked and prayed about it, sung about it—perhaps have even made a formal written consecration of yourself to God; but still you have felt that, after all, all is not given up. Oh, then, *this day* let the work be completed! Cry out,

> " Thy ransomed servant I,
> Restore to thee thine own ;
> And from this moment live or die
> To serve my God alone."

2. *The earlier this consecration is made, the more acceptable will it be to God.* True, the Lord will graciously receive the middle-aged and the aged, but he loves to receive the young. O, ye young men and women! it is this early consecration which will make your lives beautiful and sublime. It will not only save you from a thousand snares; but it will crown you with a thousand blessings. Come, while the dew of youth is upon your brow, and elasticity is in your limbs, and the life-blood leaps and tingles in your veins; and let this great work be done to-day. But none of us can begin earlier than *now.* Let not another moment pass, but now and here lay your all upon God's altar, and he will accept the sacrifice.

3. We should make this consecration to-day because a *whole lifetime* is *none too much to devote to God.* Had we done this at the very earliest dawn of our responsible being, and had every day, hour and moment been faithfully employed in his service, would it have been any too much? And if we begin now, and employ all our powers for the glory of God, all our future days, and throughout the countless cycles of eternity, will that be too much? And yet many years passed away before some of us surrendered our all! Yea, how many are there now before me who have not yet done this work!

Hasten, then, with your gift to the altar. Everything is in readiness for you.
The cleansing blood, the sanctifying Spirit, the immutable promises and the
attendant angels, are ready just now to hold you as a sealed and sanctified
follower of Jesus.

4. To do this work to-day will settle a question which has kept you in agi-
tation and trouble for years. You cannot dismiss it from your mind. It
stares you in the face wherever you look. If you open your Bible it is
pressed upon you there. If you go to pray, the Holy Ghost brings it before
you there. If you sing, nearly every hymn speaks of it. If you regard God
your Father, you see his claims upon you. If you look to the cross of Jesus,
you hear him say, " All this I have done for thee; what hast thou done for
me?" Thus has it been for years gone by. You have resolved, and resolved,
again and again, that you would do it. And then when the moment has come,
you have hesitated, squirmed, halted, delayed. Now let the question be
settled, *once and forever.* " This day the covenant I sign," etc. If this is
done then the question is settled forever. It will be easy to repeat what has
once been thoroughly done. And your soul will exult in the blessed assurance, "My beloved is mine, and I am his."

Who, then, is willing to consecrate his service this day unto the Lord?
How many of this vast throng, deeply convinced of the rightfulness, the
reasonableness and the necessity of doing this work, are ready to do it now?
Do not say, " I am not prepared to do it now." What! are you not prepared
to do right? Must you wait longer to consider whether you will be honest?
I press the claims of my God upon you. I call upon you for a decision.
One moment now of halting, hesitation, or refusal, may mar your whole
Christian character and blight your religious life. O, that there may be mul-
titudes, multitudes, this day in the valley of decision! O, you *will* do it!
Yes, *we* will give up all to thee, O Lord! Father, Son, and Holy Ghost,
witness to our surrender, and seal our sacrifice. Now apply the blood. Now
Holy Ghost, descend!

The sentences we trace on these pages give but a faint idea of the fervor
and force of oral address. Brother Dunn labored under a powerful pressure
of influence from God, and in directness of appeal, stirred the better sensibil-
ities of a very large and profoundly interested audience. The defects of
religious character were so pictured that hearts cried out for the living God
to cleanse and make them new. The light poured on soul-consecration enabled many to make a full surrender, and making it, they were speedily brought
into liberty.

TUESDAY AFTERNOON.

SERMON BY REV. GEORGE HUGHES.

" Where is the Lord God of Elijah ?"—2 Kings 2 : 14.

Elijah, the faithful prophet of God, had been suddenly translated from earth to heaven in a chariot of fire. In this termination of his career God put special honor upon his devoted servant. He had passed over Jordan accompanied by Elisha. As they came to the river he smote the waters with his staff, and they stood up on either side, making a clear path for them to pass over to the other bank.

As they went on and talked together, behold there appeared a chariot of fire and horses of fire. The prophet entered the chariot, and a whirlwind swept him upward to his heavenly home. Elisha, gazing upon the on-rolling chariot bearing his honored master to the celestial city, was constrained to exclaim, "My father, my father, the chariot of Israel, and the horsemen thereof!" Taking up the mantle of Elijah, he returned to the Jordan, and, smiting the waters, he cried, "Where is the Lord God of Elijah?" The same miraculous result was realized as in the former instance, the waters being divided, and Elisha crossing over to enter on his life-work.

The text is selected for practical purposes, and we inquire—

I. When may this inquiry be made, with the certain expectation of a satisfactory answer? There are various occasions when it may be satisfactorily propounded, but we shall simply refer to one, an occasion of transcendent interest, illustrated in the singularly glorious life of Elijah—viz., *the hour of sacrifice.*

The prophet, under divine direction, showed himself to the wicked Ahab. He called for the assembling of Israel, and also for the four hundred and fifty prophets of Baal, and the four hundred prophets of the grove, that the question of the authority and dominion of the Lord Jehovah might be definitely settled.

When the Israelites, in connection with the prophets of Baal, were assembled, the challenge was made by Elijah, "How long halt ye between two opinions?" &c. ; and the proposal for the offering of a bullock, and the God that answered by fire should be declared to be THE GOD. The result is well known. The God of Elijah was shown to be the one true and living God.

In the light of this portion of Old Testament history, we remark that a satisfactory response to the inquiry, "Where is the Lord God of Elijah?" is dependent upon the offering of a sacrifice corresponding to that of Elijah. Note its prominent features :

1. It must be a whole sacrifice, like the whole bullock offered by Elijah. God requires this. Unless there be an entire offering of ourselves to God, there can be no answering tokens. Any degree of mental reservation will mar the offering. Many, presenting their sacrifice, wonder why there is not the descending fire. Here is the difficulty,—the offering is not entire. There is

a test presented, which challenges the submission of the will. I may be a very little thing, and yet involving the vital question of submission—*entire* submission.

2. The sacrifice must be laid on the altar. Elijah's altar was carefully prepared. It was the altar of the Lord—his by special appointment. It had been broken down, and was now builded again, composed of twelve stones, representing the twelve tribes.

We have an altar—already prepared—never broken down. It is divinely prepared—an efficacious altar—which is Christ. A sacrifice laid thereupon is well pleasing to God, and must be accepted.

3. It must be entirely separated from human dependencies.

Elijah fully guarded this point. There was the water of separation—barrel after barrel, poured upon the sacrifice, and every human hand taken therefrom. There it lay upon the altar, divorced completely from all human endeavors or dependencies. There is a difficulty at this point, in the case of many now in offering themselves to God. They are seeking salvation by their own effort. All this must be abandoned.

4. It must be definitely presented to God. Here we notice in the case of Elijah, deliberation. It was the hour of evening sacrifice—the accepted hour. *Solemn address to God.* The terms and the manner both solemn. His eye toward heaven, his appeal to the Lord God of Abraham, Isaac and Israel.

The exercise of true faith—indicated by the removal of the sacrifice utterly beyond human dependencies—and the calmness of his address to God. Thus must our sacrifice be characterized.

II. The satisfactory character of the answer given to this inquiry—Where is the Lord God of Elijah?

Mount Carmel afforded a sublime demonstration of the character and dominion of the Lord God of Elijah. And there are multiplied demonstrations in connection with the sacrifices of God's people.

1. The answer was peculiar in character. An answer of fire—an all-consuming fire, in two respects. 1. As to the victim itself; and 2. As to the outward connections, consuming the stones of the altar, and licking up the water in the trenches. This beautifully symbolizes two things in regard to full salvation. 1. The entire consumption of inward impurity, and the absorption of the whole being by God himself, and the full devotement of every faculty to the divine glory. 2. The entire consumption of all outward sinful connections, represented by the altar and the water in the trenches. The work of justification cuts the sinful connections grandly, so that sin does not have dominion, effecting a decided change in the whole spirit and life. Entire santification intensifies this separation from the world, and gives an elevated tone to the whole character and life.

2. The answer was overwhelming in effect. In the overturning of skepticism —skepticism among the people of God. All the people when they saw the fiery demonstration, fell on their faces: and they said, "The Lord, he is the God: the Lord he is the God!" So the skepticism now existing in the Church is to be chased away by the spirit of burning—the holy fire resting upon and consuming the subjects of full salvation.

In the destruction of false religion. The Baal prophets and worshipers were destroyed. So the Baal-worship of the modern Church is to be utterly consumed. Ritualism, and every form of false worship is to be consumed by fire.

3. The answer was sudden. The fire leaped over the heavenly battlements, in answer to Elijah's prayer and faith. So when we have the sacrifice truly on the altar, the answer of fire will not be long delayed. The Lord will avenge his elect speedily.

4. This revelation of Elijah's God gives marching orders, and marching strength.

Elisha, now the representative of God's people, proved this at Jordan. As he inquired after the Lord God of Elijah, he was at hand to reveal his power, and to open for him a channel through the waters. The Church now has her Jordans to cross. The ministry has such calls. What is to be done? Shall the cry be: "Where are the Lexicons, where are the Cyclopedias, the Philosophies of the ages, the Sciences?" Rather let it be, Where is the Lord God of Elijah? And an open channel shall be presented. So the Church in various departments has her Jordans to cross, to meet the demands of the times. Let her cry, Where is the Lord God of Elijah? And she shall not stand on the bank wondering or confounded, but shall triumphantly pass over, and fulfill her glorious destiny.

We need here an answer to the question: Where is the Lord God of Elijah? We have had it in part, but let us look for a complete demonstration, a fiery demonstration.

TUESDAY EVENING.

SERMON BY REV. C. F. TURNER, Presiding Elder.

" *Mighty to Save.*"—*Isa.* 63 : 1.

The text is predicated of Jesus Christ. It could not be of any other. for, "There is none other name under heaven, given among men, whereby we must be saved." All the angels in heaven, with their combined wisdom and power, could not save a single sinner. But Jesus can save all sinners who will come unto him for salvation. He came into this world for this purpose, and is fully able to accomplish his glorious work. Man by nature is deeply fallen, and exceedingly sinful. Humanity needs a mighty Saviour. The necessity has been graciously and fully met. Man may be saved. Saved from sin and wrath, and raised to heaven to enjoy its perfect bliss forever.

> " Jesus the name to sinners dear,
> The name to sinnors given,
> The name that charms our guilty fears
> And turns our hell to heaven."

Mighty! Almighty to save! The appropriate topic suggested by the text is

I. *The Almightiness of Christ to save sinners.*

He is almighty to save. This is claimed for him in the book divine of truth eternal. This he claims for himself. The claim we propose to establish and illustrate. In the foundation upon which it rests there are three essential elements.

1. His Divinity!

Take from Christ his Divinity, and you take from humanity all hope of salvation. We need a divine Saviour. Nothing short of omnipotence can save us. Christ is divine, therefore omnipotent, and consequently able to save to the uttermost, all them that come unto him. This blessed truth is clearly and impressively taught throughout the sacred Scriptures, and was most perfectly illustrated by Christ himself, when on earth, as he healed the sick, restored the blind to sight, and the lame to soundness by the word of his power. As he raised the dead to life, and then went down into the realm of death himself, and conquered the king of terrors in his own empire, and came forth a divine conqueror on the morning of the third day.

> "Some take him a creature to be,
>   A man or an angel at most,
> Sure these have no feelings like me,
>   Nor know themselves wretched and lost.

> "So fallen, so helpless am I,
>   I could not confide in his word,
> Unless I could make the reply,
>   That Christ is my Lord and my God."

One of the greatest statesmen of this country was asked by a skeptical friend, what he thought of the Divinity of Christ. He replied, "I believe him divine; if I did not I could not trust my soul in his hands, for it will require Omnipotence to save me." Thus may we all feel. But satisfied and impressed that Jesus is divine, we confidently and safely trust in his almightiness to save us unto the uttermost. But essential as is this to our salvation, we are not saved by simple *power*. If this could have been, Jesus would not have tasted death for us. We must be saved in harmony with all the attributes of God and all the elements of the divine government; hence the second element in the foundation of Christ's almightiness to save, is

2. The completeness of the atonement he has made for us.

We have been redeemed not by power simply, but by *price*. A price beyond all price, even the precious blood of Christ. "Without shedding of blood there is no remission," but Jesus shed his blood for us. The price by Justice demanded was paid down and the covenant of grace therewith sealed. Now, God may be just and the justifier of all who believe in Jusus. Redemption's price was in harmony with the magnitude of humanity's offense, both were infinite.

> "The debt that sinners owed,
>   Upon the cross he paid."

But as we are not saved by simple power, so we are not saved by simple price, nor by the combination of power and price; hence the third element in this glorious foundation, viz.:

3. The efficacy and perpetuity of His intercession.

"He ever liveth to make intercession for us," and can "therefore save to the uttermost." "If any man sin, we have an advocate with the Father, even Jesus Christ the righteous." The death of Christ procured our redemption ; his intercession secures to us the benefits of that redemption. Without such intercession, the Father could not be long-suffering towards us, and we should be cut off. Nor could we have the help of the Holy Spirit to work in us enabling us to will, and do, and thus to work out our own salvatiou. But Jesus pleads. The Father spares. The Spirit strives. We repent, and believe, and Jesus saves. O the efficacy of his intercession! He pleads, not our innocence, but the infinite merits of his own blood! How can he but prevail! And this intercession is perpetual. " He ever liveth to make intercession."

A few years ago I visited a prisoner under a charge of murder. I attended the trial. His advocate was one of the most learned and eloquent I ever heard. The client had full confidence in his advocate, and the advocate seemed to make his client's cause his own. The pleading closed. The jury retired. We waited with great anxiety. They returned. The prisoner arose in his place. The jury was called to give the verdict, and replied—" Not guilty !" We gathered around the advocate and his acquitted client, and rejoiced' with them that the case was gained. A short time after I visited another prisoner soon to be tried for the same offense. He was an old man, and I pitied him much. The trial came. His advocate was as learned and eloquent as in the other case. The client had confidence in the advocate, and the advocate was fully confident of success. The pleading closed. The jury retired. We waited long and anxiously. They returned. Their verdict was called for, and they replied " Guilty !" We wept in pity for the old man condemned, and congratulated not his advocate, for his earnest and eloquent pleading had failed. Thus it is with advocates, in human courts of justice. To-day they succeed, to-morrow fail. But our Advocate in Heaven's court has never lost a case properly committed to his care, and never can, for he admits our guilt, and pleads the price by justice demanded in our behalf, and while he thus pleads,

> " The Father hears him pray,
> His dear anointed One,
> He cannot turn away
> The presence of his Son."

God be praised for such an Advocate !

Where, then, shall we find the limitation of God's power to save? With these elements blending, and harmonizing, his power is almighty !

But this power is exercised in harmony with the divine will, within the limits of the covenant of grace, which contracts to save all who repent and accept Christ by faith, as their personal and sufficient Saviour. He that believeth shall be saved.

(1.) *Personal Guilt*, therefore is not a limitation. Though our sins in multitude be as the sand's of ocean's shore, and in magnitude as mighty mountains, they may all be forgiven. Hear the words of one who had been a vile persecutor. " It is a faithful saying and worthy of all acceptation that Jesus Christ came into the word to save sinners, of whom I am chief." But O, how gloriously Jesus saved Saul of Tarsus, and made him Paul the Apostle ! The salvation of any sinner is a miracle of grace, but what a stupendous miracle to save the most guilty who are nearest the pit of destruction ! But it is written, " If *any man* will confess his sins, he is faithful and just to forgive him his sins and to cleanse him from all un-righteousness."

(2.) *Personal Moral Pollution* is not a limitation. The whole head may be sick, the whole heart faint, from the crown of the head to the sole of the foot, no soundness, but wounds, and bruises, and putrifying sores that have not been closed, neither bound up nor mollified without ointment, but Jesus can make us every whit whole. "Come now and let us reason together, saith the Lord; though your sins be as scarlet, they shall be as white as snow; though they be red like crimson, they shall be as wool." A wondrous power! But failure here would be fatal. If Jesus cannot save us from all moral pollution, he cannot save us at all, for "without holiness no man shall see the Lord." But the blood of Jesus Christ cleanseth from all sin. Could we draw aside the veil and look into heaven upon the white robed, we should doubtless see many whose sins have been of the deepest dye, and who were brought from the greatest depths of moral pollution. But the Almighty to save, brought them up, and washed them white, therefore are they before the throne. Could they speak to us, they would say "He saved us, surely he can save any; fear not; his power and willingness avails." Nor does he need the help of death, or his near approach, or purgatorial flames. He can do the work himself, and do it now. What a reflection upon Christ to say, He can save from all sin in death, or just before, but not in time to give us opportunity to illustrate to a wicked world, by a holy life, the mighty power of Jusus to save from all sin. He can save us now, for to-day is the day of full salvation.

> "Sing then of his mighty love,
> Mighty to save."

(3,) The temporary reign of death over our bodies, is not a limit. Death is a conquered foe; permitted to reign over our bodies for a time. But Jesus went into the grave and conquered the King of Terrors in his own realm, and became the first fruits of them that slept. When he rose—

> "Then, then I rose; then first humanity
> Triumphant past the crystal ports of light—
> Stupendous guest; and seized eternal youth—
> Seized in our name e'er since 'tis blasphemous
> To call man mortal, man's mortality
> Unalienably sealed to this frail frame,
> This child of dust. Man all immortal hail."

All we lost in Adam we shall regain in Christ. "As in Adam all died, even so in Christ shall all be made alive." "This corruptible must put on immortality. So when this corruptible shall have put on incorruption, and this mortal shall have put on immortality;" then shall be brought to pass the saying that is written, "Death is swallowed up in victory. O death, where is thy sting? O grave where is thy victory. The sting of death is sin; and the strength of sin is the law. But thanks be to God, which giveth us the victory, through our Lord Jesus Christ." *Mighty to save!*

Application.—In the combination of elements considered we have as clear and impressive evidence of the willingness, as of the almighty power of Jesus to save sinners; and come to the following conclusions:

1. The experience of the Church ought to be in harmony with the provisions divinely made for our salvation.

2. Any experience below the standard of salvation from all sin, is not in harmony with these provisions. There is a sad and humiliating discrepancy which greatly hinders the Church in the accomplishment of the glorious work of this world's conversion.

3. That the Church may be clothed with power to accomplish her blessed mission, harmony should be restored, and on the banners of the Church should be inscribed in letters of living light—*Holiness unto the Lord!*

4. Hence the propriety of making a specialty of holiness in this dispensation of the Spirit. These last times so near the approach of millennial glory.

> " Hasten, Lord, the perfect day ;
> Now thy every servant say,—
> I have now obtained the power,
> Born of God to sin no more."

5. The subject is full of encouragement to all who desire to be saved. Jesus is able and willing to save, and to save this hour. Hear him saying, " Come unto me all ye that labor and are heaven laden and I will give you rest." Come by faith, and he will give you rest from sin. Come test the power of his precious blood to cleanse from all sin. But come now, for to-morrow, to thee, may never be. *Now* is the accepted time—the day of *salvation.* Come to the *Mighty to save !*

AFTER THE SERMON.

During the delivery of Brother Turner's sermon a degree of enthusiasm had been awakened, which frequently found expression in "Amens" and the exclamation "Hallelujah!" At one passage the preacher asked the whole congregation to repeat in concert with him, "Mighty to save!" When he closed, under great excitement, Mr. Inskip rose to exhort. He enjoined upon every Christian before him solemnly to do whatsoever God should make plain to them as their present duty. He said, " I believe the hour is now at hand when the mighty baptism shall come upon this encampment. The great mental conflict through which I have been passing indicates to me the hour of victory is now upon us. Are you willing, every one of you, to do your duty, whatever it may be?"

Voices all through the audience—" Yes."

"God may send you forth, either alone or by twos, or in larger numbers, through the congregation, or to the tents, or to those who may be standing around the circle and on the outskirts of the camp, to invite and plead with sinners to come to Jesus. Will you do it?"

Scores reply—" Yes, we are ready."

"Be in earnest, then; and as you go, and where you go, say to every one, 'Come to Jesus.' I believe five hundred souls may be converted to-night. Now, are you ready?" Yes, they were ready. "Then get out from this altar. Clear a large space here. Open the way." Seeing persons lingering and talking, he thundered, "Get out of the way there, I command you! Don't be offended. We must see this through. Be still. I charge you to be quiet. Move on, and bring them in. Let sinners come and kneel here. Here they come!" Then was sung—

> "Come to Jesus, come to Jesus,
> Come to Jesus now;
> He will save you, He will save you,
> He will save you now."

A meeting of great activity followed, and many of those who came weeping for sin received pardoning grace; whilst those who went forth exhorting and persuading the impenitent, found access to hearts which melted under their appeals, and God was glorified in bringing wanderers back to his family and fold. The effect of such a movement, also, upon those who sprang to the work, was most blessed in an increase of light and liberty to their own souls.

EIGHTH DAY.

WEDNESDAY MORNING.

At the first sound of the bell on Wednesday morning, the encampment was aroused, and the early meeting brought out a large number of those who were awakened the previous night to feel the burden of their sins. The members of the National Association were all astir, attending to those who claimed their first sympathies—penitent souls. Believers, too, were at the altar seeking purity, and a glorious scene was experienced, in the display of converting and sanctifying power.

THE 8 O'CLOCK SERVICES.

Brother Gray, after reading a Psalm, made the following remarks: "The clearest and most acceptable form of faith is that of accepting God's promises, and waiting patiently for their fulfillment. The Psalmist said, 'I waited patiently for the Lord, and he inclined unto me and heard my cry.' I want some soul to receive the touches of the divine life in full salvation during this morning's meeting. Let us remember that the more we pray, the more we shall be blessed. O blessed Jesus, help us! Let us all come before God in supplication."

Then followed in rapid succession nine prayers, the time occupied in all being about fifteen minutes.

The spirit of devotion manifested in the prayers found expression in the song:

"I love thee, I love thee, I love thee, my Lord;
I love thee, my Saviour, I trust in thy word;
I love thee, I love thee, and that thou dost know,
But how much I love thee I never can show."

" Now," said Brother G., " we will have a short season for experience. Let your testimony be, not of the past, but how you are moving in the divine life this morning. The very first thing, when the light saluted my eyes this morning, I was constrained to say, 'Glory to God!' The baptism of last night was still resting on me." Singing—

"The blessing by faith I receive from above,
O glory! my soul is made perfect in love," &c.

In about half an hour, ninety persons testified to the work of salvation, as wrought in their hearts by the Holy Ghost.

HOLINESS AND TOBACCO.

When Brother Bell, of New York, and Brother Fish, of Philadelphia, delivered their testimonies against the use of tobacco, Rev. W. H. Boole arose and said: " I want just here, to put you on your guard against keeping the money in your pockets which comes from the abandonment of this abominable practice. There are some things that might as well be said here. I think it is not worth while to take up the time in addressing ladies in reference to the wearing of jewelry, &c. If they take Jesus for their portion, all right; if they prefer jewelry, they don't want Christ. It is a simple question. But, in regard to tobacco, you know it to be an inexcusable indulgence."

A brother—"I want to say something just here."

Brother Inskip—"Never mind, let Bro. Boole go on; he has 'struck oil' here."

The speaker then referred to the enormous waste of money in the use of tobacco, giving facts and figures to show that it is a most expensive as well as filthy indulgence. He then said: "Men are constantly provoking God, by putting the money in their pockets, which his salvation has brought them, in saving them from their vile habits. When the Church and world shall see that you do more for the cause of God, by the abandonment of your habits, then they will have the more confidence in the genuineness of the work as wrought in you.

"But, about this tobacco business, I want to say, no man ever got the witness of his full salvation, if he had been a victim to this habit, who can say that he received the blessing without its taking away the passion for tobacco. Every sanctified man on the continent will assent to that "

Bro. Inskip—" Bro. Boole, tell us right here, what is the effect on our justification, when we have the light of the present before us, on this question."

Bro. Boole—" When I come to the point of refusing to follow the light which shines around me, I lose my light of justification. If a man is convinced that it is wrong to use tobacco, he cannot do it and retain his justification. A man must walk up to the point of light that he has. I cannot think that any Christian who has attended through this series of meetings, is now, after all he has seen and heard, still indulging in this practice. (A voice: 'Yes, there is.') O let us have clean work.' Leave off this tobacco."

The question discussed was evidently an interesting one to all in the congregation.

Immediately upon the close of Bro. Boole's remarks, Rev. W. Post, of Western New York, then stepping forward, spoke at considerable length on

HOLINESS AND FREE MASONRY.

He said: "I feel moved by the Holy Spirit to speak. Bro. Boole has said much, and truthfully too, respecting the loss the Church sustains by the practices, and conformities he has mentioned. But, I desire to say, impelled by a sense of duty, though I would not on any consideration afflict any of Christ's little ones, that there is an evil, not yet referred to here, before which all the evils mentioned, dwindle into insignificance; one which, beyond them all, prevents the onward march of holiness in our Church. I have laid reputation and all, on the altar of God, and would willingly die for the Church, which I love as my life. I love my brethren; therefore, bear with me while I state my conviction that the greatest evil is oath-bound, secret organizations; Godless, and Christless; Godless because Christless; blasphemous and infidel; another religion than that of the Bible; whose origin is from the bottomless pit. I know whereof I affirm, being also in communication with some of the best minds of the country touching this matter. We find in a Masonic Ritual (Sickler's,) the first three degrees involves, 'all that the soul of man requires.' In another it is said in substance, if not word for word, that Masons living up to Masonic principles, 'are free from sin.'

"This is the thing' we have to grapple with, and contend against. In support, by a brief address, of certain resolutions, which I presented at our former E. G. Conference, Masonry was delineated and denounced, and certain expositions made, which induced a young minister—a master Mason—of another Conference, who read it, to say, the man is a Mason who delivered that address, because there are points in it understood only by Masons. This tended to confirm me that I knew something about Masonry. Besides, after I had delivered it, a Royal Arch Mason who had not been in the Lodge for many years, called on me and said: 'Bro. Post, I am glad you said what you did; every word of it is true, and when it becomes necessary you may use my name.' A Mason, now on this stand, said to me yesterday: After I obtained the blessing of sanctification, I sent word to the Lodge, ' when I wish to come back, I will let you know.'

"Now, brethren, if there can be found any where in any Masonic Ritual, up to the thirty-third degree, that faith in Christ Jesus is taught as a condition of salvation, I will at once and forever cease my aggression. I thank you, brethren for your kindness, and would say, I am all the Lord's, and love my blessed Jesus."

The delivery of this outspoken testimony was not endorsed by the National Association. The President said: " We do not want you to understand that Bro. Post has the full sympathy of this Association on this subject; some among us do not think as he does. There are many good men who think differently from our dear brother, but I know his heart is right, and with many things he said, I am myself in sympathy; but it is not profitable for us to discuss such matters, we think, in this meeting."

DR. LOWREY'S SERMON.

At 10 A. M., Rev. Dr. Lowrey preached from 1 John 5: 10. We can give but a bare synopsis of his clear exposition of this text.

He said: To believe is to have—to have a double blessing, to wit: salvation and a knowledge of salvation. These two elements can no more be separated than the sun can be separated from his rays, the rose from its fragrance, or the live heart from its pulsations.

A Christian is a composite number including two factors, faith, and its witness; and we can no more make a Christian without these parts than we can make an equation, without equal quantities, or a balance without equal weights. Faith in its actings is a duality, including cause and effect, substance and proof, a witness giving testimony to the conscience. The evidence of Christian purity is not from without, but from within. It is subjective, not objective. The process of arriving at a knowledge of the spiritual estate, is that of introspection and mutual analysis. The method, philosophically considered, is empirical, not deductive. A Christian therefore depends on experience, and the attestations are made to the heart in secret session with God.

The proposition of the text is that a believer is certified of his condition, and certified within himself.

By whom, and what, does a Christian know of these things? If such knowledge is attainable, it must be divinely communicated. A man may fancy, presume, and delude himself into a conceit of his excellence, but he cannot produce a conviction of the knowledge of salvation in his own mind, that will carry with it the consolations peculiar to a saved state. A partisan may be enthusiastically happy, a sinner daringly confident, and the arrogant pretender may be self-complacent and assured; but none can be positively certified, in the evangelical sense, of the soundness of his hopes and joys, until God seals him with the Holy Spirit of promise.

Competent evidence of a saved state must be a witness possessing these indisputable attributes; that is to say, supernatural, peculiar to Christianity, and adapted to every condition.   Pardon is an act of the Divine mind.   How can this be known, except by a direct revelation from God to the heart.   If the witness be something possessed in common by saints and sinners, it would be impossible to distinguish between a hilarious sinner, and a triumphant Christian. The speaker illustrated this point, by a prodigal child receiving equal favor with the other children.   He can only know the truth of his relation by some special, discriminating act.   So we must receive a token of favor altogether extraordinay, a recognition of sonship limited to Christians, and hidden from the world.

The witness must be adapted to every order, intellect, and diversity of condition.   It must carry conviction alike to the strongest and weakest intellect, to the darkest heart, and rudest specimen of human kind.   Any other witness, would be a class monoply, make God a respecter of persons, and show a serious defeat in the redemptive plan.

Is such a witness the privilege of believers, and does it enter as an element into Christian experience?   Let us examine: Is it possible?   It must be that he who made the mind and renews it, can communicate truth to its perceptions. What philosophical objection can there be to the hypothesis that God can, and does correspond directly with the heart?   Such a witness is probable.   Is it consistent with our ideas of God that he will dispense pardon, and yet do it secretly, that he may keep the justified man under a false sense of condemnation? Can the stream become sweeter than the source?

Such a witness is necessary to justify the representations of Scripture touching the magnitude and perceptibility of the change wrought in conversion.   Is Christian life a dream, an oblivion, a state of insensibility?   Does conversion so paralyze perception, abolish consciousness, and dethrone judgment that we cannot discriminate between life and death.

Finally, such a witness is certain, because it is promised of God, and actualized in the experiences of Christians, according to the Scriptures.

It is not a blind, unknowing feeling that something delightful has transpired in the department of our emotions, but a discriminating knowledge of the quality and origin of the work done and blessing bestowed.   It involves a new faculty of discernment.   The Christian's ken penetrates where the purblind sinner can have no insight.   He can detect a diamond, or pearl of great price, where the unbeliever sees nothing but mud.

In the acquisition of a knowledge of salvation there are three degrees: first, a change; second, a witness of the Spirit; third, the confirmatory testimonies relating to the genuineness of the work, and the credibility of the supposed witness of the Spirit.   These are blended together as the colors in the rainbow.

The assurance is like a beam of morning light peering in at our window, greeting our waking eyes, making our surroundings visible.   Evangelical truth and divine services become sweet, grateful and festive to the moral desires, like the finest of the wheat and honey from the rock to the appetite.

The second degree in the acquisition of this knowledge is the witness of the Spirit.   His work is twofold—to do, and to tell of doing.   He supplements the assurance with his own internal offices.   He locates himself in the heart as an abiding Comforter; He holds communion with the soul, keeps it in peace, replenishes with strength, sheds the love of God abroad therein, and carries on the work of refinement and holy culture without limit, as it is written, "He shall give you another Comforter," &c.   These fruits of the Spirit are not indigenous to the soul. They are exotics—importations; not a wild, casual growth, but the product of design and culture.

But how are we to know that this supposed knowledge of salvation is not a conceit, a fictitious belief, a delusion? This problem is solved by our mutual state and the character of our external conduct. It is by this we test the genuineness of the work and the validity of the supposed witness.

The mind is so constituted that it takes cognizance of its own operations. I can determine with absolute certainty whether my tastes are pure or vitiated; whether my feelings are exalted or groveling; whether my affections are refined or debased; whether my motives are righteous or wicked. When, therefore, I am conscious of an entire reversal of my sordid affections and propensities, and the Divine Spirit whispers, this is salvation, then my new exalted feelings, tastes, affections and motives rise up like so many unimpeachable witnesses. to establish the credibility of the testimony. Nothing spurious ever incorporates into itself elevating forces and love of sanctity. Pure Christianity alone antagonizes all sin. When my tastes, therefore, crave purity and loathe impurity, I know I am saved. "Hereby know we that we dwell in Him, and He in us, because He hath given us of His Spirit." Another test is external conformity to the law of God, not because it is an obligation, but because it is a pleasure. You may always tell a spirit by its element. The Christian does not find his element in the sinks and sewers of iniquity, and the sinner does not find his element in the sanctuaries and services of the Lord. By these supernatural and yet rational evidences the Christian is settled in the belief that he is saved; and so long as he remains faithful, the witness continues fixed and bright, like the stars of heaven, that shine on and on with undimned lustre through the ages.

What are the unfoldings of philosophy, the discoveries of science, or the results of travel and research, when placed in competition with the certitude of a present redemption; a sensibility of the fact; faith made fast in the wounds of the crucified; and a hope which couples the soul with immortality. Such knowledge is the candle of the Lord, lit by the Holy Ghost, to illume the midnight of man's condition.

WEDNESDAY AFTERNOON, JULY 30.

SERMON BY REV. F. HODGSON, D. D.

"And she shall bring forth a son, and thou shalt call his name Jesus, for he shall save his people from their sins."—Matt. 1: 21.

I suppose it is impossible for anyone to read the Scriptures without noticing the very conspicuous place assigned to the Messiah. He is represented as the Angel of the Covenant, of the Old Testament, who gave the law from Sinai, and led the children of Israel through the wilderness to the promised land.

13

It was part of the plan of human redemption that the Son of God should become incarnate. His coming was predicted by the prophets, by Moses, Isaiah, and others. The latest prediction of his coming was by the angel's announcement in the text, who not only declares that the proper time had come for the fulfillment of the prophecy concerning him, but dictates the name he shall bear: "Thou shalt call his name Jesus, for he shall save his people from their sins." This is its origin—not of the name, for that had been given before, but of its application to him.

The names of Scripture are usually—if not invariably—significant of something, of some event or attribute; and this is particularly the case with the names of Deity. This is true of the names of the Son. He is called Immanuel, God with us; Christ the annointed of God; Jesus; Saviour. We see in the text we have not only the name given, but the reason for it, and that a very special reason, namely, that he is called Jesus, because he saves his people from their sins.

I propose to make some remarks upon the salvation which he has come to effect. I have no thought of presenting anything new, or in a new way. I have, of late, been led to reflect upon the preachers and preaching of the olden time, and shall follow the old method the rather, in this discussion. I shall call attention, first, to the salvation of the text; and secondly, to the way in which Jesus saves his people.

I. *We shall consider the salvation under several familiar distinctions.*

1. The salvation of the text is salvation from the guilt of sin. You may say this is common-place enough: but if it were taken out of our doctrine, what should we do? Should any one of you be charged with a criminal act against the law of the land, O how eager you would be to employ the best counsel. If, upon the trial you should be convicted, how glad you would be for the pardon of the executive to be extended to you. Is it too much to say that this is nothing, as against the conviction of the soul for sin, when the sentence is suspended from execution by the pardon of God in this salvation?.

2. It is salvation from the power and control of sin. We transgress against the law of God because we choose to do it, but when our violations of God's laws are forgiven, though there may be no desire to commit sin, there may still be the tendency to depart from God; hence, the apostle Paul draws a distinction between sin dwelling in us, and sin committed by us. "If the tree be good, the fruit is good; if bad, the fruit is bad." The Saviour told the Pharisees that it was not so much what a man was outside, but what he was from within, that made the character of the life; and that "Out of the heart proceed evil thoughts, adulteries, murders, thefts, false witness and blasphemy." God must overcome the tyrant that occupies the citadel of the heart. There is a deep theological truth in the line—"He breaks the power of canceled sin."

3. It is a salvation from the very presence of sin in the heart. If the Bible said nothing about this, if its testimony was neither for nor against the destruction of sin out of the heart by the salvation of God, what would be our reasoning on the subject? We would say, if the Lord Jesus Christ, is manifested to take away sin, then it is fair to presume that its presence, as well as its power and guilt, must be removed by the atonement which he hath made.

But, are we not left to the indications of reason, for "The grace of God which bringeth salvation, hath appeared to all men, teaching us that, denying ungodliness and worldly lusts, we should live soberly, righteously, and godly, in this present world: looking for that blessed hope, and the glorious appearing of the great God, and our Saviour, Jesus Christ, who gave himself for us, that he might redeem us from all iniquity, and purify unto himself a peculiar people, zealous of good works."

The great plan of salvation, whether considered in its spirit, or symbols, is intended to make men holy. If God cannot do this, then the foundations on which the whole structure is builded crumbles under my feet. In accordance with this idea the apostle sweetly prays: "And the very God of peace sanctify you wholly, and I pray God that your whole soul, and body, and spirit, be preserved blameless unto the coming of our Lord Jesus Christ. Faithful is he that calleth you, who also will do it."

4. It is a salvation from the consequences of sin—not from all the consequences—certainly from the penal consequences. There are some conditions of things that the grace of God will not save the sinner from. A man may, in his youth, be profligate, and his errors may involve his health so as to destroy it; he may squander his patrimony; does he recover his lost health, or does salvation bring back into his hands the estate which his wickedness has bartered away? There are forms of sin which do special damage to the reputation. The victim of his vile passion whose name he has blasted does not have her character restored, nor her reputation secured from the ruin he has caused, by his repentance and salvation. These acts are embarrassments upon his plans: wherever he goes he is pointed at, as resting under suspicion. He must submit to long forbearance and patient endurance, to rejection on the one hand, and suspicion on the other; but, by a consistent course of conduct, he may, after a long time of trial, wipe away the stain that he has brought upon himself. Nevertheless, his deeds go with him wherever he goes. Can he, by the possession of grace in the heart, bring up from their bed in perdition, those young men whose lives his evil influence has ruined! It may be that he brought the gray hairs of his father or mother down with sorrow to the grave: will repenting over their cold graves bring them back to him again? So the backslider, who has gone away from God; can he bring himself back to his former position as a consistent member of the body of Christ? Although God will give deliverance from the penal consequences of sin, he never will give back the powers that have been lost by the destruction of natural forces or character.

Of this we are assured, that if we accept the salvation of Christ, it will deliver us from the guilt of sin, from its power and control, so that it shall not reign in our bodies; from its presence in the heart, so that all evil shall be banished from our nature; and from its consequences—deliverance from hell, from the grave by the resurrection of the body, and admission at last to the kingdom of heaven.

II. *How is this to be done ?*

1. Mainly by the atonement which delivers us from under the curse of the Adamic law. But if God should bring us out from under the Adamic law, and make no provision for satisfying the demands of that law, would it not be a reflection on him? Hence the atonement is a vindication of

that law, and puts before us a condition in which God may be just, and yet the justifier of him that believeth. I will illustrate this subject so that you may observe its connection with regard to the Christian doctrine of salvation. First: In regard to our pardon.

Suppose you or I were convicted of murder. We may hope for pardon; but in the absence of any provision for the same that will honorably meet our case, would we pronounce the Governor who signs the death warrant, a man who delights in blood? Is that the apprehension? Now just here is the difficulty. If he pardons me, he might as well pardon every other person. I am just as guilty, and am no more entitled to his clemency. Now suppose some friend interposes, and upon examining the case it is ascertained that the provisions of the law will, under certain conditions, be just as fully met by my pardon as by my execution. The friend tells me: I saw the Governor in your case, and by compliance with certain conditions made in pursuance of the law he will pardon. I say, is the Governor good enough to grant me the benefit of those conditions? Then I will accept them with all my heart.

The greatest interests of the divine government are all met by the provision of Jesus Christ in his atonement. By the shedding of blood there is remission. I want to accept it—for the law is magnified; and I am not only pardoned, but absolved. There's the breaking of the power of canceled sin.

If God should pardon a man for the sake of the atonement of Jesus Christ, we should feel that the Church is obliged to open its doors and take him in; and no one so pardoned can by any right interpretation of the law of God's government, be excluded from such communion. There is in the precious doctrine of the atonement provision for this entrance into the society of the believers, and elevation to sonship with God and heirship with Christ. There is that which tends to change the sinner's heart; there is a sanctifying element and a tendency to appropriate the blood of Jesus Christ, which cleanseth from all sin.

This is done again by the Holy Spirit. It is the Spirit's office and prerogative to change the heart of man, to renew him in the image of Christ. This is clearly taught in the Word. "The wind bloweth where it listeth, and ye hear the sound thereof, but cannot tell whence it cometh nor wither it goeth: so is every one that is born of the Spirit." The Spirit is the immediate cause of our justification and sanctification. This is done in part by the truth— "sanctify them through thy truth;" but to accomplish the result, there must be the direct influence of the Holy Ghost on the understanding and heart.

Here a question may arise: If the Holy Ghost is the direct agent of our sanctification, why do you attribute it to the blood of Christ? I answer the blood is the cleansing agent. "If we walk in the light as he is in the light, we have fellowship one with another; and the blood of Jesus Christ cleanseth us from all sin."

While some persons have a clear evidence of their acceptance, all do not. Some are very clear at first, others not so; yet they could say, "I know that I have passed from death unto life." I was brought out of darkness into light; but not first into midday. Have you a clear evidence of your acceptance with God? God prepares you for a deeper work of purity by throwing light on your defects. Are you in a very high state of grace but still without the fullness of the love of Christ? Will you say you cannot get the blessing of holiness here before you are instructed by the light of the Holy Spirit through the Word? Let us take a view of the matter : You come to the Word and to the Holy Ghost. But the Holy Ghost would say : I can do nothing without the blood. No wonder that now you triumph. When the light is given to see the stain of sin, and you by applying to the blood are cleansed, the Spirit behold-ing it, says the blood is on that spot. We need, therefore, have no diffi-culty.

Now let us in conclusion offer a few reflections ; and 1st, We are per-mitted to see in this subject the power of names. Suppose an American citizen is away from his home in the midst of a strange nation ; the very mention of his nationality is a passport to his protection. There is no name like that of Jesus. Whence is this ? Separate it from its associa-tions, and it is no more than any other name. It is not because of its euphony, for many names sound as well to the ear. Nor is it because Jesus means Saviour, simply. This is not sufficient ; Joshua means that. There have been a great many saviours. Washington was the saviour of his country, and his name is held sacred in the memory of the people ; but the name of Jesus towers above them all.

Here then is the solution. His name is the greatest name that ever was spoken, because he saves his people from their sins. None of the saviours we have mentioned could do this ; but he can and does, and the power of his name is celebrated in sacred song. "Our prophet, priest, and King." How then should we venerate his holy name ? Profane it not ; revere it, utter it with the utmost respect. Believe and be saved.

———

At the conclusion of Dr. Hodgson's sermon, Rev. J. E. Searles took charge of the meeting. He adverted to the theme of the hour, and, in illus-tration of the power of prayer, told the following story of a wounded boy, which occurred during the late civil war: He was found asleep at his post by the officer of the day, and, being reported, was court-martialed; and, according to military law, was sentenced to be shot. The sad tidings reach-ing his mother's ears, she at once sought a change of the sentence and the discharge of her boy. She made her way to the President's house, persist-ently pressed down all opposition, until at last she got an audience with Mr. Lincoln. She fell at his feet, made known her petition, and pleaded for the life of her son. The plea prevailed, and the President sent a relay of soldiers and a pardon for her son, restoring him, exonerated, to his mother. The son was told that he was free—that he could go home. He said, "No! I'll stay and show my gratitude to Mr. Lincoln and my country for giving me back my forfeited life."

Oh, mothers, pray for your sons and daughters, and present your plea in the name of Jesus!

Sinners were then invited forward, and quite a number responded to the invitation, and presented themselves at the altar. Seekers for full salvation, responding to the invitation, followed on, and kneeling, asked for pure hearts and the baptism of the Holy Ghost.

AT HALF-PAST ONE

The usual services were held in the Landisville pavilion, led by Rev. L. R. Dunn. There was great liberty in prayer, heartiness in singing and holy unction in experience.

Among others, Rev. I. M. See said: "I want to testify, because I am a Presbyterian by name"—here pausing a moment, Brother Dunn finished the sentence by adding—"And a Methodist in fact." "I don't care," Dr. See resumed, "what you call me, but I do care what you call this blessed experience. I do not like to see people ashamed to call this blessing by its proper name. I was twelve years in the ministry without this full salvation —living, indeed, a life of prayer, and so burdened with my many sins and failures, that I was pleading constantly that God might fulfill his promise, and give me deliverance. He sent heavy affliction on me. I sank down— down—into the depths of despair. But one name used to comfort me. It was the name of Jesus. In that condition I made such a consecration as I never made before. In looking about me, I found I had loved my wife more than God. I had to consecrate that wife, and, as Brother Earl said, attend my wife's funeral before the time. I had to give up Willie and Eddie and Mamie, and I gave Him all. I had been afraid my health of body would fail; but now I gave my body to God. The future used to trouble me, but I gave that up. It seemed so strange that I. M. See was to have no more anxiety. I have sweet songs in the night. I used to have long winters and short summers. Now I live in the tropics, and have no winter at all, but the fruits of the goodly land continually. There is, indeed, a rest to the people of God—a perpetual Sabbath-day keeping. Like one of old, I take the word of God and eat it."

Brother Bell, a missionary from Water street, New York, said he had much to be forgiven, and consequently loved much. "You can hardly realize how deeply I was sunken in sin. My being here is an evidence that the salvation of Christ Jesus is equal to any case or condition. I live my religion at home. I would not give two straws for a religion that did not make home sweet, and show itself in the treatment of the very dog and cat, as Rowland Hill used to say. I cannot say that I like to hear anybody call this world a 'waste, howling wilderness.' It is the best and sweetest world that I ever lived in, and I want to stay in it a long time yet. I am saved from fastidiousness and partiality. At our mission we have men with red shirts and with none, but I bid them all welcome; and if there is a million-aire present, I ask him to stand aside and give this poor man a seat. My voice is sanctified to God. At the midnight hour I go through the Fourth Ward in New York city, and sing of Jesus and his love in places where others would hardly show their heads, and God melts these hard hearts. I cultivate a cheerful disposition. To the wretched burglar I say, 'Look and live;' to Mary Magdalene, 'Look and live;' to the murderer, 'Look and live.' And they do look, blessed be God; and they find salvation."

The emotions awakened by this brother's talk we cannot attempt to describe.

Rev. A. Atwood exclaimed, "I am glad I have lived to see this day! I used to look about in my anxiety and say, 'O Lord, what will become of the Church?' Now, this National Camp-meeting is doing such a work that the love of spirituality is rising more in one year than in seven formerly. This full salvation makes me so happy in my home. When I sit down at the table with my wife, I look around and say, 'I never saw such a pleasant place as this. Do you suppose there is any one else as happy as we are?'"

Singing—

> " All glory to the dying Lamb.
> I now believe in Jesus;
> I love the blessed Saviour's name,
> I love the name of Jesus.
> Sweetest note in seraph's song,
> Sweetest name on mortal tongue,
> Sweetest carol ever sung,
> Jesus, Jesus, Jesus."

THE MINISTERS' MEETING.

At 6 P.M. Rev. J. E. Searles took charge, and Brother See invoked the presence and refining fire of the Holy Ghost on the kneeling company.

Brother Searles then remarked: "There are three things that we want. We need knowledge, purity and love. This is an excellent trinity." Refer-ring to his own experience, he said, "I was truly converted, and learned to set the Lord always before me. I lived in his fear, and prayed in my closet by the hour for grace to overcome the risings of sin in my soul. Yet I had no other idea than that I must always remain so. But when I went to Cali-fornia with the National Association, under this Tabernacle I had a mighty struggle. It lasted day after day. I had argued against this second blessing in the Preachers' Meetings. Now, could I go back on myself, and give up all my objections? I shall never forget the way Bro. Inskip took me in hand. With a voice as sweet and tender as a mother's, he said, 'Come, let us all go into the pool together.' Then he inquired, 'Do you now believe

that the blood of Jesus Christ his Son cleanseth from all sin?—cleanseth
me? I could hardly venture to say this; but, reverently I rested on the
promise of God. I was afraid of working up my feelings, and that the impression would die away; but, on the 6th of May two years ago, I was conscious of being filled with God and heaven. I said to my wife, 'I do believe
I am thoroughly sanctified.' I had been one of the timid ones, but this has
made me bold in witnessing and working for Christ."

A Baltimore minister said he had been again and again baptized with the
Spirit, but Satan would always be ready to whisper, "Now, look out; you
know how liable you are to fall into sin. If you make a loud profession, and
do not live up to it, you will bring disgrace upon the cause you love so well;
keep quiet." Thus he failed to confess distinctively this sanctifying grace,
and lost it. "I came here," he continued, "to obtain such a blessing as
would settle and fix my wavering soul forever. Last night I wandered off
into the woods, and at the foot of a large tree I knelt and prayed that God
would fully save me, and take the roots of sin out of my nature. The Divine
Spirit was poured out, and I was unusually blessed. I am not yet satisfied.
I want thorough cleansing and clear experience."

Brother McFarlane, of Yonkers, N. Y., said he had contented himself
since he came on the ground with listening and drinking in the sweet joys
which abounded here at every service. The place he lived in he named
"Sweet Home," as a memorial of what God had done for him. Jesus occupied the guest-chamber, and was always present at the sweet hour of family
prayer, and when his dear name was celebrated in song. He had precious
rest of soul.

Brother Foote, alluding to the cases of our brothers Barker and Bell, both
of whom were amazing monuments of Divine mercy, in being brought up out
of a horrible pit, said he had more reason than either of them to be thankful
to God for the way in which he had been led and kept. "God," said he,
"saw such a germ of wickedness in me, that, to prevent its development, and
all the harm it would have done, he was pleased that I should be born of a
Christian mother, and converted at an early period of my life. He saw what
depths of iniquity I was capable of reaching, and prevented it. Glory to his
name! I was sanctified early in my ministry, and this was an incalculable
blessing. Oh, let me exhort young ministers to get this blessing!"

"All ministers," said Brother McDonald, "whether young or old, should
have it—and may have it now, if they desire it, and exercise faith."

In this meeting, Rev. Dr. Levy, in relating his experience said: "I denounced this doctrine, which I now uphold. I was more excusable than you
Methodist brethren, because I did it in ignorance.

"A sister in my congregation professed sanctification, and I took occasion
to tell her that I thought there was a great deal more consistency in living

right than in professing so much. She was a good sister, and when I become convinced of my error, I at once thought I offended her, and at my first
opportunity would make amends.

"The 'sanctificationists' as we called them were beginning to make a stir
among us, and I and another minister agreed to open our batteries simultaneously against the dogma. I went to my study and made a careful preparation.
There was a deacon, a good brother, in my charge with whom I always took
tea on Saturday. I said to him at the table, 'Dr. Fish and I, are going to
preach to-morrow against this new fangled doctrine of sanctification.' He
looked grave and troubled, and at last said solemnly, 'I think any minister
has mistaken his calling when he preaches against anything that has for its
only object, the making of people better.' I wilted down under the force of
that logic. When I went home I burned the sermon, and never preached it.

"After the blessed Lord brought me into the enjoyment of this sweet experience, I met the dear sister of whom I have just spoken, and I said to her :
'Sister I want to ask your forgiveness for my cruelty towards you.' She did
not recall it until I told her the circumstances ; and when I finished by saying, I am now wholly the Lord's, we had a gracious time of congratulation.
Bless the Lord !"

Rev. Dr. Lowrey said : "I was converted in 1833, received the clear evidence of adoption in 1842, and the evidence of sanctification in the same
way. The spirit reported the fact to my consciousness. Methodist preachers
stand in very intimate relation to this subject, it being presented to them
both in our examinations and theological training. So long as I retained my
justified state, I hungered for holiness. I read Wesley's Plain Account of
Christian Perfection, I was committed to this subject before I was ordained.
Bishop Morris, questioning me before the Conference, asked, 'Are you going
on to perfection ? Do you expect to be made perfect in love in this life ?
Are you groaning after it ?' To these questions I answered ' Yes.' I was in
the habit of praying and fasting then. I hungered about three months in
this way, when the Lord Jesus Christ fully saved my soul.

"I made two mistakes. When I was converted, I did not confess it for
more than about two years, except to one person. I therefore lost the evidence of my conversion. I made the same mistake in regard to sanctification. Several years ago I felt that this would not do, and I resolved I would
find my lost treasure. I did like the woman in the Gospel who was in search
of the lost piece of silver, I swept the house and continued seeking until I
found it."

Dr. Hodgson of Central Pennsylvania Conference stepped forward and
said: "I came here not to see my friends, though I am in the midst of them.
I came here to be blessed with the communication of the divine fullness. I
came here to be entirely sanctified. I have preached this old Methodist doc-

trine. I have believed it with all my heart; and there was a time when I would have fought for it. Now there is nothing on earth I so much desire, as this blessing. Pray for me."

Bro. Osborne here stated, that under a mighty sermon, preached by Dr. Hodgson at Red Lion, Delaware, he was convicted and led to the Saviour. Scores of others were present, who had been thrilled under his ministry, and the general prayer was, "Lord, bless Dr. Hodgson !"

EVENING SERVICES.

The interest was so absorbing at the Preachers' meeting, that it required considerable bell-ringing to call the people who lingered in the Tabernacle, out to public worship.

The grounds were beautifully lighted. A clear, starry sky, with a silvery moon above, lent enchantment to the scene. During the day, the congregations had been larger than usual, many strangers having arrived to stay until the close of the meeting. A more imposing audience than that before which the preacher of the evening stood up to declare a message from God, he had probably never seen.

The preacher was our stalwart brother, Rev. Wm. Bramwell Osborn, a man who, in the pine forests of Cape May county, N. J., as an itinerant preacher, first became exercised about a "deeper work of grace," in his own heart. His native energy availed him to the extent of finding "full salvation." He thereupon began to labor "on this line ;" and by what many of a more timid temperament regarded as of doubtful propriety, agitated the holding of a camp-meeting for the express purpose of promoting gospel holiness. At his instance, the first National camp-meeting was proposed and held, the METHODIST HOME JOURNAL, of Philadelphia, becoming an early and serviceable ally in the cause.

He is also responsible for another vagary, as it was termed at its inception—the founding of Ocean Grove, from which pleasant retreat he was called by Episcopal authority to assume the charge of a section of the work as Presiding Elder, in the State of Florida. Relieved from service there, he appeared among his co-laborers of the National Association, a few days previously, and now it came his turn to preach.

Brother Osborn is gifted with a commanding presence, and the voice of a Stentor. He took up the cry of the Prophet of old, when addressing the Church (Isa. 57: 1,) and made a fearless onslaught on the sins and idolatries of modern times. What the Church of God ought to be—her light having come, and the glory of the Lord having risen upon her, he faithfully portrayed. What she is, worldly, weak and inefficient, he had ample illustration at hand to show. He spared not. The exceeding broad requirement—to be pure and holy—to practice charity, self-denial and benevolence, was made apparent. Men's various subterfuges, and women's nonsensical fashions were exposed with indignant remonstrance, mingled with humor and satire, and we hardly think it possible one sinner, or formal professor, escaped a scathing.

His own experience, intermingled with the word of exhortation, gave piquancy to the occasion; and as he pointed to the mercy seat where a pardoning God waits to receive and bless the penitent, and the glorious provision made in the "fountain opened," the congregation were ready to enter into the spirit of his favorite hymn as he sang—

> "O bliss of the purified, bliss of the free,
> I plunge in the crimson tide opened for me;
> O'er sin and uncleanliness, exulting I stand,
> And point to the print of the nails in His hand.
>
> O sing of His mighty love,
> Sing of His mighty love,
> Sing of His mighty love,
> Mighty to save."

This sentiment recalled the leading theme of the preceding evening, and again all who had hearts to feel, and a voice to plead, were urged to go out after the unconverted, and persuade them to an immediate surrender to Christ the Saviour.

The meeting was attended with marked results in the salvation of souls, and up to the hour for general silence, the song and shout of the newly born of God sweetly blended, making the woods vocal with heavenly melody.

THE COLORED PEOPLE'S MEETING.

An event of the evening was the meeting conducted by Sister Smith in the large board tabernacle, for the benefit of the colored people, quite a number of whom were in attendance as waiters, and some as visitors at the encampment.

At the very opening of the services the lively and impressible nature of this class began to exhibit itself. The singing was so full of soul-stirring power, that it soon attracted a large crowd of white spectators and participants. In prayer there was a considerable margin of eccentricity, but entirely characteristic and sincere.

As far as it was possible or prudent to do so, Sister Smith kept her congregation under good control, walking up and down among those who were kneeling and seeking salvation. Her design was to show them the simple way to be saved by faith, and to testify to all, from her own past experience, that they might partake of the water flowing out of the smitten rock in the desert, which rock was Christ.

"This pure stream," she said, "would give them new life, and wash all their guilty stains away."

> "The fountain lies open,
> The fountain lies open,
> There I'll bathe my weary soul."

In the experience given there was a quaint pathos and tenderness that touched very deeply the sympathies of their white brethren and sisters looking on. A very aged woman said the blessed Lord had called her to take up the cross and follow him seventy years ago; and he had been her friend ever since, and was better to her now than ever before. "The land was heaving into view," she said, and she was "waiting for the chariot of Israel to come along and take her to the place of many mansions."

A younger person rose to speak, and asked all to pray for her old aunt, who sat there without any hope in God. She wanted to see her converted then and there, for soon, she argued, it will be with her too late, and the door will be shut forever.

This brought all to their knees, and, while prayer was offered, the aged aunt professed to find the Lord, and many others, with her, were powerfully blessed. Then was sung—

> "My sins are washed away
> In the blood of the Lamb;
> My sins are washed away
> In the blood of the Lamb,
> Glory to the Lamb," &c.

Shouting, with these humble souls, means always an accompaniment of clapping of hands and lively bodily exercise, such as walking and leaping and praising God.

It was near midnight when these demonstrations entirely ceased, and, to the credit of the authorities, nobody interfered to break up their meeting or enforce the rules of the ground.

Most welcome to those who had attended camp-meetings in Maryland and Virginia, in former years, was the sensation of falling into unconscious slumber, with the full chorus of a happy band of colored people sounding in their ears—

> "Hallelujah to the Lamb,
> Jesus died for every man," &c.

The old usage was to let them have the last part of the night service, and begin as early in the morning as they pleased, which was generally at the break of day. Sinking to sleep, therefore, and the first waking moments, were associated with these pathetic, and often expressive and beautiful melodies.

It is said of the excellent Governor Bassett, of Delaware, that he always pitched his tent as near to that part of the ground devoted to the black people as he could, so that he might enjoy, to the fullest extent, the harmony and deep religious sentiment of their camp-meeting songs; and he never complained if they sang and prayed and shouted all night.

NINTH DAY.

THURSDAY MORNING.

Reaching this point in the narrative of the proceedings, we are admonished that the matter on hand, unless abbreviated to some considerable extent, will exceed the limits prescribed.

Among the readers of these pages will be many who were participants in all the services of this, the last great day of the feast. Its scenes, doubtless, were so indelibly fixed on their memory, that they will readily perceive the omission, where we pass over thrilling experiences, and present only an abstract of the successive services of the day.

A more lovely morning it seemed, never dawned on the world than this last day of July, 1873. So deeply were the people imbued with the spirit of praise, that a doxology was in every heart and on every tongue, as the opening heavens and the rising sun, called them once more to devotion.

Father Coleman, at the five o'clock service, encouraged all to expect greater things. Compared with the soul-capacity God had given us, and the boundlessness of his power to fill and bless, it might be said comparatively : " Hitherto ye have asked nothing ; ask and receive, that your joy may be full."

The largest portion of time, and interest, he contended, should now be devoted to " impotent folk," who had not succeeded in getting into the pool. They must be saved to day—they should be saved this morning. Let those who have faith help them. Every moment is precious.

The rapidly passing time was filled up with brief testimonies, and the usual singing and prayer at suitable intervals.

The spirit of the occasion then followed the people to the restaurant, where, during the breakfast hour, the place presented a spectacle of wonderful interest. People praised the Lord ; those who had remained unconverted were brought under conviction, and waiters, while busy at their work, were weeping with godly sorrow for sin, or joining in the stanza :

> " My God is reconciled,
>   His pardoning voice I hear,
> He owns me for His child,
>   I can no longer fear.
> Jesus paid all—all to him I owe,
>   Sin had left a crimson stain,
> He washed me white as snow."

A prayer offered at the opening services—that nobody might come on the encampment during the days then ensuing, without being brought in direct contact with spiritual influence, had been answered in uncounted instances, and in no case more specifically than at this juncture. It would seem that, as in the "upper room" at Jerusalem, so here, "they were all filled with the Spirit." The conversation at table was of "refining fire." Groups here and there under the shade of the forest trees, were rejoicing together in "the abundance of peace." Whenever a person confessed discouragement or doubt in a meeting, he was noticed, and followed after by twos and threes, who engaged him in private conversation, and never slacked their interest in his case until he was enabled to "step out fearlessly on the promises," and go forward with new confidence and joy, in the way of holiness.

"I never saw the like of this," was the oft repeated remark. "Everybody you meet begins to speak of Jesus, and his uttermost salvation. Every group of persons you overhear talking, are interested in the one subject. An irreligious man, drifting in here finds nothing congenial to ordinary modes of life, and must soon get away, or ' go down ' and pray to be converted."

If there were exceptions to this rule, they were found among the " case-hardened" members of Christian families, who become familiar with such scenes.

AT 8 O'CLOCK

The congregation assembled in front of the main stand was very large. Rev. J. B. Foote had charge of the exercises. For some days past this brother's presence and voice was seen and heard in every meeting. Tireless, he seemed, in the activities of the occasion. His rest was labor; his joy, to see such numbers in the valley of decision, and catching the earnestness of his own spirit, pressing towards the mark—perfect love.

The meeting was opened by singing-

> " There is a gate stands open wide,
> And through its portals gleaming,
> A radiance from the Saviour's side,
> His wondrous love revealing.
>
> "O depths of mercy can it be,
> That gate stands open wide for me—
> Stands open wide both night and day—
> Stands open wide for me? "
>
> " O blessed Spirit lead me in,
> And let me falter never,
> Make me a victor over sin,
> I'll praise Thy name forever." &c.

" Well," said the leader, " if the gate now stands wide open, lets go right in—clear in, and down to bed-rock, out into clear light, and up into pure air. God grant we may get this day, the last day of our meeting, the most solid, the clearest and purest experience of all we have yet received."

The answer was a prolonged "Amen."

Sister Amanda Smith was called on to pray, and was followed by Bro Foote; the fervor increasing every moment.

After singing again Bro. F. said, "It is appropriate, as we are now nearing the close of our meeting, to inquire after our exact whereabouts. The voyager crossing the ocean, as he approaches the port, examines his condition, and finishes any necessary matter preparatory to landing. The business man making preparations for some new enterprise on the day preceding its commencement, reviews his propositions to see if all is ready. So ought we now endeavor to know how far we have advanced in our searchings and preparations. Have I made a full surrender? Am I cleansed from all sin? Have I received the Holy Ghost, and do I possess the full endowment of power? Let us speak to these points as near as we may. We might call this a *position meeting*."

There was no hesitancy. The stand was crowded with ministers, and every man of them seemed ready to testify.

Some deference, however, was shown to those who had not spoken previously.

Rev. Bro. Long, of the Pittsburg Conference, Major, of Philadelphia, Dunn, of Newark Conference, in rapid succession, defined their position, some of them growing enthusiastic to a high degree, as they recalled the glorious circumstances of their full salvation in Christ Jesus.

Responses increased, showing the lively attention given by the audience.

A narrative of his early life was given by Bro. Bell of New York, describing the evil associations, which like hooks of steel bound him to vicious habits and reckless pursuits. But he was rescued by grace, and now counted it his greatest happiness to

"Tell to sinners round
What a dear Saviour he had found;
To point to His redeeming blood,
And say, Behold the way to God."

The facts and incidents of his mission life in the dens of vice in Water street, were of a thrilling character. With such evidence as he gathered daily, showing the saving and purifying power of the gospel, he could not doubt God, and exhorted all present to believe for a perfect and complete salvation.

With unwonted energy the congregation joined in that happy refrain from the Sabbath-school:

"I am so glad that our Father in heaven,
Tells of his love in the book he has given,
Wonderful things in the Bible I see,
This is dearest that Jesus loves me.
I am so glad that Jesus loves me,
Jesus loves me, Jesus loves me,
I am so glad that Jesus loves me,
Jesus loves even me."

"I feel," said Brother Foote, "a warm affection for Brother Inskip and the brethren of the National Association, although I cannot speak of being incited to seek holiness by their ministrations. I entered into this experience before I ever saw or heard of any one of them. Now, I want to say that this experience came to me after six years of service as a Christian, during which I did not backslide. I was first converted when little less than thirteen, but took a new start at the age of sixteen, from which time on I never neglected a class or prayer meeting through any indifference, and never failed to take part either in praying or speaking, except once; and for that I did not feel condemned at all, for the whole six years, up to the time at the age of twenty-two, on the 9th day of July, 1848, when I entered into this blessed state of triumph and rest.

"It was in a class-meeting. I had been most earnestly canvassing this whole subject for weeks, and, especially the few preceding days, I had the fiercest struggle of soul over the question of a full consecration and a full cleansing. In this state of mind I went as usual to class; not in condemnation for any transgression—not with any sense of guilt—but with a feeling of sinfulness and humiliation and depression almost unbearable. The class leader asked me to open with prayer. I turned to refuse, but remembered that, although I had been often asked to pray in such meetings, and at the family altar, and in Presbyterian prayer meetings—for my parents were Presbyterians, and I had often gone to their meetings—and had never declined, I would not decline now. After prayer, to my great grief, he called on me to lead the class. Now, I never was a class leader in fact; yet I was sometimes called on to assist in this way, and had never refused; and so, somehow, I dare not now. It seemed as though I never heard the old brethren of the class say so much about entire sanctification as they did then. There was one influential man, a banker, not remarkable for his piety, I thought, yet that night, in the most tender and touching manner, he expressed his interest in this special subject, and wished he and all the others might enjoy it.

"How could I give any advice to him? I only spoke of myself; and so I continued again and again confessing my own deeply-felt need, my longing, and at length my willingness to surrender wholly to Jesus, and fully accept him as my 'all in all.' I can't give the details, or describe my feelings just then; suffice it to say, that just as I stood under the pressure of deep emotion, trembling and silent, the gentle voice of a precious sister broke out in singing—

"I believe it, I believe it, just now."

Jesus at that moment took full possession, and everything contrary to his will receded. I know that, not in a backslidden state, I received a distinct and instantaneous cleansing from all sin and a baptism of power on my heart; and I received it by simple self-abandonment, and faith in the all-efficacious merit and love of Jesus Christ.

"Next day I wrote a full description in my journal, covering a number of pages; and, some months ago, I hunted up the old journal, to see if my experience at that time agreed with the theory I have become established in after years of mature investigation, and I found it was genuine and orthodox, according to the Bible and Methodist standards. I wish I had been more steady and definite, and always pronounced on the subject; but, thanks to God, for eight years past I have enjoyed a steady, precious light shining into my heart, and I am glad to testify that my experience does corroborate the doctrine of entire sanctification, as a distinct and instantaneous blessing, 'receivable now by faith.'"

Brother Inskip here came to the front, saying the uniform and unvarying testimony of all who had spoken was to the same end—sanctification, a distinct and instantaneous blessing, to be received by faith, and hence to be received now.

"Who will receive it? The matter is simplified to this point—'whosoever will.' If there is no existing antipathy to holiness—if you really want this full salvation—it is free. You can by faith, this moment, appropriate all that the promise of God signifies. Let all who sincerely want the fullness come forward, and spend awhile, in this place of consecration and prayer, and have the victory that comes by believing."

Dr. Hodgson, being on the stand, rose up among the first, and, proceeding to speak, everything was hushed to hear his words. He said: "I have been present at a great many camp-meetings, and have generally attended with a view of preaching one or more sermons. But I did not come to this meeting to preach sermons; nor did I come here to enjoy social intercourse with my friends. *I came to be blessed.* You know what that means. That is what most of you came for. I want a blessing. I am conscious of a want beyond what I have in my present experience. I dare not say I never experienced this special blessing; I dare not say I enjoy it. I propose to go down, and I do want your prayers."

He grew touchingly earnest as he continued to speak of his feelings, and deliberately stepped down off the stand, followed by a long line of preachers, whose hearts were melted by such an unexpected movement, and tears were running from many eyes.

Just before Dr. H. knelt down, he turned and waved his hand to those standing around and still on the platform, saying, "I want you all to understand that I do not regard this as going down in any sense of humiliation. I don't feel that way at all—rather a high privilege."

The moral effect of this short, simple address, and the movement by which it was accompanied, was perceptible on all present. The few ministers and prominent laymen who had kept aloof from the altar, and spent their spare

14

hours disputing about modes of operation and technical points in phraseology, and whose self-respect, as they thought, would be compromised by the admission that any man's dictation was entitled to their attention, appeared to be nonplussed.

Here was a really great and strong man—one on whose carefully-matured judgment and discrimination they had relied to expose the flaws and illogical assumptions of those who were associated in the "holiness movement"—now on his knees as a seeker of "this blessing." They evidently felt uncomfortable, but would not yield to the force of any new convictions which may have seized them, and their voice was not heard in the hymn or shout, which told the listening earth and the bending heavens—

"Washed in the blood of the Lamb!"

We cannot better describe the meeting of this morning than as a "Modern Pentecost." The power was experienced in more than one hundred and twenty hearts. God was apprehended as graciously near, and nobody that we noticed among the rejoicing throng were more happy in an assured sense of the Divine favor than those who saw in all that transpired a direct and signal answer to their own prayers.

Before Brother Barker's address, Dr. Levy offered thanks to the blessed Saviour, who had been in the garden here, gathering lilies—alluding to the conversion of one hundred and forty-five children; and, using the beautiful figure from Canticles, he added: "We have found a place in thy loving bosom, let us now reach up and enjoy the kisses of thy lips."

<hr>

THURSDAY, 10 A. M.

ADDRESS BY REV. JOSEPH BARKER.

The announcement that Rev. Joseph Barker was about to speak at 10 o'clock excited pleasurable anticipations, and drew out a very large congregation at that hour. A hymn was sung, and Dr. Levy offered a deeply affecting prayer.

The hymn, "Jesus, lover of my soul," followed, notices were given, and Brother Barker was introduced to the audience, and proceeded to say:

I am to-day going to tell you my own experience. I am a believer in the doctrine of holiness, the profession of which is enjoined on us as a duty, presented as a great privilege, and a requisite for admission to heaven ; to be obtained by faith in Christ, to be sought and obtained now, and to be enjoyed forever. God make me to realize it fully, and keep me ever in its enjoyment !

I shall read to you the following passage : " As a shepherd seeketh out his flock in the day that he is among his sheep that are scattered ; so will I seek out my sheep, and will deliver them out of all places where they have been scattered in the cloudy and dark day." Ezekiel 34, 12.

There are some people who begin Christian life well, who seek and find the Lord early in life, and move right on in a straight direction toward heaven ; their path is the path of the just, which, as a shining light, shineth more and more unto the perfect day.

Others for a time have run well, but stray away and wander into doubt and unbelief. This was my case. You ask, "How happened it that you fell under the influence of doubt and unbelief?" I will tell you. But there are several forms of skepticism, which arise from various causes. It arises sometimes from habits of vice, from a love of forbidden pleasures— men choosing darkness rather than light, because their deeds are evil.

Again it comes through other causes. Thomas was a doubter ; so was John the Baptist. His feet were well nigh gone, because darkness was over him and hung in clouds around the providence of God ; he was disappointed in Christ. So people are constantly inclined to doubt in hours of affliction, not understanding the mysteries in nature, in history, and in ourselves, that we cannot solve.

I was not led into unbelief from any of these causes. I never fell so low as to chew tobacco, drink beer, etc. If you allow a little leaven of bad feeling to get into your mind, in time it will go through your whole nature; and this, in part, is the explanation of my fall. I got bad feeling toward my brethren, and then I grew cold.

I will tell you how it all happened. As a young minister I wanted to feel that I was right in my belief ; to assure myself I went through and through the Scriptures. I discovered some things that my brethren never taught, which I thought vital, and I could not leave them out. I found if I was to bring my mind to receive these things, I must make alterations in my teachings. I did so. Then the brethren whispered, and muttered complaints. I defended myself as best I could ; this provoked controversy, and acrimony. I was a practical preacher ; I would not preach speculative or controversial sermons; I wanted to press Christians onward in the way to heaven, and I could not do that without sifting the Church of those who ought not to be there. My brethren could not think it right for me to do this, and in this was a cause of grievance.

I wanted to make things very plain, but I had to deal with English folks and queer communities. I saw members in the Church that could fail seven times and yet be sustained as though their action was all upright. In my own Church, among members and leaders in it, I would talk discipline, and that made fresh trouble; and yet I saw where forty men had to go out of an American Church on account of imprudences in life, to one on account of bad conduct. The Church of which I was a minister was a small body, not Wesleyan. My brethren thought I was impracticable, and hence I became more and more obnoxious to them.

At this time I became the publisher of a periodical, in which I fully expressed my own views ; it was called the EVANGELICAL REFORMER, and soon obtained an extensive circulation. But before Conference came on I saw that I was to be brought into relations of opposition ; charges were brought up against me. I was arraigned before Conference ; not yielding to their demands, I was expelled. I was not so far sanctified as to bear these things with a Christian spirit, and I found myself in a condition of hatred toward my brethren.

The farther I got from that kind of people, I thought, the better. I became greatly excited, and excitement in a wrong cause is a dreadful thing. I have two friends who once were canvassing for votes. One of them said, " Who's John Miles going to vote for?" Being answered, he said, " Then I'll go the other way." Miles had defrauded him in a business transaction. I saw some ministers and Church members go by the houses of the poor, paying them no attention, but making their calls upon rich men. The feelings being changed, change everything. Everything we do is tinged with it ; every sermon grows more severe with the work of exposure and denunciation. All this time a man may be the same that he ever was, but we fail to recognize it. I had this weakness. If any of you think you have it not, you may set it down that you have a double portion of it.

That I might preach without salary, I learned the art of printing. I wrote and published extensively. I went on investigating matters with a view to ascertain their full bearing. My brethren withdrew from me, and being bold and outspoken, I drifted away from Christ.

I found myself drawing near to Unitarianism, and they gladly came near to me, to help me on my downward way. Unitarianism is not one thing but everything, from a close proximity to Christianity to the most violent form of infidelity. Those nearer the truth may drift the farther from it, and yet by that system be accounted good disciples. It is a bad stream. I came in my progress near to utter deism. Then I got into politics, and found myself in a whirl of double excitement. I was prosecuted by the government, was thrown in prison where I remained eighteen months. In the midst of all this my health failed.

I resolved then that I would come to America. My family now began to entertain the suspicion that I had drifted away from Christianity. Arriving in this country, I bought a large farm in central Ohio, where I might have done well and lived at ease. I became an old fashioned Garrisonian Abolitionist, and entered heartily into association with its leaders. Of that company all were infidels but one. I became a Woman's Rights advocate. I might have enjoyed myself if I had been prudent, but I obtruded my opinions on my neighbors in lectures until I excited their indignation and scorn. In my last lecture the young men resolved that they would reward me. They therefore surrounded the place, having first supplied themselves plentifully with rotten eggs. I took a different course homeward than they expected, and by mistake they gave their father the eggs. But I was not to get off so easily ; they pulled down the fences of my farm, and subjected me to many annoyances. They determined to make me move. So I sold out my farm, and bought property thirty miles farther west among a people called "Come-outers" Here, because I would not lead the life of abandon, I became a source of trouble. They were the vilest sort of men, these infidel persecutors. I moved again, this time going far into the wilderness of Nebraska, then twice as large as Pennsylvania, and having, through that vast territory, only about 2,000 inhabitants. Here I was therefore safe. I settled and devoted myself to the improvement of my property.

It became at length to be suspected that I was returning to a better life. I began to be quiet, for here I had rest and opportunity for thought, and from that settlement, so far removed from the life I had been living, God's good spirit began to work upon my heart.

I now saw how much I had lost by my course of life; the world looked dark and dreary to me; I wished I had never been born. I was tempted to relieve myself by a fatal step. Suicide is the one consolation and last refuge of a poor infidel. God kept me from it. I found that infidelity did not meet the wants of my soul. Any man of heart wants more than it can furnish; he wants a Father, a Saviour, a Holy Spirit. I found therefore more difficulty on the side of infidelity than Christianity. I saw a man could not be good away from Christ and the Bible. The more I got to know of infidelity, the more I despised it. Out in this vast wilderness I felt strange thoughts come into my mind. Then the influence of my family came over me. I felt that my children were believers under the shadow of an unbelieving father. I recalled the earnest entreaty of my mother, " Joseph, don't leave God, or deny your Saviour."

Then again affliction came upon my family. One of my children died, and O, I thought of the time when I could have prayed, but now it seemed I could not.

I was involved financially. In three weeks I lost $50,000.

Being invited to lecture, I went to Philadelphia, and was there engaged for three months. I said to those of my old associates who gathered around me, we can't make folks good by infidelity. Then I went again to the churches, but finding no rest for my troubled spirit, I said "I'll go to my native country, and there I'll publish a periodical in which I will investigate in the most thorough manner this whole subject." I left Philadelphia and started for England. On board the vessel my daughter said, " Father, when you go to England, don't think of such a thing as writing against Christianity." I landed in safety, and in a short time connected myself with a paper which I did not like; my family found out where I was, and it gave them distress. In a little while an infidel book was put in my hand for review. I opposed its filth and pernicious sentiments, and it created dissatisfaction.

I then started a periodical of my own. I said in my very first issue, that I had resolved to review Christianity; to examine the character of its founder, and try to ascertain the true nature and real value of his teachings and his spirit.

I kept that resolution. When I came to read the Bible over I found something good in every step I took. Passages which had suggested objections on former occasions now presented themselves in a different light. I went through the book of Job, and it melted me. I was astonished at the vastness and depths of the wisdom of the Book of Proverbs, the salutary influence of the teachings of the prophets, who were men of clear vision, of great wisdom and amazing powers, whose aim was to make men true and good. So I passed on until I came to the Gospels. Then I got sight of Jesus of Nazareth; that view melted my whole soul. I wept; moistening with my tears the book in which I was reading, and the paper on which I was writing. I saw in him first the perfection, the grandeur, the glory of all human excellency; and I drew his portrait accordingly, and sent off the articles to the press. My daughters, when they read the proofs, said: "Father is coming right again." I had no thought of getting into close quarters with Jesus the Christ; but as I looked upon him my soul was drawn by a powerful attraction, and he looked on me. Then he reached out his hands and took hold of me, and I took hold of him. In the grapple for life, he saved me!

From that day to this I have been working for God in England and America.

All glory to God, and everlasting praise be given to the Father, Son and Holy Ghost! He hath done all things well. I own his hand even in temporal affairs; for the $50,000 worth of property which went down to nothing, has been greatly increased in value of late, and I shall have enough and to spare.

And now, I may in conclusion say, my tongue and pen, my time and talents, my property, family, and life, belong, and shall be devoted to Jesus while I live.

With an interest almost breathless the preachers and people heard him through. As he neared the close, and referred to the power of the gospel of Jesus in transforming his nature, and the loving look, and mighty hand of the Saviour extended to him, and the way he took hold of the strength of the Divine Son of God, that he might be saved, every individual within hearing experienced at the same instant a touch and thrill of holy power. The speaker could not proceed much farther, and wisely closed his straight-forward story in the very midst of this excitement.

Bro. Inskip gave a signal and the whole audience sprang to their feet singing—

> "All hail the power of Jesus' name,
> Let angels prostrate fall;
> Bring forth the royal diadem,
> And crown him Lord of all.
>
> "Let every kindred, every tribe,
> On this terrestrial ball,
> To him all majesty ascribe,
> And crown him Lord of all."

As the noble strains of "Coronation" rose, the pent up feelings of the people found expression in the song.

Recalling them for a moment, Mr. Inskip said, "What might appear extravagant at ordinary times, becomes proper at others. He for once appreciated the wish expressed in the verse of the first hymn—

> "'O for a thousand tongues to sing,
> My great Redeemer's praise;
> The glories of my God and King,
> The triumphs of his grace.'"

He had no sooner uttered the words than the singing burst forth again, all joining in the aspiration. Then followed the next stanza—

"My gracious Master and my God,
Assist me to proclaim;
To spread through all the earth abroad,
The honors of Thy name."

The third was sung with undiminished zest, and repeated once or twice by direction of the leader, when all attention to order broke down. The faces of the great multitude were turned heavenward, and a light brighter than the noonday sun flashed over the scene. It was rapture—bliss—heaven—a "joy unspeakable and full of glory."

Ministers, aged and young, were embracing each other in the stand; some had fallen on the ground overpowered by ecstatic emotion, and the people were all in glorious confusion, each in his own way heightening the general joy.

Dr. Hodgson, who had gone out a little before into the boundless ocean of perfect love, now shouted, with his face shining, " This is the time for ' Hallelujah!' " '

" Hallelujah" became the watchword, and rolled from every tongue. The dinner hour was forgotten, and on this tidal wave of power it was estimated that many souls were borne into that haven of soul-rest they had been previously seeking.

The scene, in every respect, was most extraordinary. Nothing like it had ever occurred in the experience of a number of the people and ministers present.

THE AFTERNOON.

Baptized as were the people at the morning services, and remembering that the series of meetings during the afternoon and evening were to be final, every place was crowded, and every hour marked with extraordinary interest.

At 2 P. M. the experience meeting in the Landisville tent, and the children's meeting in the great Tabernacle, were under full headway. Groups were also gathered at various other points, speaking or listening to those who, filled with wonder and joy, were trying to express their new realizations of the love of Jesus, and beseeching others to "present their bodies a living sacrifice, holy, acceptable to God."

Lest the unprecedented excitement of the day might divert in any degree the public mind from prayer and faith, Rev. Wm. H. Boole, at the usual hour for afternoon preaching, took the congregation in hand. Great interest centred in this service. Many souls, it was safely conjectured, by some lurking prejudice or forbidden pleasure, were still in the gall of bitterness, cleaving to a doubtful indulgence, which would rob them of the rich communications others were enjoying, and they might return to their homes no nearer salvation than when they came.

A season of great grace like the present, if not used with honest intent to make one better, might react to make him worse, and plant thorns of regret in his future experience.

To strike the last prop of hesitation or self sufficiency from under persons of this class, and bring them to a decision and full surrender of themselves to God, seemed to be the aim of the preacher. He commenced by saying:

"I have no set discourse before me, but I want to say that it is not yet high tide. It is several hours to high water. God intends to make this the most mighty and glorious meeting ever held in this country. Cast up the highway; gather out the stones. Prepare ye the way of the people!

"There is an impediment somewhere. There is a shore-line that must be cut. See one of the ocean steamers as it lies fast at the wharf. Cast off that bow-line. Cast off the quarter line. The bow of the vessel is in the current, but the stern-line is still fast. 'Let go that stern-line!' cries the captain. Too tight to unloose? Then cut it. It is done, and away the steamer goes. Now you have thrown off every line but one. The Captain sees it; and if he will help me to stimulate your will, and you take the axe and cut the line, you will go out with many others into the broad ocean of peace. But you must know what you want. It will not do for you to say, 'Lord help me;' you must know what you want, and ask definitely.

"You have been told that you must be clear in justification, that you may have a good foundation for entire sanctification. This is a good general principle; still your knowledge may go ahead of your faith, and you may have both blessings this afternoon. I have an example in David. He had backslidden, and he cries, 'Have mercy on me, O God,' &c.; then, 'Create in me a clean heart, O God, and renew a right spirit within me.' Here are both blessings. Now, you may put both these in your consecration—sign the deed of your whole self to God; do it once and forever.

"The way of God's blessing me you are not to meddle with. Let God have his own way. Your will must be given up; this hinders many. Some are full of joy; you may not be.' If it comes in a gust of power, or in a quiet way, say 'Amen.' 'What may I expect when I am blessed?' You may have the Holy Spirit. I believe that several times I have secured the blessing of heart purity. I know that I loved God, but I opposed this doctrine; yet I gave no man credit for loving God more than I did. God brought the light to shine deep in my nature, and I found a nest of vipers there. This was a new discovery, and I went to my closet: I put everything I had upon the altar, and my sins I cast away. I did not think of putting my sins upon the altar. Then I began to believe that God did accept me. I did believe that if God required me to be holy, he would indeed make me holy; and I said 'I will have it.' I lived ten days on the promise, 'Man shall not live by bread alone.' If any one had asked me, 'Are you blessed?'—'Yes.' Yet I was not fully saved. After ten days God came in a mighty surge of fire, that shook my soul through and through.

"I need not say how I lost it; professors of religion stumbled me out of it. Still this was no excuse for me. I began to seek it again; and I did not fix any way, or thought that I would have it one way or another. I began to plead, 'If we confess our sins, thou art faithful and just to forgive our sins,' and 'what things soever ye desire when ye pray,' etc. I pleaded these promises, and believed them, and went to bed, and in about twelve hours after, God flooded my soul again, and I was constrained to praise him mightily.

"I had attained a higher sense of purity than formerly, and now had three distinctive communications: 1. The baptism of fire; 2. The baptism of love; 3. The baptism of joy.

"There are some things which you must do before you are sanctified: you must cleanse yourself; you must put away all filthiness of the flesh and of the spirit; you must give up the last thing. What idol is in your way? A wealthy man said, 'If I find that my business interferes with my religion, I will give it up.' He had ten thousand dollars invested in the beer business; he found it was wrong, and he gave it up. Now, there is something that hinders you; it may be your business—it may be the evil constitutes a habit; and you have run in these ruts. Now, you must give them up, even if you die. You may ask, 'Can I be so saved from it that I shall be as free as if I never had these habits?' 'Yes.'

"I knew a man in California who tried to gain the victory over the habit of tobacco, and he thought it would take away his life. He was told that God had power to cure this evil. He made up his mind to have it settled, and God took the whole appetite away.

"The Doctor said he was astonished. I have seen scores of such instances. You must not experiment upon God. You must trust the promise, but you cannot claim the promise till the conditions are fulfilled. I knew a man who ate opium enough to kill two hundred men. He came to the altar for prayer, and had a mighty struggle. He confessed his fault; he began to give it up, and was in great distress, saying, 'My God! what shall I do?'

"'Why, give up your sin.'

"'Why, I shall die if I do.'

"'Then die if need be.'

"Why, there is no sinner that God cannot save. You are nobody for God to save. He would take a thousand of such sinners, and save you in ten minutes. This man came to the altar one Sabbath night. I said, at the close of the meeting, 'There shall not another prayer be offered for you, unless you say you will give up that sin, even if you die.' As solemn as though he was signing his death warrant, he said, 'I will never take any more if I die;' and, in a few minutes, God saved him gloriously. In a week or two he said, 'I don't feel any appetite for this evil;' and, after five years, he still declares that he has never felt this appetite since.

"So there is some evil habit in your case, and you must cast it off.

"Some of you say, 'I can be saved now, but can I be kept saved?' I say. 'Yes.' God can carry on his own work without any of your help. Just look at that white pebble in the stream. It is kept pure by lying in the stream; and just so you may lie still in the fountain of salvation, and be kept clean all the time.

"Salt Lake City, among its wonders, has a crystal stream always flowing from the eternal snows. The teams may come along and the waters be soiled; but on, on the current flows, and the stream is soon pure again; so God sends the stream that makes glad the city of our God, and if you stay in it you are kept clean.

" I want to say further that it is not the lack of faith, but it is a lack of exercise of the faith that you have; the faith that justifies is the faith that sanctifies. I would not ask you to increase my faith till I had used all the faith I had.

" I used to think that faith was a special gift. I believe that every Christian has the faith by which he might be sanctified. 'What things soever ye desire when ye pray, believe that ye receive them, and ye shall have them.' Ye shall have it after you believe; it never will become an actuality till you take it by faith. If you have asked God for what he has promised to you, believe that God will fulfill his word; there is nothing else that I can do; wait on God and let that thing alone. I am not responsible for the fulfillment of another man's promise; take the promise to pay, and go on rejoicing. God is responsible to fulfill his own promises, only trust him. Don't you feel any anxiety yourself? 'No;' and now God's express train is never behind time. If Satan should hinder the messenger, then he would put on more speed, and reach me before I was in want. I trust God, like the little canary bird that sung on a day and a half, without a seed—sing on. You come seeking the great blessing, and you have faith to lie down upon the promises, and you are under a threefold obligation to believe. 1st, to your own soul, you are under obligation to eat the fullness for your own self; you must eat and be filled. God wants to make you all millionaires in his kingdom.

" 2d. You are under obligation to God. No wonder God does not set his glory before you. Half a character is not set forth in the Scriptures. God would change you from glory to glory; you are under obligation to God to receive this baptism. Let nothing hold you back. Get it.

"3d.. For the sake of the dying multitudes before us get it! get it!"

Brother Inskip: "Let all who will have the blessing now, kneel down." (Hundreds knelt down.) "If there are any of you that do not expect it now, I charge you to rise up." (A voice; "I will not rise up.") Silent prayer followed.

"Are you believing?"

"Yes."

"Can you believe to the uttermost?

"Raise up your right hand. Do not tell an untruth; you said you would take it by faith, and you have not done it.

"Don't doubt. Any man that believes at all hazards, and will not doubt, raise up your hand.

"Say it now; 'I will not doubt.'"

"I *will not doubt;* I won't doubt. Say it all over the camp 'I will not doubt.'

"Now we will go a step farther, and say, 'I will believe;' put your whole will to it, and say 'I *will* believe.' Hold up your hand and say it. Go a step farther; you cannot doubt, go on; you can't go back, go forward. 'I do believe, I do believe.' Hold up your hand: 'I do believe.'

"I believe God saves me now; stick to it. You that say, he saves now, and will believe as long as you live, raise your hands. What will you say when you rise? Will you still say, 'I believe.'"

After silent prayer, he said: "Sing—

"'Here at the cross, where flows the blood,
That bought my guilty soul for God;
Thee, my new Master, now I call,
And consecrate to thee my all.'"

This remarkable service helped many into light. Streams of grace came down, and the multitudes went away under the most solemn pledges to abide by this act of consecration as long as they lived.

THE LAST PREACHERS' MEETING.

At 6 P. M. the Tabernacle was once more a scene of solemn and joyful service. God, angels and men were deeply interested in its heart-moving meditations. The hour had come for a final decision on the part of any preacher who up to this time had hesitated to take his position squarely on the platform of personal holiness. But few in such a case as this, were left, and they were ready to say—

"Tho' late, I all forsake
My friends, my all resign;
Gracious Redeemer, take, O take,
And seal me ever thine.
"I am coming, Lord; coming now to thee,
Wash me, cleanse me in the blood that flowed on Calvary."
"Come and possess me whole,
Nor hence again remove;
Settle and fix my wavering soul,
With all thy weight of love!"

Bros. McDonald and E. Davies led in prayer, after which the former, who had charge of the meeting, said:

"It is a very delightful thing for a minister to enjoy religion, and a great privilege to sit under his ministry. I would rather sit under the ministry of such a man, if he had but little learning, than the most learned man without it. I have a pastor who enjoys religion, and I love to hear him preach. He tells us if we love to hear him as much as he loves to preach to us, we must be the happiest people on earth. He has an experience to tell in every sermon, and although it is not according to common usuage, yet he turns his pulpit into a witness stand, and testifies of the grace that saves to the uttermost."

A brother here remarked that the man to whom Bro. McDonald referred, was Dr. Steele. "I heard him at several camp-meetings last summer, and there is always an unction attending his word. I believe that the crowning baptism of the Holy Ghost on us ministers will enable us savingly to impress the unconverted, and lead them to Christ. It is not only the spirit of love, and purity, and self-denial, but the power that brings sinners to God; hence there were three thousand converted on the day of Pentecost."

He proceeded to speak of President Finney, and the wonderful endowment that man possessed, saying: "I want this power, that may be conveyed by a look, or a word; that will pierce like a sword, break the heart like a hammer, and burn like fire. Heart-purity is only the alphabet of full salvation. After this, God can fill and furnish the soul, and beautify it with all the graces of the Spirit."

A brother said: "That is what I want. I came here to obtain all that there is for me. I feel that I am saved—wonderfully saved; but I pray God to fill me."

"When I entered the car to come here," said a preacher, "I wanted to be alone with Jesus. As two lovers, happy in each other's company, so Jesus has been with me, and keeps my mind and heart in perfect peace."

"I came here in a dark, indefinite state; but now all is light. Oh, how I have mourned that I could not heretofore feed the best part of my flock. Now I am just beginning to live. I have grown more during the last few days than for many years before."

Others in a similar strain proceeded to acknowledge the benefits they had derived from this meeting, and their purposes to go home and trust Jesus while they held up the banner of gospel holiness.

With prayer, and mutual pledges to be faithful to God, and the doctrine of salvation from all sin, and a last farewell in view of the probability of meeting no more until the Judgment morning, the Preachers' Meeting here closed, and the crowd of deeply interested spectators took their way to the circle, where the final public services were about to be held. There let us follow them.

THE CLOSING SERVICE.

When it was intimated that the religious services of the meeting would close on Thursday night, the interest, steadily rising all day, reached a climax of intensity.

The population of the surrounding towns and country seemed to have been transferred to the camp ground. When the time for preaching was announced by the bell, a vast congregation was already seated in front, and crowds came pouring in from every avenue to swell the expectant throng.

As many ministers as it could hold filled the stand; and, after a familiar hymn had been sung, the venerable Father Coleman, who during the entire progress of the meeting had taken his share at the laboring oar, and seemed as fresh as when it began, offered a simple and comprehensive prayer for special help in this hour of need.

For the last time the Secretary read his list of "Requests for Prayer." Mothers wanted their children converted. A medical doctor on the ground was a subject of supplication, that he might accept Christ and be saved to-night. The children of "a father who never entered the house of God" wanted that father awakened and made a Christian man. And so the reading ran. Silently the whole audience rose when asked to do so, and each case was laid before the Heavenly Father.

In a few introductory words the President introduced, as the preacher of the evening,

REV. DR. NAST, OF CINCINNATI.

The Doctor, in the midst of much excitement, found, as might be supposed, a good deal of embarrassment in giving free and full expression to the ideas that filled his mind, and the emotions which stirred his heart, in a tongue foreign to him; but he made himself understood, as he read and applied the words of the apostle (Gal. 2: 20), "I am crucified with Christ; nevertheless I live; yet not I, but Christ liveth in me; and the life which I now live in the flesh, I live by the faith of the Son of God, who loved me, and gave himself for me."

He said he could not have consented to address the people on such an imposing occasion but for the lessons of faith taught by Brother Boole in the afternoon.

"It is an act of faith in Christ for me now to preach, and I trust him to help me, as I do to save my soul. If Christ speaks through one of the weakest of his servants, all right. I only want to glory in the cross. I know I have your prayers. If, like Peter, I begin to sink, I shall cry, 'Lord, save me!'

"After all I have heard and seen here, I think I am about the hardest case among you. This morning you had a converted infidel to speak to you, but he was a grand believer in comparison with William Nast. For three years I walked in the desolation of thick darkness. I recall with deep interest the 17th of January, 1835, when, near Danville, in this State, I grappled with the monster Despair.

"It is different these times. There is not so much struggling as believing. We had not so much light then. I was at a meeting some time ago at Bucyrus, Ohio, and, stopping with a German family, the sister said to me, 'They make no account of getting religion now-a-days; just believe; come to the Lord Jesus Christ; ask what you need; He will save you; and that is all. In our times we mourned a good deal, and prayed, and thought if we were blessed after days or weeks of effort, it was a great thing' I told the sister, 'After all it was present faith, and not struggling or praying, that met the conditions of the gospel.'

"But I have gotten off the track. O how much trouble I gave the Lord and the Church to get me right side up! When I was converted (I had been for some time a praying man) I was blessed at the family prayer; yet at night I was at the mourners' bench again. The brethren got tired seeing me hanging on to doubts and fears; but the mothers stuck to me, and continued to help me by their sympathy and prayers. I was in a love-feast, and all around appeared so lovely, as if they had washed their robes and made them white; but I looked at myself as so unholy, I could have crept through a hole in the floor. I admired holiness, and used to preach it; but, I fear that as long as we were fond of smoking, we could not read our title clear.

"I was in this way when Bro. McDonald came to Cincinnati to hold a meeting. I thought, now is my time. A German brother got sanctified out West, and began to publish flaming articles through the *Apologete* (Dr. Nast's paper) and I was greatly troubled. I thought, now we will have a breeze; I must put on the brakes.

"But I wanted it, and it seemed the Spirit led me. Bro. McDonald called on me to pray the very first night of the meeting, and then I gave myself away to be forever the Lord's. He had to pour upon me one baptism after another; and even in my dreams I was interested in this matter of purity more than any other. I felt as Bishop Hamline describes, when the blood seemed to come all over him, cleansing every part of his nature. O glory be to his name; I know his blood cleanses me now!

"I find I am not preaching you a sermon. Well, I couldn't preach you an eloquent sermon if I was to try. I don't want to be of that kind; but let the Lord use me just as he wants to.

"Now let us turn and look at the words of Paul—'I live by the faith of the Son of God, who loved me, and gave himself for me.'

"What is more natural than that we should love one who died for us? Jesus gave himself—this means, he paid the debt. He died for sinners, that he might save them and then live in them. What sort of a life is this? It is a life of faith—the faith of the Son of God. Whatsoever is not of faith is sin. There is no other way for us to be made free from sin, but by faith. This admits us to the heaven of love, and through it we get to the heaven of heavens.

"Look at the arrangement to make us partakers of the divine nature. Christ was incarnated, and we are ingrafted in him. No man can adopt Paul's language here, unless he has power over sin. Its dominion is broken. You have to die before you get this life. As sure as you have to die to get into the other world, you must die unto sin, to get the Christ life. Some of us have been half dead and half alive. This is a poor arrangement. Notice persons dying naturally. They cling to life. The tide ebbs and flows; but at length they give up, and are dead. So through the law, Paul died, that he might have the new life, and live unto Christ. "By his stripes we are healed."

"Healed! Yes, all our surroundings are changed. The world may look down on this proceeding, but that is of no account. If we suffer with him, we shall also reign with him.

"When I came to this camp-meeting I thought—what a privilege to be here! I shall never forget to-day at noon, and the other night. If any are yet in their sins, God have mercy on you! There is power here to save you to-night. And brethren—there is a power to enable every one of us to live better than ever before. We must hereafter let this light shine on the pathway of others, and save all we can in the name of Jesus before we die. The next time we meet will be at the Judgment. May the Saviour in condescending grace, bless us all. Amen."

A LAST APPEAL.

Rev. J. S. Inskip, following Dr. Nast, said—"There are two periods which always excite tremendous sensations in my heart—the beginning and close of a meeting like this. I have gone through those sensations at the commencement and we now have reached the close. After all that has been done here, I feel some regret that we have not done more; and yet the Lord may do more for us to-night than all before this hour. O Lord, convert every sinner throughout the camp; and sanctify every believer here! (Amen! was shouted by a hundred voices at once.)

"If we were in the condition we ought to be, there would be an all-conquering moral power here to-night. I am in sympathy with the idea that this tremendous responsibility resting upon us, is to a great extent pervading all minds. Some here may be ready to exclaim, 'The harvest is past, the summer is ended, and we are not saved.' But you are not lost; and if not saved, you may be saved to-night. O sinner, if you pass through such a scene as this unconverted, you will go out into night eternal, where there is no morning; no hope. O ye gay and wanton triflers, hear this last call and turn to Christ. Fly, fly to-night, to the open arms of mercy. O believers in Jesus, why such hesitation on your part to go out and persuade the unconverted to seek after God! We ought in some way or other to bring five hundred sinners to the Saviour to-night. Let the watch-cry of the camp be 'The sword of the Lord and of Gideon!' and be assured this meeting will wind up with a baptism of fire. Come on here, and let us get to work in earnest. We want no dress parade, or scientific music. Backsliders are all around us, and it is no wonder. The Church is asleep. We do not intend to divide the Church, but with the help of God, we will go on preaching holiness, and praying holiness, and singing holiness, and talking holiness, until we get on the ramparts of the new Jerusalem and help to shout 'Hallelujah, the Lord God Omnipotent reigneth!'"

The speaker, at this point was under very strong excitement, and the answering shouts from a congregation catching his enthusiasm, rolled up in volumes of sound. To quiet the apprehensions of those who might suppose he was going beyond his strength, he said he was "hooped and bound, and could not blow up until the Lord's time."

He was thankful, in reference to his own conversion, that he got in early; and it was no namby-pamby affair. His father opposed him, and would not countenance his holding meetings, lest his sisters, too, should 'turn fool,' as in the old gentleman's estimation, he had. He finally had to leave his home, on account of professing religion.

He was happy, singing as he took his little bundle and started over the hills to find another home. An old Quaker lady comforted him, and his good class-leader stood his friend. He was quickly sent for to return home. His father had been taken sick. When he went in, his mother—a queenly woman who taught her children to pray and revere the Bible—told him the state of the case. The father was under conviction. He had been heard praying, and now asked the boy he had driven away in his wrath, to call in the neighbors, and intercede with God for him. He was converted, and father and mother are now in heaven, while he was going on the way to meet them again. Closing this interesting narrative, he then shouted:

"Clear all this space in front for the seekers. Come on; and while you kneel here enter into solemn covenant to be wholly the Lord's. Let Christians again go out and speak to everybody they find unsaved, and invite them to Jesus to-night."

This general order was instantly obeyed. Away went the preachers and people in search of unconverted friends or strangers, and returned at intervals, bringing penitents to the altar.

All were filled with thankfulness for the mighty influence exerted by the meeting. It was nearly eleven o'clock when the final doxology was sung and the benediction of the Father, Son and Holy Ghost invoked upon the people, now, henceforth, and for evermore.

At length quiet reigned. The great meeting was over. "Visions and dreams," it is presumable, were entrancing after such a day of salvation. Its memories shall remain

"While life, or thought, or being last,
Or immortality endure."

www.ingramcontent.com/pod-product-compliance
Lightning Source LLC
Chambersburg PA
CBHW031953040426
42448CB00006B/346